For all those who suffer from grief and resentment,
and with deep gratitude to Steve Andreas
who taught me how to elegantly resolve
these human afflictions.

TABLE OF CONTENTS

INDEX OF EXERCISES AND EXAMPLES

FOREWORD

We humans come into this world with a brain that is one of the most complex and versatile computers known. It comes without any user's guide, and with only a few rudimentary programs installed, but with a prodigious ability to learn. From the moment we are born, and perhaps before, we develop and acquire new programs, often without our conscious awareness as we respond to our environment, our parents, and others around us.

Most of these programs work quite well. However, we also learn some programs that don't work well, and when confronted by a problem we often become preoccupied by what doesn't work, and lose sight of all those that do. Well-intentioned helpers often add to this misery by blaming and judging us for our failures. Psychiatry has an extensive 980-page manual of mental disorders labeling people who can't get their mental programs running in resourceful ways. That same manual has not one single page that tells how to resolve even one of those disorders!

Many of these diagnostic labels come with their own assumptions: that very little can be done to resolve the problem, or that the problem can only be resolved by years of difficult and painful therapy. When the therapy isn't successful, clients are often abandoned as "resistant." Rather than the helper admitting, "I don't know how to help them," they assume that the person "can't be helped," or just "didn't want to get well."

One alternative is to tinker with the computer itself and change its electrochemical processes with powerful drugs – or even electroshock. These "treatments" are only marginally effective, and often have powerful side-effects that interfere with all the other programs that were already running quite well. Drugs also run the risk of making people happy and content while they continue to do terrible things to themselves and one another.

Rather than focus on investigating failure, it is much more useful to discover how people successfully resolve problems. Most therapies focus their work on the content of a person's experience, rather than how their programs result in success or failure. When people resolve their problems what changes is not the "problem" itself, but the underlying process of how the "problem" is represented in their mind. The solution is often ridiculously simple, and often people will tell you exactly how they did it.

I was born not knowing and have only had a little time to change that here and there.
— Richard Feynman

Beware of eloquent labels and descriptions of problems masquerading as solutions to problems.

It's fairly easy to spot wrong answers; it's often more difficult to spot wrong questions.
— Steve Andreas

For example, when someone says, "Oh that used to be a problem, but I put it all behind me," we discover that the person has literally put the memory image behind them in their personal space, where it is hard to notice, and no longer bothers them. When you discover a solution like this, it is ridiculously easy to teach someone else exactly how to enjoy the same solution.

Rather than study people who were stuck in their grief, we studied people who had rapidly resolved a significant loss. We discovered how they thought about the lost person in a way that resulted in joy for having had the incredible luck to have known them. Then it was a simple matter to teach others who were grieving how to hold the lost person secure in their hearts so that they were forever with them.

We did the same for people who had been successful in forgiving someone who had done "unforgivable" things to them, and again we are able to teach this process to others whose lives are corroded by chronic anger or resentment. Believe it or not, people can be taught how to resolve deep-seated grief or resentment in one session of an hour or less, and these are two of the key programs that Rob presents in **Restoring Hope**. While these may seem like bold claims, I invite the reader to do the exercises in this book, and find out how well they work.

Some readers may need to suspend their judgment and assumptions about how people can change when they use the exercises to explore their own and their client's experiences. There is no magic or slight of hand; everything is exactly as it appears. However the results are often so magical that both client and coach are left in a state of awe at the internal creativity and healing power within each of us.

While Rob describes the exercises in easy-to-follow sequential steps, it is important to do them **with** a person rather than **to** a person—and with compassionate caring and respect, as you help people learn how to use their minds to create healing by adjusting their mental programs.

I invite you to not only enjoy reading this book, but to experience the deep satisfaction of being able to help yourself and others resolve their difficulties rapidly, restoring them to hope, and to a satisfying life.

Steve Andreas
http://www.steveandreas.com

We can't solve problems by using the same kind of thinking we used when we created them.
— Albert Einstein

Don't worry, just because you keep an open mind, your brains won't fall out.

How many people use the latest software on their desk computer yet don't know about the latest software for the computer in their head?
— Unknown

Acknowledgments

My purpose in life is to be helpful, humorous and healing. While I now am an Episcopal priest, psychologist, and executive coach, I have not ventured too far from being the mechanical engineer that I first was by profession and training. I am by nature practical and utilitarian. If you find this book too much of a user's guide, and lacking in theory, then I have probably been very true to my core purpose. I want to make things better, and get frustrated with books and ideas that are essentially statements about how things **should be** better rather than teaching the specifics of how to actually **make them** better.

It is ironic that I have written several books, because I am not a reader. Personally, I think most books on theology and psychology should be registered with the FDA as sleeping aids. While I do not find reading all that helpful, I am an avid learner and take incredible delight in discovering practical ways to make a healing difference in the lives of the people I encounter. My primary mode of learning is going to workshops. I particularly find the "hear one, see one, do one" method of teaching to be my most profound way of learning.

My secondary mode of learning is to teach, and to demonstrate the skills I am teaching. It is in these real-time exercises that I have discovered the truth of what I am teaching and the subtle variations that need to be incorporated to incarnationally engage with the unique individual who has entrusted themself to my care. I particularly enjoy those magical moments when the teacher-pupil dichotomy is transcended and together we become learners and co-creators of that person's future. To all those who have been willing to take a risk and go on that voyage of discovery with me, I am truly grateful.

This book is the result of these two learning processes. My primary teachers in the past few years have been Steve and Connirae Andreas[1], innovators, developers, and exponents of Neuro-Linguistic-Programming, (NLP). The grief and forgiveness processes are directly taken from their work. I am also grateful to Steve for his technical and editorial advice while writing this book. Andy Austin[2], another NLP exponent, is largely responsible for the idea that painful memories involve a disruption of perceived time.

Several other teachers, who were students of Milton Erickson,[3] have also had a significant impact on my work. Stephen Gilligan[4] introduced me to the idea of compassion being made up of tenderness, fierceness, and mischievousness. This understanding has transformed my

The place God calls you is the place where your deep gladness and the world's hunger meet.
— Frederick Buechner

Personally I'm always ready to learn, although I do not always like being taught.
— Winston Churchill

Never doubt that a small group of thoughtful, committed citizens can change the world. Indeed, it is the only thing that ever has.
— Margaret Mead

I love quotations because it is a joy to find thoughts one might have, beautifully expressed with much authority by someone recognized as wiser than oneself.
— Marlene Dietrich

If I have been of service, if I have glimpsed more of the nature and essence of ultimate good, if I am inspired to reach wider horizons of thought and action, if I am at peace with myself, it has been a successful day.
— Alex Noble

understanding of the healing, and sometimes bizarre, communication patterns of Jesus and other contemplative healers who employed what the Buddhists call "crazy wisdom." Bill O'Hanlon[5] taught me the necessity of ensuring goals were always positive and Steve Lankton[6] introduced me to the concept of accessing and associating resources that became incorporated in my $A \Rightarrow B$ model of change.

The last teacher I want to acknowledge is Edith Stauffer[7]. Early in my ministry this delightful lady introduced me to the power of forgiveness. She taught me the demand characteristics of resentment and how to transform demands into preferences, and to surrender people into the unconditional love of God, as a way to forgive. I have incorporated Edith's approach to forgiveness into Steve and Connirae Andreas' process on forgiveness.

Because most of my learning has occurred at workshops, I find it difficult to cite specific books or references such as you might find in an academic publication. Instead, I would refer you to these teachers' body of work in the reference section, and also encourage you to attend any seminars they offer.

Throughout this book I have used numerous quotes and call-outs to capture and express the thoughts and ideas I am presenting. Many of the quotes are pithy statements, or "meditation starters" that tease my imagination to consider new possibilities or ways to think. My primary sources of quotes are web anthologies such as www.thinkexist.com or www.wisdomquotes.com.

To the multitude of thinkers and authors who have shared their thoughts in ways that inspire me to see things differently or just get me to think, I am grateful. Where possible I have endeavored to provide the original author; however, some of these quotes have become part of mainstream conversation to the point that original sources and exact statements are lost. Side quotes without attribution are the products of my imagination, inspired by reflecting on daily living and helping others.

I am also grateful to my editor Elizabeth Farquhar for ensuring that I make sense to others and to my artistic consultant Christine Ambrose for her help with the cover design. Lastly and not least I am grateful to my beloved Kim who is the temporal manifestation of the eternal loving kindness in my life.

With Gratitude and Love
Rob Voyle

Introduction

You and I are going to spend the rest of our lives in the future. Hope is the ability to look into the future, see a future that is life-giving, and realistically know that we have the resources to achieve that future. Unfortunately, many of us are unable to work on creating our desired future because we are weighed down by grief and resentment over things that have occurred in our past. When we are grieving or resenting we are hope-less. This book is a practical guide for restoring you and others to a place of hope.

My Intended Audience

This book is written for clergy, coaches, psychologists, spiritual directors, and counselors who desire to incorporate their spirituality into their healing work. As a priest and healer I will use the stories of Jesus the healer to illustrate the principles and strategies of healing I am describing. I invite you, the reader, to incorporate the stories of your spiritual guides into your understanding of restoring hope.

Personally, I do not care for the many titles ("priest" or "psychologist" or "coach") that apply to my work. I think life and the healing arts are about people coming together to discover the healing potential that resides within each of us, not about an "expert" imposing healing on someone. If we are to be experts in anything, it is to help people discover their own expertise. However, in writing this resource I found I needed labels to distinguish the helper from the person being helped. So, for simplicity's sake, and since this book focuses on helping people develop the skill of forgiving and resolving grief, I have called the helper a "coach" and the person being helped the "client."

Practicing Within Your Comfort and Competence

While egalitarian by nature, I do recognize the need for expertise and continue to hone my skills as a helper and healer. The strategies that are presented in this book range from conversational perspectives to specific processes that require varying levels of competence and confidence. Having taught many helpers in a variety of settings, and acknowledging the breadth of my intended audience, I know that my readers will vary in their level of expertise and their comfort with engaging in some of the processes. While challenging you to grow your skills, I also encourage you to stay within the realm of your competence and comfort. When either of those is reached, please refer the client to someone with the necessary ability to restore them to hope.

I look to the future because that's where I'm going to spend the rest of my life.
— George F. Burns

We are here on earth to do good for others. What the others are here for, I don't know.
— W. H. Auden

The second kick of the mule has no educational value.
— Unknown

Restoring Hope: Time Doesn't Heal Anything

Many people in the midst of distress such as grief or hurt are told that "it will take time" for the person to heal. Yet I have known people who have carried resentment for thirty years, or traumatic memories of the Second World War for over sixty years, with little relief. If time did heal, then these people would have been well and truly healed years ago.

It is not time that brings healing. Healing comes from what we do during that time. This book is based on discovering the strategies that people have engaged in to find healing. Many of us have actually done these strategies without being consciously aware of what we were doing. Restoring hope is about discovering these unconscious processes and doing them consciously with those hurts we have not yet resolved.

We cannot change our past. No amount of grieving or resenting will change the past. All we have of our past is our memory. While we cannot change our past, we can change how we experience our memories of the past. We can also choose what we allow from our past to inform our future. When we help people to consciously transform their memories and have control over how they allow their past to inform their future, we help them grow from being helpless victims of their past to people who are living fully in the present moment as they work to create their desired future.

A Realistic Hope

Genuine hope is not based on a fantasy of how you would like the future to be. It is based on both an image of a preferred future and a reality-based awareness that we have the resources to achieve that future. Passively "hoping" the future will be better is unhelpful. Imagine someone living in an abusive relationship, hoping that their abuser will change. That kind of hope is very unhelpful and even dangerous. Giving up hope that the abuser will change is a helpful first step in the person taking charge of and responsibility for their own life. Finding the resources to move out of the relationship and growing out of their victim consciousness is essential to establishing a sense of personal assurance and a realistic hope.

Don't Give this Book Away!

If you know someone who is suffering from grief or resentment, don't give them this book! Instead, use the processes in this book with the person to restore them to a place of hope. Knowing about grief and forgiveness will not help – doing the processes will.

You don't get to choose how you're going to die. Or when. You can only decide how you're going to live.
— Joan Baez

And by hope I mean blues-inflicted hope that is morally sound; hope learned and earned in the harsh realities of daily struggle; hope that remains on intimate terms with death; hope that is life-renewing and opposed to the cheap optimism of market-driven America where Disneyland is sold as heaven on earth.
— Cornel West

Knowing is not enough; we must apply. Willing is not enough; we must do.
— Johann von Goethe

Overview

This manual is divided into five sections:

1. An Introduction to the Appreciative Way

   The core foundations of Appreciative Inquiry are presented and related to the task of resolving grief and resentment.

2. The Nature of Hope: Core Concepts, Resources and Processes

   In this section, a basic understanding of the nature of hope and several core resources are presented. The resources include an understanding of unconditional love and compassion. In the processes sub-section, the reader will explore the ways they represent or structure experiences in consciousness and how these processes can be used to create healing.

   The Appreciative Way and Core Concepts will then be applied to:

3. The Resolution of Painful Memories

4. Resolving Grief

5. Forgiveness and the Art of Resolving Resentment

For each of the applied sections I will provide two primary strategies to resolve painful memories, grief and resentment:

- A narrative approach which focuses on the content of a person's experience and the perspective from which the content is viewed.

- A structural approach to resolve these same issues. The structural strategies are likely to be new to many readers. They reflect the genius of the approach that Steve and Connirae Andreas have pioneered. These structural strategies provide ways to rapidly and sustainably resolve a wide range of human distress.

In addition to the processes for use with individuals, I will also present processes to work with organizations, such as a congregation that is dealing as a community with issues of pain, grief, and resentment.

Experiential Learning Exercises

Restoring hope by resolving grief and resentment is achieved by doing. If you are grieving or resenting, you can read and understand the steps in this book, but unless you actually do the steps you will remain in a place of grief and resentment. Throughout this book I have presented exercises to create a set of resources to facilitate the healing process. The exercises serve two purposes:

- To help the reader experientially understand a concept or strategy.

- To help a coach implement a specific strategy with a client.

*In three words
I can sum up everything
I've learned about life:
it goes on.*
— Robert Frost

*All the things we
take for granted
once were nothing more
than a figment of
someone's imagination.
We need to focus on
what we need to do
to make our dreams reality
rather than consider why
we can't achieve them.*

*Tell me,
what is it you plan to do
with your one wild and
precious life?*
— Mary Oliver

Learning the Strategies

Some readers may find that they can do the exercises by themselves on their own. Personally, I usually need someone to lead me through them, even when I know what the steps are. To facilitate your learning I have created a set of resources that are available at: www.appreciativeway.com/hope.html.

- Audio recordings of all of the exercises. You can use the recordings to lead yourself through each of the exercises.

- Hard copies of the exercises.

As you are learning and working with clients, you may find it helpful to download the exercises and use them to guide you through a process. Many clients have reported that the coaches' use of a script gave them confidence that something specific could be done about their distress. Because the exercises are often conducted without reference to the content of a painful experience, I also encourage you to practice the steps with peers or colleagues in both formal and informal learning contexts.

Using the Exercises With Clients

Each exercise has the same format:

- Instructions for the coach are in plain text.

- Text in italics is a verbatim script for the coach to use with a client. Adapt these scripts so that you are working with your client and not doing a procedure to or on the client.

- A "..." indicates a pause to allow the client to complete the step. The pause may also be used by the coach to adapt the step to the specific needs of the client.

When leading a client through the exercises, you do not need to explain the theory behind the process. For many people it is easier to understand the process after doing the exercises, because the steps and results are profoundly different from what people have traditionally been taught about the nature of grief and resentment.

More importantly than serving as a guide for the process, your presence as a coach during the process validates and bears witness both to what the person has experienced in the past and in their present healing process. Your acceptance of the client is an important part of healing the alienation that people experience when they have been hurt or are grieving. I trust the exercises enable you to be a healing presence for the people you care about.

1: INTRODUCTION TO THE APPRECIATIVE WAY

The Appreciative Way is a way of being and doing in the world. It is a synthesis of:

- Appreciative Inquiry
- The work of Milton Erickson and his students
- Contemplative Spirituality

Appreciative Inquiry

Appreciative Inquiry was developed by David Cooperrider[1] in the mid-1980s. It was developed as an organizational development process that uses shared storytelling to discover and build on what is best about an organization. From an appreciative perspective, organizational development occurs from intentionally creating and working toward a clear and compelling vision of the future that embodies the strengths and core life-giving values of the organization. This is in direct contrast to many problem-centered approaches that see organizational development occurring only as the result of a continual identifying and fixing of problems.

To "appreciate" has several meanings:

- to pay attention to
- to value
- to grow

To "inquire" means:

- to seek information
- to ask

All of these meanings are present in the work of Appreciative Inquiry. In the process of asking questions we are paying attention to something. Within the appreciative approach we are very deliberate in what we appreciate (pay attention to) because we know that what we inquire into will appreciate (grow). This is expressed in the second assumption of Appreciative Inquiry: "What we focus on will become our reality." When we focus on what is working, what is working will grow. Likewise, when we focus on problems or what is not working, we find that these problems will grow rather than be resolved.

This does not mean that we ignore problems. However, rather than focusing on the cause of the problem, we focus our attention on the solution to the problem. We focus our attention on what we want *more* of, rather than on what we want *less* of.

> *Appreciative Inquiry is based on a reverence for life ... More than a method or technique, the appreciative mode of inquiry is a means of living with, being with, and directly participating in the life of a human system in a way that compels one to inquire into the deeper life-generating essentials and potentials of organizational existence.*
> — David Cooperrider

> *Think of Appreciative Inquiry as a new conversation, as a search engine for the positive core of a system, as a convergence zone or "space" creating a multiplier effect in the area of human imagination and intellectual capital.*
> — David Cooperrider

The Work of Milton Erickson

Milton Erickson was a psychiatrist who, in the latter years of his life, lived and worked in Phoenix, Arizona. By most standards he was very unorthodox in his approach to his patients; however, in response to his methods, patients often made rapid recoveries. He was a founding figure in the use of hypnosis in clinical settings. In contrast to others who used formal hypnotic inductions, Erickson was more inclined to use naturalistic trance states and communication patterns to help people access their unconscious resources.

Unlike Freud (and as seen in much of psychology), Erickson did not view the unconscious as some dark, mysterious, angst-filled place that gives rise to primitive and destructive urges. Rather, he viewed the unconscious mind as a treasure trove of resources and wisdom that a person could access to create a fulfilling life. Erickson also developed and employed many therapeutic strategies such as: utilizing or prescribing the symptom; creating confusion and transformation through the use of paradox and ambiguity; and using parables or storytelling to open people to new possibilities.

As a healer I have always been fascinated by the healing stories and transformational processes that Jesus used. Jesus didn't just pray for people but engaged them in bizarre conversations (*John 4:7-38*), or only taught in parables (*Matthew 13:10-17*), or spat on the ground and made mud to put on a blind man's eyes (*John 9:1-12*). It was only after studying Erickson's work that I began to gain some insight into what Jesus was doing in these Gospel stories, and was able to replicate some of Jesus' healing strategies in my own work.

Erickson had a foundational influence in the work of Jay Haley and strategic family therapy, Bill O'Hanlon and solution-oriented therapy, Steve Andreas and Neuro-Linguistic-Programming, Stephen Gilligan and self-relations therapy, and numerous others, such as Steve Lankton and Jeffrey Zeig who have kept alive Erickson's healing ways through their writing and teaching.

Contemplative Spirituality

Religion and spirituality have to do with how we are connected to that which is greater than or transcends ourselves. Religion is based on the question, "What must we do to please God?" The ultimate goal is atonement, or to be one with God, and this state is granted in response to our performing some task such as believing correctly, or being born again, or performing some good works.

In contrast to religion, spirituality is about how we are already connected to that which is greater than ourselves and that which is life-giving. Spirituality is about waking up to, and manifesting, what already is. Atonement is not some future goal – we are already one with God. The task of life is to wake up to this reality that already exists and, from this place of oneness, manifest God's love here on earth.

One way to differentiate spirituality from much of what passes as religion is to compare two neighboring Native American tribal societies, the Navajo and the Hopi, who have very different cosmologies that gave rise to very different types of religious practices.

Within the Navajo cosmology, there is no God or gods that can be appealed to influence or intervene in human events. The Navajo expression *hózhó* means "to walk in beauty." It has some parallels to the Christian idea of "going in peace." When a person is injured or has suffered some tragedy, they are no longer walking in beauty and need to be restored to beauty. Depending on the nature of the adversity, a trained *Hatałii* (medicine man) would conduct one of the many healing ceremonies to restore the person to *hózhó*, the natural harmony and beauty of all things.

In contrast, in Hopi cosmology the people can appeal to many spirits that can influence or change the natural course of events. For example, the rain dance ceremony is performed to call upon the rain spirits to send rain to water the land and crops. If the rain spirits are satisfied with the quality and sincerity of the dance then they will make it rain. Great emphasis is placed on performing the dance correctly so that the rain spirits will be pleased with the performance and reward the people with rain.

Many Christians live the "Hopi" way of asking what we must do to please God so that God will bless us. For many, having correct beliefs is the way to please God; for others, it is performing acts of mercy and self-sacrifice. Suffering is often seen as an indication that God is displeased with the person. To end the suffering, the person needs to repent of their sin that caused the suffering. And sometimes God is treated like a cosmic janitor that is essentially ignored until some calamity occurs – God is then called upon and expected to clean up after the person has messed up.

Contemplative spirituality is more akin to the "Navajo" way. Although we believe in God, we do not believe that God is subject to human manipulation. The task is not to please God and get God to bless us

The task of life is not to get God to love you or to try and please God. The task of life is to wake up to the fact that God already loves you and is pleased and go into the world and make as much noise with that love that you wake up those who are still sleeping.

Finally, whatever is true, whatever is honorable, whatever is just, whatever is pure, whatever is lovely, whatever is gracious, if there is any excellence, if there is anything worthy of praise, think about these things.
— *Philippians 4:8*

but to become one with and manifest the blessing that already exists. Prayer is not seen as a way to change God's mind but to change our mind to the mind of God and to see things the way God sees things. This is the heart of contemplation: to see life through God's eyes, and to look with the eyes of Love. What we find is that when we change the way we look at things, the things we look at change.

This understanding of contemplative spirituality informs how we engage in the process of restoring hope. For example, forgiveness is not simply something we do. Rather, since we are one with God, whose nature is to forgive, forgiveness becomes beholding people in that forgiveness that already exists. Instead of struggling to forgive we become one with all the forgiveness in the universe which is naturally being extended to all of humanity.

The Appreciative Way Synthesis

While these three approaches are distinct, they do share some underlying commonalities that allow them to be integrated and used synergistically to create strategies to restore people to a place of hope. All three approaches are essentially positive in their view of humanity and place considerable importance on what we focus on.

A Positive View of Humanity

The Appreciative Way is essentially optimistic and has a positive view of humanity. This positive view of humanity – made and blessed in the image of God – contrasts with the "total depravity" theologies of many religions. Although Appreciative Inquiry and Erickson would not use theological language to describe humanity, they see people as resourceful, having within themselves the potential and ability to live creative and fulfilling lives. The task of all three approaches is to call forth that inherent creativity and goodness from people.

The Importance of Focus

The second assumption of Appreciative Inquiry says, "What we focus on becomes our reality." In Buddhist thinking this understanding of focus is called "right seeing." Enlightenment is primarily about seeing things differently. The world doesn't change when a person becomes enlightened – and yet while nothing has changed, everything is different. Likewise, there are many occasions in the Bible when the reader is admonished to "behold" that is, to look or pay attention to certain things. The Ericksonian approach provides many practical ways to reframe, or focus differently on, perceived problems.

When we change the way we look at things, the things we look at change.
— Unknown

The glory of God is a fully alive human being
— St. Irenaeus

What you focus on becomes your reality.
— Second Assumption of Appreciative Inquiry

or put another way:
What you water with your attention will grow.
— Unknown

Instructions: This exercise explores what you habitually focus on when you go about your daily life.

1. *Take a few moments and look around the room you are in. Memorize everything you see in the room as though you were going to be quizzed at a later time on the contents of the room ...*

2. *Now look around the room and make a mental note of everything that is red in color ...*

3. *Next, look around the room and make a mental note of everything that is blue in color ...*

4. *Finally, look around the room and make a mental note of everything that is green in color ...*

5. **Debrief.** Did you discover that despite the fact that you had initially observed everything in the room when you were directed to focus on a color, things began coming to the foreground, or "leaping" off tables or walls into your consciousness?

   This exercise demonstrates part of the second assumption of Appreciative Inquiry:

   ### "What we focus on becomes our reality."

   Because we are bombarded by so many stimuli we learn to screen for certain things rather than being overwhelmed by too much input. This makes decision-making more efficient, but it runs the risk that we may miss certain things.

6. *Now take a few moments and think about where your attention goes when you enter a new situation, or go to church, or to work. Does your attention go to:*

   > *Is there a problem?*
   > *What is wrong?*
   > *Who is to blame?*
   > *How long has it been going on?*
   > *What do we need to do to prevent failure?*

   Or does your attention go to:

   > *What is working?*
   > *What is life-giving?*
   > *I wonder what we will achieve?*
   > *I wonder what the future will bring?*
   > *What do we need to ensure success?*

7. *In your daily life what do you screen for or focus on?*
   Do you focus on problems, or on possibilities?
   Do you focus on who is to blame, or do you focus on solutions and what needs to be done?

8. *What do you need to be love-based, hopeful, and open to possibilities?*

The Appreciative Way Of Creating Change

The Appreciative Way synthesis can be summarized in the **A ⇨ B** model for creating sustainable change.

BASIC A ⇨ B CHANGE MODEL

All intentional change can be understood as a process of helping people get from one place **A** to another desired place **B**. The task of the coach is to help them discover and access the resources they need to achieve the desired outcome. Large scale changes are actually a set of nested and chained smaller **A ⇨ B**s to achieve the overall **A ⇨ B**.

To facilitate this change process we need to know three things:

1. Where we are starting from.
2. Where we want to end up.
3. The resources we need to get there.

Because how we focus on things pre-determines our outcomes, we need to pay attention to how we focus on each of these elements.

The Starting Point

To help someone make a change we need to know where they are starting from. However, contrary to popular opinion we don't need to know why, or who, or what, is to blame for their being at this starting point in order to help them achieve their desired goal.

When dealing with a problem situation, rather than focusing on the cause of the problem we need to focus on how the person is "currently doing" the problem. We need to define specific current behaviors and attitudes that can be changed and need to be changed. For example, the person may be resentful towards someone for a past injury or insult. The past event is no longer the problem; the problem is how they are resenting in the present moment.

Endlessly talking about the past will reinforce the current resentment rather than relieving it. As the reader will discover, it is entirely possible to help someone resolve significant distress from trauma and resentment without knowing anything about the initial injury.

You have to be very careful if you don't know what you are looking for because you may not find it.
— Adapted from Yogi Berra

Appreciative Inquiry gets much better results than seeking out and solving problems. We often concentrate enormous resources on correcting problems. But when used continually over a long time, this approach leads to a negative culture… or a slip into a paralyzing sense of hopelessness. Don't get me wrong. I'm not advocating mindless happy talk. Appreciative Inquiry is a complex science designed to make things better. We can't ignore problems — we just need to approach them from the other side.
— Tom White

This lack of interest in the origins of problems is seen in Jesus' response to his disciples' question about the cause of a man's blindness: "Was it his sin or the sin of his parents that caused him to be blind?" Jesus rejects this line of thinking and sees the situation as an opportunity for the glory of God to be manifested in the man's healing (John 9:2-3).

The only time an understanding of cause is helpful is when it directly leads to the identification and accessing of resources to create a solution to a problem or achieve a goal. Unfortunately, we live in a society that is obsessed with the idea of blame, which leads to time and money being spent on creating eloquent descriptions of problems masquerading as solutions to the problems.

A Parable of How Eloquently Unhelpful We Can Be

Several years ago I attended a professional continuing education seminar for psychologists on forgiveness. Over five of the six hours were devoted to describing all the bad things, such as elevated stress hormone levels that can cause heart disease, that could occur if a person was resentful. The last hour was spent on an admonition that we need to forgive, and that when we do, stress hormone levels would decline.

The sophisticated research was eloquently presented with Powerpoint graphs and charts, but at no point during the entire presentation was resentment or forgiveness ever defined, nor were we taught **how** to actually forgive. At the end of the day I was no more equipped to help clients than when I had begun. In fact, in some ways I was now more of a menace to my clients as I knew the terrible things that would happen to them if they continued in their resentment, but at best all I could do was make them feel guilty for not forgiving. A thirty-minute description of what resentment is and how it is ineffective in achieving goals, followed by five and a half hours of teaching on what forgiveness is and how to help clients forgive, would have been more helpful to me as a clinician.

The Desired Outcome

In the Appreciative Way we focus on creating our preferred future. We pay attention to desired outcomes and continue to work, often iteratively, until a desired outcome is achieved. When we create goals, we need to ensure first that our goals are positively stated and then that our strategies are actually achieving that desired outcome.

Fix the problem, not the blame.
— Catherine Pulsifer

We need to discover the root causes of success rather than the root causes of failure.
— David Cooperrider

Appreciative Inquiry is an articulated theory that rationalizes and reinforces the habit of mind that moves through the world in a generative frame, seeking and finding images of the possible, rather than scenes of disaster and despair.
— Jane Magruder Watkins

When we think of Jesus' mission, did he come to give us less death, or did he come to give us life? When we are working with resentment or grief, we are not seeking to help the person have less resentment or less grief. We are working to help the person achieve a state of forgiveness and hope.

Jesus didn't come to give us less death. He came to give us life, – so much life that we could share it abundantly with others.

In some cases healing processes are paradoxical. What works in one situation may have the opposite effect in another situation. Rather than paying attention to the intention to heal, the coach needs to pay attention to the outcome and continue to modify the process to achieve that healing. If the client's distress increases in response to a strategy, then it is likely that it will reduce if the opposite or paradoxical strategy is used. Erickson was a master at the use of paradox and doing the opposite of what people expected. Buddhists call this paradoxical approach "crazy wisdom." Jesus was continually doing the unexpected, such as offering forgiveness rather than judgment, or healing on the sabbath.

If at first you don't succeed try something else.
— Unknown

Transformational processes of healing are often confusing. Problems often exist because they are viewed from a stuck place of certainty. We literally can't see an alternative and become certain that there is no solution. These unexpected actions of crazy wisdom evoke doubt and confusion in the midst of certainty, and open minds to the possibility of alternatives. Eliciting and managing confusion is often an essential part of creating desired outcomes.

Persistence until the objective is achieved is essential if we are to create sustainable outcomes. Initially, when Jesus healed one man who was blind, the person could see but people looked like "trees walking around." This was unacceptable to Jesus the healer, and he kept working until the person was able to see correctly (*Mark 8:22-26*). When using the grief and forgiveness protocols, getting complete relief is the goal, rather than "some" relief. The processes may need to be iteratively "tweaked" to achieve that objective.

I wish I was a glow worm, A glow worm's never glum. 'Cos how can you be grumpy, When the sun shines out your bum!
— Unknown

Discovering and Accessing Resources

A resource is anything we need to achieve the goal. Resources may be material, psychological, or spiritual. They include skills and motivational attitudes that we need to pursue and achieve a desired outcome. This manual is essentially a set of resources to help the reader facilitate the process of restoring hope in the midst of grief and resentment.

When pursuing a goal the focus is always on "what we need" to achieve the goal rather than on "why we can't" achieve the goal. Problems are viewed as situations that have insufficient resources allocated to them. Failure to achieve a goal is viewed as an indication that we need additional resources.

While goal- and future-oriented, the Appreciative Way does not ignore the past. The past is seen as a treasure trove of resources that can be "remembered" and used by the person to create their preferred future. To be able to create a goal in consciousness, a person must have had some prior experience of the goal state. Consequently, the first place we look for resources is inside the person's past experience. The seeds of a person's preferred future have already been planted in the past. If a person wants to experience peace, then we can explore how they have known peace in the past and use these experiences as a foundation for a more peaceful future.

In the organizational development use of Appreciative Inquiry, people are invited to share stories of their best experiences of the organization. In these stories of their best, they discover the resources they need to both imagine and create their organization's preferred future. When working with individuals we do not necessarily need them to tell the story of resourceful times "out loud" but simply to remember and immerse themselves in their story. Once immersed in the story, they can begin to imagine what they need to do to use these resources to achieve a desired outcome.

While future-focused, the Appreciative Way understands that resources are accessed and life is lived in the present moment. Creating a future is about what we are doing in the present moment. The art of contemplation is to discover how the preferred future is already being manifested in the present moment. Qualities such as love and peace are timeless. We can't get them tomorrow, we can only experience them now. For this reason, we don't want to make a timeless quality a goal to be achieved at some future time. Rather, the timeless quality is a current resource that we can use to inspire and energize action toward the goal.

Ensuring Change is a Blessing

It is often said in church and psychological circles that people don't like change. I don't think that is true, and in many situations people welcome change. It's the kind of change that causes people to welcome or resist it. What we need to do is ensure that our changes

---

Life can only be understood backwards; but it must be lived forwards.
— Soren Kierkegaard

We need to discover the root causes of success rather than the root causes of failure.
— David Cooperrider

A problem is nothing more than a situation that has insufficient resources associated with it.

People don't want to be changed, they want to be blessed.
— Stephen Gilligan

are a blessing. From the **A** ⇨ **B** perspective a blessing is any final outcome **B** that is more valuable than **A** plus the cost of the resources to achieve **B**. People will resist any change when they cannot perceive the outcome as more valuable than the starting point or worth the effort and resources to achieve it.

Notice that the issue is a perception of value and not some objective measure of the value. People will cling to resentment when they value the safety it appears to provide and when they perceive forgiveness as a state of vulnerability. Rather than fighting to overcome the resistance, we need to explore the deeper issue of safety and provide alternative strategies that are more effective for the person to stay safe. From an incarnational perspective which I will discuss later, it is important to work **with** the resistance, not **against** the resistance if we want to ensure that change is experienced as a blessing.

Ensuring Changes are Ecological and Sustainable

Creating change is rather pointless if we can't sustain the final outcome. Often we are conflicted when we set out to create change. Part of us may want the desired goal and part of us may not. This can occur because we have values that are in conflict. For example, I value personal freedom, but I also value being in community. Sometimes it appears that to be in community I need to give up some freedom in order to accept community norms. Similarly, part of us may object to forgiving someone because the act of forgiveness violates our sense of justice. If we do not resolve this inner conflict, the change is unlikely to be sustainable. We may feel like we have forgiven only to find that the resentment returns.

One of the most powerful strategies I learned from Steve Andreas was prior to embarking on any change process we need to seek and satisfy any objection we have to making the change. What we want to do is satisfy the objection and not overcome the objection. When we overcome an objection we get ourselves "by the scruff of the neck" and force the outcome on ourselves. This does violence to ourselves and the violated part is likely to sabotage our future endeavors. Seeking and satisfying objections is a way of ensuring that our decisions are internally ecological.

We will use the strategy of seeking and satisfying objections in each of the change protocols. Before implementing a change we ask the client if any part of them objects to the change. After they provide an objection, we ask that same part what would satisfy the objection.

There is nothing so useless as doing efficiently that which should not be done at all.
— Peter Drucker

Are all hearts clear?
— Quaker Discernment Practice

The only change outcomes that will be sustainable are those that result from greater self-acceptance.

The objection and its satisfaction then need to be explored to create a specific satisfaction that will genuinely satisfy the objection.

When satisfying objections, we want to go beyond simple ideas of compromise – which often leave people feeling compromised rather than free to engage in new behaviors. This may require exploring deeper values to find a point of commonality, or it may require exploring whether the current behavior, such as resentment, is an effective strategy to achieve a goal such as justice. When a satisfaction is discovered then we can add it to the list of resources that the client will need to access to achieve their goal.

We also need to ensure that the satisfaction is within the client's locus of control. A satisfaction can never be that someone else changes, or other external events change. Other people and external events are beyond our control and we will not find it helpful to make our actions dependent on people or things we cannot control. For example, if a client said they object to forgiving because the other person hasn't changed, they may have a very long wait – or they may never experience the freedom and healing that comes from forgiving. When dealing with these external events, it is often helpful to engage the client in a conversation about how they want to wait until the external events or people change.

In addition to considering the internal ecology of a change, we need to consider the external environmental ecology of our changes. As we develop new skills we need to ask if there are circumstances when it would not be wise to act in the new way. For example, as part of a forgiveness process you may need to learn assertiveness to protect yourself. As you develop your assertiveness skills, you need to have the freedom to be (or not be) assertive, depending on your environmental circumstances. It may be entirely appropriate to be assertive with a demeaning boss but inappropriate to be assertive with someone who has a gun to your head and is demanding your money.

Ensuring Change is Just

As we make changes we need to consider how our changes will impact others. We need to pay attention to whether the pursuit of our goal will deprive somebody of what is life-giving to them. We may abhor the strip-mining of our physical environment, while at the same time we may be "strip-mining" the psychological and spiritual environments of our family, employees, or volunteers. When others

*All change
is a balance between
safety and development.*
— *John McWhirter*

*If our blessing
comes at the expense
of another
it is not a blessing
it is theft.*

*The white man's happiness
cannot be purchased by
the black man's misery.*
— *Frederick Douglass*

in our environment are deprived of what is life-giving they are likely to resist our plans, and either openly confront or covertly sabotage our actions. Ensuring that others can live with our actions is a simple matter of justice and ensures that our goals are ecological in the material, psychological, and spiritual environments. To build a life of hope we need to ensure that our hope is not built on the deprivation of others.

The Importance of Acceptance

From my perspective, the deepest longing of the human soul is acceptance. Yet rather than living in the realm of acceptance, we often experience alienation. We are alienated from ourselves, from others, and from the source of our existence. Changes that result in increased alienation are inherently unsustainable. To create sustainable outcomes, the entire change process needs to be covered by an umbrella of acceptance.

To intentionally create change we need to accept that we are at **A**. If we cannot accept that we are **A** then we will be in a state of denial and we will be unable to engage in a change process.

When dealing with the death of a loved one it is clear that the person's death was not a desired outcome and is a change that is not a blessing. However, it does become the new starting place to build future blessings. Accepting the reality of the person's death will be a necessary first step in the path to healing.

While we may not like being at **A**, we do need to accept that we are at **A** with an attitude of love or compassion. Hating ourselves for feeling resentful or grief-stricken will keep us trapped in those feelings rather than being able to move to some alternative. Only when we have the freedom and self-acceptance to stay at **A** will we have the freedom and love to journey to **B**.

Many people who are dealing with an undesired habit stay stuck in their habit because of their self-hatred. For example, a person may hate themselves for being overweight. They say they will love themselves when they achieve their desired weight. Unfortunately, what they have also learned is to eat as a form of comfort when they are rejected. In the light of their self-rejection, they will eat to find comfort. The goal can never be to **get** love. It is **in** love, love of ourselves and others, that we journey to the goal.

As coaches we need to give people the freedom and acceptance

What I see is not what I am looking at but what I am looking with. And so my first and principal duty ... is to find my eyes of love.
— Dan Jones

We come to love not by finding a perfect person, but by learning to see an imperfect person perfectly.
— Unknown

He drew a circle to shut me out. Heretic, rebel, a thing to flout. But love and I had the wit to win. We drew a circle that took him in.
— Edwin Markham

to stay where they are. We don't need to give them the added burden of our rejection for being where they are, nor are they here simply to satisfy our personal objectives for them. One strategy to offer acceptance is to view people from the place of understanding that what they are doing is the best they know how, in their current context, to meet a perceived need. This is not offered as an excuse for past actions, nor as an excuse for continuing the behavior, but is a simple observation formed from the understanding that if the person knew how to do something differently to meet their needs, they would. Our task as coaches is to help people learn more effective, efficient, and ethical ways to meet their needs.

Notice that this understanding is context-driven. Many people have learned that resentment is a way to stay safe by putting emotional distance between themselves and a person who has hurt them. While they may know how to forgive in some contexts, there are other contexts in which they still find it impossible to forgive.

Telling someone who is grieving or resentful that they shouldn't feel that way is a statement of alienation. You are telling them to not feel what they are feeling, which is akin to saying "don't be yourself." The same is true if you are telling yourself that you shouldn't be grieving or resentful. In that process you are alienating yourself from the part of you that is distressed. Rather than telling someone not to feel something, we need to accept the person and the feelings and then help them resolve the feelings.

In addition to self-acceptance, we also need to accept that the current state **A** has not deprived us from the source of our life. When dealing with the death of a loved one, the fact that we are still alive when they are dead means that we have not been deprived of life. What we have lost is the person we shared life with, but not the source of our life. The classic movie line, "I love you, I can't live without you," is a statement of incompetence and inability to live fully rather than an expression of being in love with someone.

We also need to accept that staying at **A** may eventually deprive us of life, but the fact that we are still alive today means we have the opportunity to turn to that which is fully life-giving. However, being afraid that we may eventually die if we continue on a certain path is highly unlikely to motivate us to change. The fear of lung cancer rarely helps people stop smoking; in fact, it may cause the person to continue to smoke as they have learned that smoking is a powerful way to anesthetize their fear of dying. Rather than being motivated

Acceptance Meditation

Just like me, this person is seeking happiness in his/her life.

Just like me, this person is trying to avoid suffering in his/her life.

Just like me, this person has known sadness, loneliness and despair.

Just like me, this person is seeking to fill his/her needs.

Just like me, this person is learning about life.

Just like me, this person is doing the best they can.

— Unknown

Love doesn't make the world go 'round; love is what makes the ride worthwhile.
— Franklin P. Jones

by a fear of death, we need to be motivated by a desire to live – and not just to live, but to live fully.

The Appreciative Way is Incarnational

All sustainable change is an inside job. When change, even good change, is imposed upon people it is likely to be resisted because it violates a deeper value of freedom and autonomy. When working as a coach, we need to join with the client to co-create with the client their preferred future. Joining with a client is a profound way of creating an atmosphere of acceptance which is a key foundation for the healing process.

Creating a connection with the people we are helping is essential in the healing process. We join with people where they are and walk with them to their preferred future. This is in contrast to approaches that "drag" the client to the coach's perspective, or where the coach tries to impose healing upon the client, who is often perceived by the coach as being resistant.

Erickson placed great emphasis on joining clients, especially through the use of the client's language and pace, as part of the healing process. Once he had joined with the client he was able to invent a unique therapeutic strategy to meet the needs of the particular client he was working with. In this joining process he was working "with" the client rather than "against" the client. This process of joining dissolves classic psychotherapeutic understandings of resistance.

Similarly, in Jesus we see the "Word" who came and lived as one of us rather than the "Word" who came and imposed salvation on us. He did not rely on a "one size fits all" approach. Jesus treated each person as unique and responded to each person individually. He joined with people in their lived experience and used that as the basis for his transformational conversations.

This incarnational approach will be important when you are helping people resolve grief and resentment. While I will outline very specific approaches to resolving grief and resentment, they need to be used incarnationally. **Don't fit the client to the exercises – adapt the exercises to fit the client.** Slavery to the exercises will not bring freedom or healing. Use the underlying principles to incarnationally innovate healing processes to meet the specific needs of the individual you are helping.

*Namaste:
I recognize that within each of us is a place where Divinity dwells, and when we are in that place, we are One.*
— *Hindu Expression*

Jesus did not come and impose salvation upon us. He came and lived as one of us.

Blessings that are imposed will be resisted and the person offering the assistance will be perceived as arrogant.

Let's hold rigidly to a flexible plan.

Locating Resources to Create Change

A person's performance of any task is dependent on multiple interrelated factors that are both external and internal to the individual. External resources are resources located in the environment. They may be tangible things like money or material, or intangibles such as location or community attitudes. Internal resources are the person's skills to perform the task and the person's motivation to engage their skills to achieve the goal.

To improve performance a person can change their environment, their skills, or their motivation. These factors are neither discrete nor independent. For example, we are usually more motivated to use well-developed skills that are likely to result in successful outcomes. The environment may also negatively or positively impact our motivation and ability to perform a skill.

When coaching a person we can use these three factors to help decide what resources the client needs to access to achieve their objective. For example, they may need to access environmental resources, or the internal resources of developing a skill or improving their motivation. The most efficient and effective place to intervene is where the most benefit for the least amount of effort can be achieved.

To help you understand these factors, I will apply them by example to the task of forgiving someone. Imagine if the client were to say that sometimes they can forgive, but sometimes it doesn't seem to work very well. The model provides three places to intervene.

Environmental Factors

When forgiving others one environmental factor may be the presence of family members who foster an attitude of resentment and become angry with the client if they forgive someone who injured another family member. From a wider environmental perspective, our culture is not predisposed to forgiving and puts a high value on revenge. This desire for revenge is often cloaked in morally primitive ideas of punitive justice rather than restorative justice, and does little to create a just society. In such a society, forgiveness is often seen as a sign of weakness. In these situations it may not be possible to create an environmental change, and the action of forgiving may be an action in defiance of these cultural norms. The client may also find it helpful to find a subculture within the wider culture that does value forgiveness.

The greatest resource is love.
Do you have enough love to do what you love?

If you find yourself riding a dead horse, the best strategy is to dismount.
— Dakota Indian Saying

An eye for an eye makes the whole world blind.
— Mahatma Gandhi

Other environmental factors may be the ongoing presence of an abuser that continues to evoke resentment. Staying in such an environment with a naïve hope that the abuse will stop is not helpful. Moving out of the environment will be a necessary precursor to forgiving.

Developing Skills

Despite living in a Judeo-Christian culture that puts a high value on forgiveness, we as individuals are generally very unskilled in our ability to forgive. As Steve Andreas has pointed out, Jesus often taught about the need to forgive but he never taught his hearers **how** to forgive[2]. Perhaps his hearers knew how to forgive and his disciples saw no need to record the details. Perhaps they were as clueless as we are and didn't ask how because they didn't want to appear ignorant. Regardless of the reason, we need to discover how to forgive if we are to have peace and love in our lives.

Personally, it was only after I was ordained that I was taught the specifics of how to forgive, and only in recent years – many years after I was licensed as a psychologist – that I learned ways to help people rapidly resolve resentment. Without these skills I and others normalized our spiritual poverty by saying that achieving forgiveness takes time (perhaps an entire lifetime!) and that in many situations the best we could do was simply "desire to forgive."

A large part of my motivation for writing this manual was to make the basic skills of forgiveness accessible to people in the helping professions. In the forgiveness section, I will present specific examples of what forgiveness is and isn't, and the skills a person needs to learn to achieve forgiveness.

Motivational Factors

Our basic lack of understanding of what forgiveness is and how to actually forgive radically diminishes our motivation to forgive. We are not stupid. We are not inclined to engage in something we know little about and have little expectation of successfully achieving a desired outcome. What I have discovered is that when people learn how to forgive and experience the relief and healing that comes from letting go of resentment, they will become highly motivated to incorporate forgiveness into the daily fabric of their lives.

In the forgiveness section we will look specifically at some of the objections to forgiving which reduce a person's motivation to engage in forgiving others. In this section, we will explore four different ways we can be motivated to engage in a specific behavior.

The Four Motivations

What motivates you to do what you do? Are you motivated to avoid pain or to pursue pleasure? Answering this question using "the four motivations"[3] – political, economic, emotional and spiritual – is one of many ways of looking at what drives human behavior. I will review the four motivations as they relate to three things: caring for the environment, resolving grief, and forgiving someone who has offended you.

Political Motivation

Often we do what we do because we are compelled by external forces to engage in that behavior. I call this a "political motivation." Underlying this political motivation is fear; we do what we do because we are afraid of a bad consequence for not doing what is demanded of us. Eventually, resentment and outward hostility will be manifested toward the source of the fear. If we are kept afraid for too long, the fear will crystallize as hate directed toward that which is frightening us. Fear-based motivation only results in further fear-based behavior from those affected – ourselves and others. The long-term consequence of living from this place of fear is resentment and, ultimately, hostility toward that which is evoking the fear.

Because of the potential for great discrepancy between our internal values and our outward behavior, politically-motivated or fear-based behavior will guarantee hypocrisy, burnout, cynicism, hate, and overall poor, unsustainable performance.

Examples: We may decide to care for the environment and not pour our waste engine oil down the drain because we want to avoid being fined. It's simply not worth the effort to "fight city hall." In reality we are not motivated to actually care for the environment; rather, we are motivated to avoid a bad outcome such as a fine. Such motivation results in hypocrisy, because our outward behavior is not consistent with our internal thoughts and feelings.

Being compelled by others to "get over" feelings of loss is an example of a political motivation to overcome grief. Our faith tradition may tell us that we "shouldn't grieve" because our loved one is in a better place, or that we should simply trust in God, and grieving is a sign of spiritual weakness. Denying or repressing grief to preserve an outward appearance of appropriate faith is an example of a political motivation. From my perspective they are also indications of

If we want an end to terrorism, then you and I must renounce using fear as a means to motivate anyone. When we use fear to motivate others or even ourselves we have become a terrorist in their lives and in our own.

What difference does it make to the dead, the orphans and the homeless, whether the mad destruction is wrought under the name of totalitarianism or the holy name of liberty or democracy?
— Mahatma Gandhi

a misunderstanding of the true meaning of faith that results in very unhelpful, rather than liberating, life experiences.

We may decide to forgive someone because our religious tradition teaches us that unless we forgive we will not be forgiven. Here we are not really interested in forgiving another person, we are motivated by our desire to avoid rejection or punishment by God. This is similar to a parent telling two siblings to forgive each other or they will be punished. Any forgiveness that is coerced through threat is likely to result in deeper resentment rather than genuine forgiveness. We cannot frighten people into loving acts.

At the same time as some may feel coerced to forgive, others may feel coerced not to forgive. We live in a society that is radically invested in the idea of punishment. We have a retributive rather than a restorative understanding of justice. Family members may say to a person who wants to forgive, "How could you forgive that person?" To avoid the threat of familial rejection the person holds onto the resentment rather than forgive.

Economic Motivation

When motivated from an economic perspective we apply a cost-benefit analysis to the behavior in question. We will engage in the behavior if we can see that the benefits outweigh the costs. We are not simply avoiding a potentially bad thing, such as punishment, because there is a positive advantage to us in doing the behavior.

Examples: We do not pour waste oil down the drain because we realize that we can sell the waste oil to a recycling company. Clearly the motivation is not really to care for the environment but to realize a profit. Fear is no longer the compelling emotion; however, the motivation is not one of love of the behavior but of the economic benefit of the behavior. Economic motivation is extrinsic motivation. It is entirely dependent on the presence of this external reward. If the reward is removed the behavior is likely to cease.

We may decide to "get over" our grief because it is simply too painful to carry. But this type of "getting over" by numbing out the pain means that we are unable to access the good memories of being loved. Without access to these memories from the past we will find it difficult to experience love in the present moment and establish new relationships. We may also find it hard to enter into new relationships because we are afraid that this person too will die and cause us a fresh repeat of this great sorrow and pain we are experiencing.

> *I object to violence because when it appears to do good, the good is only temporary; the evil it does is permanent.*
> — Mahatma Gandhi

> *Money can't buy you happiness but it does bring you a more pleasant form of misery.*
> — Spike Milligan

> *Forgiveness is primarily for our own sake, so that we no longer carry the burden of resentment. But to forgive does not mean we will allow injustice again.*
> — Jack Kornfield

We may decide to forgive someone because we realize the resentment we carry is burning ulcers in our stomach and it would be to our personal advantage to forgive. We forgive, not out of concern for the other, or our relationship, but out of a desire for the personal benefit that comes from being free of our pain. While not the compelling motivation, fear is still present, especially in regard to the fear of our ongoing pain if we don't forgive.

Emotional Motivation

We do what we do because we find joy or emotional satisfaction from the activity. Doing the behavior is personally pleasurable and has some intrinsic reward. We do what we do because we love doing it.

Examples: From the emotional motivation perspective we care for the environment because it gives us a sense of joy to experience the beauty of the world and to leave it better than we found it for others to enjoy. We may enjoy planting trees on Arbor Day with our children because we value the beauty of the environment and want to instill that value in them so that their children can also enjoy this beauty.

An emotional motivation to resolve our grief is a desire to be able to remember our loved one with gratitude and love rather than with a sense of sadness and misery. From this place of gratitude and love we are able to use these memories as resources for building a new future and being open to new ways in which we can love and be loved.

We may forgive because we remember back to a time of joy in a relationship and we look forward to the possibility of joy in the relationship again. If we forgive the person then together we might regain the joy we had in our relationship.

Spiritual Motivation

Spirituality is about being aware of being connected to something greater than ourselves and that which is the Source of our Life. Spiritually-motivated behavior flows from the depths of our being that is one with this Source of Life. The word "enthusiasm" means to "be in God" (from the Greek en- "in" + theos "god") and spiritually-motivated actions often have a profound quality of enthusiasm. We do what we do because it is who we are, we **cannot not** do it. Spiritually-motivated behaviors result in "flow state" or being "in the zone." The behavior flows from the depths of our being in a way that leads to a humble, rather than arrogant, satisfaction and joy.

You must be the change you wish to see in the world.
— Mahatma Gandhi

If you want to build a ship, then don't drum up people to gather wood, give orders, and divide the work. Rather teach them to yearn for the far and endless sea.
— Antoine de Saint-Exupéry

The most beautiful things in the world cannot be seen with the eyes, but only with the human heart.
— Helen Keller

Spiritually-motivated activity seems effortless, energizing, and creative. While potentially physically tiring, at the end of the day, you may sleep with a deep sense of satisfaction knowing that you will awake refreshed and inspired to do it all over again. You love what you are doing and when you are in your zone you are aware that you have a greater love not only for yourself and the people you work with but for all of humanity.

Spiritual motivation generally requires some kind of transformational experience. Enlightenment, being "born again," and awakening are all expressions that relate to the transformational experiences that result in spiritual motivation. It is in these experiences that we discover the timeless or eternal nature of things like love and peace, and while we may have loved and been loved by someone in a temporal context, the essential nature of love is eternal and will never end.

Examples: Imagine that you are wandering through the giant Sequoia forests of California. You come to a huge stump left after the early loggers plundered the forest. Some trees were cut down simply because the lumberjack wanted the record of cutting down the biggest tree in the forest. As you look at the stump you feel a great sadness. It is as though part of you was cut down when the tree was cut down. In that moment you know that in order for you to survive, the environment must survive, for you are one – you and the environment are inseparable. It is from that moment of awareness that you realize that you don't "have to" care for the environment; rather, you profoundly know you **cannot not** care for the environment. This caring is not a burden of responsibility imposed by others but an expression of your connection to all things. You care for the world around you just as you care for yourself because you and the environment are one.

In the realm of the Spirit we do not grieve, because we are aware that we still have the person's love in our life today. We know that we no longer experience their physical, temporal presence, but we can experience their love which knows no time limit and over which death has no power.

We forgive others because we **cannot not** forgive. We know that at the heart of the universe is a Heart of Love and that we are forgiven, loved, and one with that Heart. It would be impossible for that Heart not to forgive. You do not "have" to love, it naturally and freely flows from that Heart to you and through you to the world.

Love empowers action. Love is never one thing. On the path of life, love is the beginning and the end, and the light along the way.

We are not human beings having a spiritual experience, we are spiritual beings having a human experience.
— Teilhard de Chardin

Love cannot remain by itself – it has no meaning. Love has to be put into action and that action is service.
— Mother Theresa

In loving, you become a living, breathing manifestation of the One Heart of Love in the universe.

The Land of Fear and Shoulds

Political and economical motivations are dominated by fear and "should" thinking. Should-based thinking is primarily concerned with how people think of us. While it may seem that we are concerned for others when we feel the pressure of a "should" or "ought," a careful exploration of our inner thought patterns will reveal that our major concern is what other people think of us. For example, much of my caring in the early years of my ministry was motivated by a desire to be seen by parishioners as a caring priest, rather than being motivated by a selfless concern for their well-being.

Fear-based motivations may result in immediate increases in performance, but over time will degrade into resentment, burnout, and diminished returns. Such behaviors are rarely sustainable because they depend on external rewards. When the external reward is removed the behavior is likely to cease. Fear-based motivations also result in resentment and hatred toward the external oppressor.

Fear is also a very poor motivation, especially when it is connected to an addictive behavior such as smoking or drinking. Most people who engage in addictive behavior do so in part to deal with feelings of anxiety. Making an addict afraid will actually drive them to their addiction rather than empower them to refrain from the addiction. Since guilt results from a fear of punishment, making an addict feel guilty or ashamed for their behavior will actually encourage their addiction.

If we want sustainable outcomes, then we need to find love-based motivations that begin with acceptance, rather than fear-based motivations that deepen patterns of alienation.

The Land of Love, Joy, and Hope

In contrast to the fear-based political and economic motivations, the emotional and spiritual motivations are love-based. Love-based motivations are sustainable because they have their own intrinsic reward that leaves people feeling purposeful, deeply satisfied and joyful.

This joy is an abiding joy that is beyond emotion. When I think of happiness and joy two images come to my mind. My wife Kim and I heat our house with a wood stove. I can create a fire with paper. It

If you try to motivate people by lighting a fire under them, all you will get is burnt butts.

A more enlightened way to motivate people is to find the fire within them and fan it.

To work without love is slavery.
— *Mother Theresa*

If you haven't found the place deep inside where you cannot not do what you do, keep looking for that which you cannot not do, and go do that.

If you don't, you will simply waste your God-given potential, rob society of your gifts, and make yourself and the world around you miserable.

burns fiercely, giving off great heat, but is soon gone. Alternatively, I can create a fire with dry hardwood. It may not blaze as high, but it becomes a large collection of glowing coals that gives off heat over a longer period of time. These glowing coals are like an abiding joy – they provide a sustaining warmth. They are not a whipped-up frenzy of happiness that will soon die down and leave you shivering. While the spiritual realm is undergirded with a feeling of emotional well-being, it also transcends emotion, just as the glowing coals transcend flames.

Think about the kind of future you want. The path to that future must be consistent with the future you desire. If we want to have love and joy in our future our path today must be the path of love. While it has become politically correct to say that "all paths lead to God," I think the basic idea is wrong. If you want to find the God of Love then you need to get on the path of love. The path of fear and resentment will not lead to the God of Love, but to the gods of tyranny and oppression.

Growing from Fear to Love

No motive is ever completely pure, depending on the context and our awareness, we are prone to all the motivations. However, in the things we spend most of our time and energy doing, we need to consistently derive our motivation from the emotional and spiritual realms if our efforts are to be sustainable.

While hope and fear are responses to how we image the future, love is about how we experience and live in the present moment. When we become afraid we need to use that as an indicator that we have lost the path of love. Re-finding the path of love, rather than trying to understand why we lost it and became afraid, becomes the appreciative goal.

In the next section I will return to the idea of "creating a path of love" after I have presented some core concepts and processes that we can use to understand our experience and develop specific strategies to restore people to hope.

The Statue of Liberty is no longer saying, "Give me your poor, your tired, your huddled masses." She's got a baseball bat and is yelling, "You want a piece of me?"
— Robin Williams

The path of fear and resentment will not lead to the God of Love but to the gods of tyranny and oppression.

2: RESTORING HOPE: CORE PROCESSES AND RESOURCES

Hope is the ability to imagine a tomorrow that you find enjoyable and life-giving and to know that you have the resources to achieve that preferred future.

To have hope we need to pay attention to three things:

- the way we image the future
- knowing what is truly life-giving
- our confidence in our ability to access resources to achieve our preferred future

While hope is how we imagine the future, the imaging is done in the present, and hope is something we experience in the present moment. In this section we will explore how we image or represent experiences in our consciousness.

To have hope we need to know what is truly life-giving and be able to distinguish it from those things that are incapable of giving life. Life-giving qualities such as love, peace, acceptance, etc. are timeless or eternal; they existed before us and they will exist after us. We experience these timeless qualities in specific temporal ways. A friend may be a temporal manifestation of the timeless quality of love and acceptance. While the friend did not give us life, we shared life with them.

To have hope we need to hold and be held by this timeless quality rather than clinging to its temporal manifestation. Idolatry occurs when we view this temporal manifestation as the source of the timeless quality. Clinging to the temporal expression of a timeless quality will result in fear of loss and grief if we do lose it. In this section we will explore how we imagine, and then we will explore strategies to distinguish a timeless quality from its temporal expression.

Having confidence in our ability to access life-giving resources in the future raises the issue of realistic hope and unhelpful hope. There is a world of difference between a naïve hope based on avoiding anything unpleasant and expecting the future to work out without any action on our part, and a hope based on the quiet assurance that comes from reflecting on our memory that we have come through tough times in the past and we will be able to meet the challenges that come our way. Because faith is often linked to hope, we will explore issues of a realistic hope, and helpful and unhelpful experiences of faith, at the end of this section.

I have one life and one chance to make it count for something ...
I'm free to choose what that something is, and the something I've chosen is my faith.
Now, my faith goes beyond theology and religion and requires considerable work and effort.
My faith demands
– this is not optional –
my faith demands that I do whatever I can,
wherever I am,
whenever I can,
for as long as I can
with whatever I have
to try to make a difference.
— Jimmy Carter

When it comes
to the future,
there are three
kinds of people:
those who let it happen,
those who make it happen,
and those who wonder
what happened.
— John M. Richardson, Jr.

Fearful Imagining

Anxiety is what we experience in the present moment when we imagine the future and cannot imagine having the resources to meet a perceived demand. The intensity of the fear response is dependent on how life-threatening we perceive the demand. While essential for protection and survival, our fear responses are often unrelated to physical survival issues. The fear of rejection may have its origins in physical survival, when it meant being banished from the tribe and consequently from basic essentials such as food and protection. In today's world, rejection is rarely a survival issue, yet it still can evoke a powerful fear response. Exploring the perception of threats and whether they are currently realistic may be helpful. Discovering the resources you need to feel assured and confident in the face of threats will be essential if you are to live hopefully.

Anxiety is always anticipatory. It is a response to a future threat, which may be years or only moments away. It is interesting to note that many people in the midst of great danger are unaware of fear. It is only after the event that they report fear. The relationship between anticipation and ongoing distress from traumatic events will be explored in more detail in the resolving painful memories section.

Hopelessness, Depression and Suicidality

Hopelessness can occur for several reasons. If we are unable to imagine a life-giving future, or alternatively if we can imagine a preferred future but have little confidence we can achieve it, then we will feel hopeless. If our past has been traumatic we are likely to imagine that similar bad things will happen again, so the future we imagine will be neither appealing nor hopeful.

While often found together, depression and hopelessness may or may not be related. Not all depressed people feel hopeless, and not all people who experience hopelessness are depressed. Aaron Beck's research on suicidality found that suicide is correlated to feelings of hopelessness and not specifically to depression[1]. Some depressed people are not perturbed by thoughts of the future and express little sense of hopelessness. On the other hand, people who may not be depressed may suddenly feel very hopeless when facing a calamity, such as the stock market crashing, and become instantly suicidal.

When helping clients deal with overwhelming feelings of hopelessness it is important to inquire about suicidal ideation and possible suicide plans, and to take steps to ensure the client's safety.

> If you believe
> that feeling bad
> or worrying long enough
> will change a past
> or future event
> you are residing
> on another planet with a
> different reality system.
> — William James

> A problem is only a
> solution that is
> not working very well.
> — Andy Austin

> I tried to drown
> my sorrows,
> but the bastards
> learned how to swim.
> — Frida Kahlo

How We Experience Our Experiences

There are three interrelated elements to the way we experience and respond to an event[2]:

- **The content of the event.**
  These are the objective facts of what occurred. They are the things that a video recorder would record.

- **How the event was perceived.**
  Consider how a blind or deaf person may have experienced the same event. Would the content of the event be different to them, or would only their experience be different? Likewise, as shown in our discussion on focus, each person experiencing the event will focus on different aspects of it. *How* the event was perceived is affected by the personal characteristics of the perceiver.

- **The meaning or interpretation put on the event.**
  Our interpretation involves comparing the current experience with past experiences, and predicting how this current experience will impact our future.

Based on these three elements we will then decide how to respond. Our response is typically made up of two components:

- an internal emotion or feeling
- an external action or behavior

For example, if a man is standing in front of us with a knife, we see the man with the knife, we interpret the event as a threat to our personal safety, we feel afraid, and we run from the man.

While I have presented this sequence in a linear fashion, the process is synergistic with multiple feedback loops. Our interpretation of an event changes what we pay attention to, which then changes our behaviors. These behaviors will also impact the event so that we are not simply an objective observer but part of the event itself. If others are in the event they will be going through their own set of perceiving, interpreting, and responding, which are also likely to impact our subsequent response patterns.

We Never Deal With Reality

From the previous discussion it can be seen that when we feel and act we are never dealing with reality, we are always dealing with a perception of reality that is then interpreted in the light (or perhaps darkness) of our prior experiences. This explains why two people or

---

The test of a first-rate intelligence is the ability to hold two opposed ideas in the mind at the same time, and still retain the ability to function. One should, for example, be able to see that things are hopeless and yet be determined to make them otherwise.
— F. Scott Fitzgerald

The problem is not the problem. The problem is all the attempted solutions to the problem.
— Virginia Satir

The map is not the territory.
— Alfred Korzybski

---

groups of people can have such radically different responses to the same event. While responding to the same event, they are perceiving and interpreting the event in different ways.

Sometimes our response to events is so rapid that there is very little conscious cognitive processing. It is only after the event that we can reflect on the experience and analyze what happened. Yet even this analysis in the present moment of a past experience is also impacted by this sequence of perception and interpretation. When telling the story of what happened we will actually be engaged in re-perceiving the event.

Changing the Way We Respond

When an event has troubling, ongoing consequences for a person they may seek the help of a coach or therapist. The troubling consequences are most likely to be either the feelings the event continues to evoke when the event is remembered, or an undesired behavior in response to the event. For example, a person may continue to feel anxious and avoid the place where the event took place, or avoid other places that evoke the same memories and anxieties. To help a client create change in response to an event, there are five areas the coach can focus on:

- The objective content of the event.
- How the event is re-perceived in the present.
- The interpretation of the event.
- The feelings the event evokes.
- Learning new behaviors.

Changing the Content

We cannot change the past. If we tried changing the actual content of what happened then we would be engaged in a process of delusion. We can, however, widen the scope of how we view the content by adding what happened just prior to the event or just after. Knowing the "rest of the story" can change our interpretation of the event.

For example, we may have felt threatened and subsequently resentful toward someone who had been angry and yelling at us. Upon learning that the person was not angry with us specifically, but had just come from a situation in which they had felt threatened, may change our interpretation of their intentions toward us. This in turn may change our feelings of resentment and we may act compassionately toward them.

Optimist: someone who isn't sure whether life is a tragedy or a comedy but is tickled silly just to be in the play.
— Robert Brault

Whatever your past has been, you have a spotless future.
— Unknown

Lots of people talk to animals ... Not very many listen, though ... That's the problem.
— Benjamin Hoff

Denying or intentionally avoiding the content of the event because it evokes distressing feelings is usually unhelpful. It takes energy to deny something. Active denial or avoidance always means that the avoided thing is in consciousness. It is like trying not to think of a purple cow. The harder you try not to think of the purple cow, the more the purple cow occupies your consciousness.

Denial also impairs social relationships with others who experienced the same event. The "elephant in the room" phenomena is a form of collective intentional denial. Such denial breaks down trust and will render the group impotent when trying to make decisions.

The specific content of the event is actually outside of the client and is beyond the client's control. While we can't change the actual content, what we can do is help the client to remember the content without distress and to make decisions and act in ways they freely choose. This means we have to pay attention to the things that are internal to the client which they do have control over, such as their perceptions, interpretations, feelings and actions.

Changing How the Event is Perceived

Most therapies pay little attention to *how* the event was perceived, and how it is being re-perceived as the person remembers the event. Instead, the focus is placed on the interpretations, or the feelings, or the behaviors associated with the event. Yet many clients actually tell their coaches that they want to "see" things differently. In such cases the client is asking for help to change the way they perceive the event.

Steve Andreas and others have shown that changing *how* we experience and re-experience an event in consciousness is a powerful strategy to change what we feel about the event and our subsequent behaviors. Changing this "how" is a foundational aspect to the strategies I will provide on resolving grief and resentment, and we will return to this process at the end of this section.

Changing the Interpretation

Human beings are meaning makers. We do not simply experience events, we compare and contrast them to other events we have experienced, and then create meaning. "The man with the knife" is interpreted as a threat which leads to self-protective measures. Without this interpretation these measure would not be taken.

Interpretation is not solely about past events; it also includes predictions about what will happen in the future. A person who has

You better cut the pizza in four pieces because I'm not hungry enough to eat six.
— Yogi Berra

Turn your face to the sun and the shadows fall behind you.
— Maori Proverb

Some people are always grumbling because roses have thorns; I am thankful that thorns have roses.
— Alphonse Karr

experienced abuse in the past may interpret the event as meaning they will experience more abuse in the future. A large part of some therapies focus on clarifying these interpretations and seeing whether alternative interpretations can be made, especially the predictive interpretations about the future. It is however hard to hold an alternative interpretation as "true" when the person is swamped with distressing emotions that conflict with the interpretation.

Changing the Feelings

Many therapies spend considerable time talking about the feelings related to the troubling event. Some of these feelings, especially feelings of fear and hate, can be self-alienating when the client says "I hate feeling this way." In this situation the problem isn't the troubling feeling, but rather how the client is feeling **about** the feeling they are having. Finding a supportive environment to talk about troubling feelings can be healing when it helps the person own and accept these troubling feelings as a part of who they are and not the totality of who they are.

However endless talking about feelings will likely lead a client to reinforce the negative interpretations and their associated feelings. Talking about being a victim and its associated feelings of helplessness will simply reinforce the experience of victimization. It will not lead to healing and transformation. To find healing, people need to move from talking about their feelings and re-experiencing these feelings.

It is a rare person who can simply change the way they feel about an event. It seems that feelings have a mind of their own. They are only likely to change if the interpretation is changed. Sometimes changing your behavior by "acting as if" you felt differently will lead to a change in feelings. While "fake it until you make it" may work, it can also be experienced as very hypocritical, and may require lots of energy to sustain the motivation before the feelings change. It is not something I would encourage.

Changing the Behaviors

This is where we learn and practice new responses and behaviors. For example, a person may learn to be assertive and grow a sense of confidence and assurance when dealing with a troublesome individual. With these assertiveness skills learned, they can rely on their assertiveness rather than resentment to provide boundaries between themselves and a troublesome individual. However, if the underlying feelings of resentment are not resolved, the assertiveness skills may be used as an act of angry aggression that continues to compound the problem rather than creating a lasting solution.

One of the common strategies to learn a new skill is role rehearsal. The person uses their imagination to respond in the new way in a future situation. However, it is difficult to image behaving in a different way when the feelings prompting the old behavior patterns are still present. Feeling miserable usually blunts a person's creativity. Without a personal sense of creativity, trying to learn a new behavior can make the task a difficult challenge. The new behaviors may feel inauthentic when done in opposition to their associated feelings. Alternatively, the new behaviors may be difficult to engage in because they are devoid of any motivating emotion.

To live in hope means that a person can imagine feeling and behaving in the future in ways that are positive and life-affirming. To accomplish this we will need to help them change how they feel, not only about their future, but also about their past, since past events can contaminate their experience of both the present moment and their sense of the future.

Re-Membering Experiences in Consciousness

Most of us take for granted the way we experience reality. We don't pay much attention to **how** we actually experience things. For example, we may see a tree, but we do not have the actual tree in our mind. What we have is a representation of the tree in our mind. Beyond the experience of the present moment, have you considered how you represent memories of past events in your mind? The word "remember" is made of two parts: "re" and "member." The word means to put back together, in consciousness, a prior experience. Likewise, when you imagine a future event, how do you image that event? How do you represent or structure that future event in consciousness?

In the following section we will explore how we perceive an event in consciousness and then how we structure or represent past and future events in consciousness. In these exercises you will develop some of the basic skills of discovering and changing how we represent or structure experiences in consciousness. Modifying the representational structure of our experiences will be a core strategy in the processes to resolve grief and resentment.

We are not interested in explaining or excusing yesterday.

We are interested in discovering the best of the past and the present in order to fuel our imaginations and gather the resources we need to build the future.

Life is one fool thing after another whereas love is two fool things after each other.
— Oscar Wilde

When people are laughing, they're generally not killing one another.
— Alan Alda

Instructions: This exercise will explore how you experience and interpret the present moment.

1. **Focus on the Present Moment**

   Take a few moments to be in the present moment. Set aside any concerns about tasks that you may need to do and simply allow yourself to become fully aware of your surroundings.

2. **Visual Senses**

   What are you seeing? Take time to look at the things in your surroundings ...

   To heighten your visual awareness become aware of everything that is red in color ...

   Now pay attention to everything that is blue in color ...

   Now pay attention to everything that is green in color ...

   Be aware of the shading and intensity of colors ...

   Focus intensely on one object and allow other things to fade into the periphery of your vision ...

   Contrast that narrow focus by taking in everything and see it all as a montage ...

3. **Auditory Senses**

   What are you hearing? ...

   Notice the quality of any sounds ...

   Are there different sounds coming from different locations? ...

4. **Physical Senses**

   What sensations are you experiencing in your body? Are you warm, cold, tense? ...

   Are different parts of your body experiencing different sensations? ...
   For example, is one part of your body warm and another cold? ...

   What emotions are you having? ...

   Notice that the label we give an emotion such as "happy" is an abstraction applied to a set of physical sensations. Can you distinguish between the physical sensations and the label?

5. **Olfactory and Gustatory Senses**

   What are you smelling? Are there multiple aromas that you can distinguish? ...

   What are you tasting? ...

6. **Reflection**

   Be aware that the reality that you are observing is not inside your mind. What you have is a representation of that reality in your mind. For example, if you are seeing a tree, you don't have the tree in your mind, you have a visual representation of the tree in your mind ...

   Pay attention to the distinction between a sensation and an interpretation of the sensation ...

   What interpretations are you making about what you observe? ...

   Are there alternative interpretations? ...
   (For example, as I write this I am sitting in my rather cluttered office. I can interpret that to mean that I am an untidy person, or I can interpret it as a sign that I am really focused and in the flow of writing.)

Instructions: This exercise will explore how you represent or "structure" a memory of a past event in consciousness. For the purposes of learning I suggest you remember a pleasant memory. Later we will explore how you represent a painful event in consciousness.

1. **The Content of the Event**

   Go back in time several years and recall a pleasurable event.

   Where did it happen? ...

   What did you do? ...

   Who were you with? ...

   What did they do? ...

   What did you do as a result of the experience? ...

   What you are remembering is the content or the story of the experience.

2. **The Structure of the Memory**

   *Pay attention to **how** you are "re-membering" as distinct from **what** you are remembering.*

   Are you recalling the event in pictures? ...

   If you are recalling the event visually:

   > *Are they still pictures or is it a video? ...*

   > *Are they in color or black and white? ...*

   > *How sharp or clear or intense are the pictures? ...*

   Are you recalling and hearing any sounds? ...

   Can you hear the conversations that were part of the event? ...

   Are the sounds clear or muffled? ...

   Notice any physical sensations that you had at the time that you are having now as you remember the event. Note any difference between remembering what you felt and re-experiencing what you felt in this present moment ...

   Are you recalling any smells or tastes that you associate with this experience? ...

   Spatial Awareness: Some people don't have clear pictures or sounds of an event but may have a clear "sense" of what happened. That sense includes things like physical location, such as, "I was on their right," or a sense of size, as in, "I sense that the other person is a lot bigger than me." Pay attention to any spatial sense that you have of the event ...

3. **Current Feelings You Have as You Remember**

   What are you feeling emotionally as you remember the event? ...

4. **Changing the Structure**

   Knowing that you can always change it back, take some time to change elements of the structure and observe what happens to your current emotion. For example: If you have color pictures, change them to black and white (or vice versa) and note how your emotion changes ...

   Change the size of the pictures and note what happens to your current emotion ...

   Change the volume of the sounds and note what happens to your current emotion ...

   Change the representation back to the way that seems right to you ...

Remembering, Imagining, and Visualization

For most people, the visual representational system is their best-developed and most resourceful sense. For example, most people can process multiple images simultaneously (as in a montage) while in contrast they find it difficult to process multiple sounds simultaneously, such as when two people are talking at the same time. Because the visual representational system is highly refined, we will use visualization as a primary strategy in the healing processes for resolving grief and resentment. However, while many people are visually adept, some people will initially find it difficult.

My Personal Struggle to Visualize

I personally do not "see" pictures, at least initially when doing these kinds of exercises. While I don't have a clear picture, of many events I do have a strong "sense" of what transpired. When I focus on my sense of different events I can make subtle distinctions between them; for example, some events seem clear while others are fuzzy.

I am also able to make quite specific distinctions in my spatial awareness of where my sense of somebody is located in my mental space. Some people "seem" very close when I remember them and others "seem" far away.

When working with clients, this sense of location will be more important than whether they can clearly visualize them. We will explore this sense of spatial awareness in the next exercise.

Strategies to Help Visualizing and Imagining

Here are several strategies to help a client who is struggling to visualize:

- Invite the client to imagine rather than visualize. Visualizing is a subset of imagining. Get them to reflect on how they imagine. Affirm that however they imagine is just fine.

- Invite the client to "sense" the presence of an individual rather than visualize the presence. Many people who struggle to visualize have well-developed kinesthetic ways of experiencing and will have a strong "sense" of another person.

- Invite the client to remember any conversations and the tone, volume, and direction the sounds appear to be coming from when they remember the conversation.

People and organizations grow toward their images of the future.
— David Cooperrider

Imagination is more important than knowledge. Knowledge is limited.
— Albert Einstein

We are all agreed that your theory is crazy. The question that divides us is whether it is crazy enough to have a chance of being correct.
— Neils Bohr

- When the client is worried that they cannot do the exercise, invite them to really worry about failing and remember other times they have failed and how terrible it would be to fail doing this exercise. When they are truly in the midst of a good worry, stop them and invite them to use the mental machinery they are using to worry in the next exercise, by explaining that "worry is pure imagination." If someone can worry, then they have the mental equipment needed to do these exercises.

Here is a brief exercise you can use to help clients identify their sensing process:

> Take a moment and remember a happy home that you have lived in ...
> As you recall that home, remember how many windows were in the house ...
> As you are determining the number of windows, reflect on whether you are walking around the inside of the house, or around the outside, to count the windows ...

Most people will be processing some form of visual representation to create an image of the house in order to count the windows. The picture they have may not be very clear, but it will be sufficiently detailed to allow the windows to be counted. Rather than evaluating the clarity of their pictures, invite the person to use their way of imagining as they proceed with the exercises.

I have found that people who cannot readily visualize can quite readily respond to this request:

> "Well, just imagine you do have a picture, such as a snapshot, and work with the picture that you imagine you would have if you were able to visualize the person."

The client can then be invited to describe the picture that they imagine they would have.

While I personally don't "get" clear pictures in my imagination, I can imagine having a picture of an individual. As I imagine having a picture I can then begin to describe the color of the person's clothes, and in this way be led into perceiving a clear picture.

In the next exercise we will explore how you structurally locate and organize experiences in your mental space.

Worry is pure imagination. Anxiety occurs when we look into the future and perceive that we don't have the resources to prevent something bad from happening.

"If you mean the demon drink that poisons the mind, pollutes the body, desecrates family life, and inflames sinners, then I'm against it.
But if you mean the elixir of Christmas cheer, the shield against winter chill, the taxable potion that puts needed funds into public coffers to comfort little crippled children, then I'm for it. This is my position and I will not compromise."
— A Congressman debating whiskey and prohibition.

Instructions: In this exercise we will compare and contrast how you structure in consciousness two people, one who you care about, and another who you do not feel caring toward.

1. **Structuring in Consciousness the Person You Care About**
   Take a moment and think of a person that you care about, whose company you really enjoy ... Think about their characteristics, or the content (they are funny, caring, creative, warm, etc.) of what you enjoy about them ...

   As you recall them, close your eyes and allow yourself to have a sense of the person. You might "see" a picture of them, or you may just have a "sense" of the person.
   Regardless of how you are imaging the person, point to where your sense of the person is located. For example, are they out in front of you, alongside you, to the left or to the right? ...

   This may seem strange at first but most people will have a clear sense of where their sense of the person is located in their "mental space" ...
   Take some time to note the location in your mental space of the person as you recall them ...

   (Note: By "location" I am not meaning where an event with the person took place, but where your sense of the person is located in your consciousness or mental space.)

   Open your eyes and distract yourself from that person.

2. **Structuring in Consciousness the Person You Don't Care About**
   Now recall a person that you don't like or really care about ...
   Be aware of the content of why you don't like them ...
   As you recall them, close your eyes and point to where they are located in your mental space ...

3. **Comparing The Difference in Structure**
   Now recall both people simultaneously and compare their locations within your mental space ...
   Notice any differences in locations ...
   Which one is closer to you? ...

4. **Reflection**
   Most people will say that the person they like and care about is closer to them, or that the person they don't care about is more distant. This parallels our common language: "I feel really close to them." Or, "We were once close but we seem to be really distant from each other."

   Sometimes people will report the opposite response: that the people they don't care for are much closer because they need to "keep an eye on them."

5. **The Language of Structure**
   The language we use to describe events often has these structural references. Taking these descriptors literally rather than metaphorically and then changing the structure is a powerful strategy for resolving grief and resentment. Here are some common structural expressions:

   I need to put this behind me.
   You seem to be distant.
   On the one hand I feel ... on the other hand I feel ...
   He's really way out.
   I need to get over this.

Representing Experiences in Consciousness

In the previous exercises we explored **how** we experience an event in consciousness, independent of the content of the event.

We have seen that the five cores senses (sight, sound, touch, smell, and taste) that we use to sense and experience a present event are also used to represent a memory of an event in consciousness.

People often report verbally how they are representing something in consciousness. For example:

- Visual: "I see how that would work."
- Auditory: "I really hear what you are saying."
- Touch or Kinesthetic: "This just feels like a solid idea to me."
- Olfactory: "I really stink at doing this."
- Gustatory: "It was a really sweet moment."

Within each modality there are submodalities, such as size, intensity, direction, location, and clarity. Different people will also have a preference for different representational systems. For example, some people are very visual and report their experiences in visual terms. Others may be auditory and can accurately recall conversations and what they have heard, while others are kinesthetic and report a "sense" of what happened.

In addition to the language they use, people may also reveal which representational system they are using by the direction their eyes move. In general, but not always, a person's eyes will move up when they are accessing or imagining visually, horizontally or down to the left when accessing or imagining sounds, and down to the right when accessing kinesthetic experiences. The study of eye movement can become quite a detailed skill; however, I have found that people can do very effective work with a client's grief and resentment without this specific expertise.

Modifying How We Structure Events in Consciousness

Since we cannot change the content of the past, we need to change how we represent the past in current consciousness to create changes in the way we feel about the past. Modifying how we structure or represent things in consciousness is a key strategy that we will use to help people resolve grief and resentment.

In the next exercise we will explore how we imagine a future event and the impact of modifying the structure of our imagery.

You can see a lot just by observing.
— *Yogi Berra*

The color of our skin may be different, but the color of our blood, sweat, and tears is the same.
— *Unknown*

Keep your friends close, your enemies closer and your wallets even closer.
— *Joette Rockow*

Representing the Future

Instructions: In the previous exercise we looked at how you represented a memory in consciousness. Now we will explore how you imagine, or represent in consciousness, a future event.

1. **Create a Goal**

   Think of something that you would like to achieve in the future ...

   Before doing the exercise take a moment and determine on a 0-10 scale how successful you think you will be in achieving this goal ...

   Imagine you have achieved the goal ...

   Tell yourself the story of how you achieved the goal ...

   *This is the content of your imagined experience. Now we will explore **how** you are imagining.*

2. **The Structure of Your Imagination**

   *Pay attention to **how** you are imagining as distinct from **what** you are imagining.*

   Are you imagining achieving the goal visually? Can you "see" yourself achieving the goal? ...

   If you are imagining the event visually:
   > *Are they still pictures or is it a video? ...*
   > *Are they in color or black and white? ...*
   > *How sharp or clear or intense are the pictures? ...*

   Are you imagining any sounds as you work to accomplish the goal? ...
   > *Can you hear conversations that were part of the event? ...*
   > *Are the sounds clear or muffled? ...*

   Notice any physical sensations that you are having as you imagine the goal ...

   As you imagine achieving the goal, are you imagining how you will be feeling? ...

   Are you imagining any smells or tastes that you associate with this experience? ...

   Spatial Awareness: Close your eyes and notice the location of your sense of the goal ...
   > *As you imagine the goal is it to your right or left, or in front or behind you etc ...*
   > *How far away from you is your sense of the goal? ...*
   > *Does it seem far away or near? ...*

   Having observed the structure of your imagination, has your expectation of success changed?

3. **Changing the Structure**

   Knowing that you can always change it back, take some time to change elements of the structure of your imagination and observe what happens to your expectation of success.

   Increase and decrease the size and color intensity of your goal images ...

   Play with making it a movie or still pictures ...

   Move your sense of the of the goal closer or further away ...

   If it seems far away, can you imagine several intermediate goals that lead to the final goal? ...

   Change the structure so that your expectation of success is at its greatest and feels right to you.

Representing Time: Past, Present, and Future

In the previous exercises we explored how we represent the present moment in consciousness by using our five senses. We then explored how we use similar processes to remember the past and imagine the future. In the exercise "representing the future" we began to explore the impact of modifying the structure or the way we represent our experiences in consciousness. Most readers will have discovered that they can increase their expectancy of success simply by changing the way they represent things in their consciousness. This parallels a common expression in our language: "I see things in a new way."

Since hope is about imagining the future, *how* we imagine will often be more important than *what* we imagine in determining whether we will feel hopeful. Aligning how and what we imagine will ensure that we can create a realistic, robust, and reliable sense of hope.

While hope is about how we image the future, the biggest influences on those images are our past experiences. Unresolved events, even though they occurred in the past, are alive in our present awareness and can negatively impact our images of the future and consequently our ability to feel hopeful. How we represent time and represent our experiences with respect to time will also be important processes to understand as we develop processes to resolve things from our past that are still alive and negatively impacting our present.

Our language reflects some of the ways we structure events in consciousness with respect to time. For example, events from our childhood may be "a long way back" while things that are about to happen are "close to happening."

In addition to having temporal experiences that are located in time, we can also experience timeless realities like love. Experiences and qualities that are not limited by time are eternal. Learning how we perceive and structure these timeless or eternal qualities in our temporal awareness will also be a core process in restoring hope.

On the next page is an exercise to explore how you structure your experience of time. This is followed by an exercise to distinguish an eternal or timeless quality from its temporal manifestation. These exercises will form a set of resources to resolve distressing memories and grief.

*Forgiveness is giving up
the possibility
of a better past.*
— Unknown

*Everything we value
comes to us in a vehicle.
Problems arise
when we confuse
the value with the vehicle.*

*Truth is eternal,
knowledge is changeable.
It is disastrous
to confuse them.*
— Madeleine L'Engle

Representing Time

Instructions: This exercise is designed to help you discover and understand how you personally organize and structure your internal experience of time.

1. **Identifying the Past, Present and Future.**
   Take some time to find three pictures in your mind:

   i. *A picture from your past (at least several years ago) of some pleasant memorable event ...*

   ii. *A picture from your present or very recent past of some pleasant memorable event ...*

   iii. *A picture from your future of an anticipated pleasant memorable event ...*

2. **Identifying the Past, Present and Future.**
   Look at the three pictures simultaneously and pay attention to how you have organized them with respect to their location in your personal mental space ...

   Have you sequenced "past," "present," and "future" from left to right, or right to left, or from back to front, or top to bottom? ...

   How do you know from their arrangement, rather than their content, that one picture represents the past, another the present, and the other the future? ...

3. **Reflection.**
   Many people, but not all by any means, will sequence the pictures left to right, past to future. Others may have the future ahead of them and the past behind them. Others may arrange time in a circular rather than a linear fashion. While it can be helpful in some situations to alter the way we structure our experience of time, that is beyond the scope of this exercise. At this point we just need to know how you represent your past, present, and future.

   If you want, you can try sequencing them in some other order just to understand how you organize your internal experience of time. Most people will have a sense of "it's not right" if they alter the sequence. After experimenting, just allow your pictures to return to their "right place."

4. **Creating Your Timeline.**
   Add more pictures to your past, present, and future to create a personal history or timeline. The future pictures will be of you doing things that you are planning to do or imagine doing ...

5. **Contrast Analysis of Your Timeline.**
   Once you have filled in your timeline take a look at the pictures and, without paying attention to their content, determine how you know something occurred before or after an event ...

   Do the pictures vary by location or sequence? Older pictures may be further out or more distant from your viewing place.

   Do the pictures vary by color? Older pictures may be smaller, faded, or less intense with respect to color than more recent pictures. Notice any other differences ...

6. **Experimenting with Your Position on the Timeline.**
   Feel what it is like to go back in time and stand on your time line, looking forward toward events that have already occurred ...

   Now go into the future to the time when you have achieved a future goal. Look back and see what you did to achieve the goal ...

Instructions: In this set of exercises you will explore the differences between an eternal, or timeless, quality and its temporal expression or manifestation.

1. **Remembering a Valued Place.**

   Think of a place that you love to go. A place that you find restful or restorative. A place that you go to get refreshed ...

   Take some time to remember that place ...

   Make note of what you value about the place ...

   As you remember being in the place, allow yourself to feel the feelings that you have when you are there ...

2. **Identify the Timeless Qualities.**

   Make note of the qualities (such as joy, peace, serenity, or gratitude) that you experience when you are in that place ...

   Allow yourself to experience those qualities now as you remember the place and the qualities ...

3. **Remember the Timeless Qualities in Other Places.**

   As you are aware in the present moment of the experience of the qualities, such as joy or peace, think of other places that you have experienced these same qualities that you value ...

4. **Distinguish the Timeless Quality From its Temporal Manifestation.**

   Notice that the timeless quality that you value can be experienced in many places, including where you are right now ...

   There is a timeless or eternal quality and a temporal way of experiencing that quality ...

   You can experience the timeless quality independently of the temporal vehicle, such as the place that allowed you to experience that quality ...

   A timeless quality is not limited to one specific temporal vehicle ...

7. **Allow the Quality to Hold You.**

   As you re-member or put the timeless quality back together in consciousness, allow the eternal quality to hold you rather than you holding onto it ...

   Allow yourself to "float" in the quality ...

   Allowing the quality to hold you will reduce your tendency to grasp the quality and turn it into an idol.

Instructions: This exercise is designed to help you distinguish an eternal life-giving quality from its temporal manifestation and then create a resource of multiple life-giving threads in your timeline.

1. **Obtain a Baseline Measure of Your Hopefulness.**

   On a 0 to 10 scale (0 being "not hopeful" to 10 being "very hopeful") assess how hopeful you feel about your future ...

2. **Identify a Life-Giving Quality.**

   Think of something that you are currently experiencing and find particularly life-giving ... Separate the life-giving quality or qualities from any specific temporal experience of it ... For example, you may currently find friendships very life-giving. Separate the quality of "friendship" from any specific friend.

3. **See the Quality as a Timeless Golden Thread.**

   See the timeless life-giving quality as a golden thread that passes through many temporal experiences of the quality ...

   For example, you can see a golden thread of friendships running through your life, through many different people. Your current friends are not your first experience of friendship, nor will they be the last, and you can imagine that quality going out into your future ...

   If you had the quality in the past you have a realistic hope of having that quality in the future. Instead of specifying the vehicle by which you want to experience this quality in the future, take time to be curious and wonder how you will experience this quality in different ways ... See the thread going from before time to after time ...

   These threads are small threads in the great "rope" of the quality that spreads out through the universe, that connects humanity with one another.

4. **Assess the Impact of the Quality on Your Level of Hopefulness.**

   Use the 0-10 scale to assess how hopeful you are now about your future ...

5. **Add Additional Life-Giving Qualities.**

   Now that you have learned the process, take some time to include other qualities, so that it is not a single thread but a strong woven rope of life-giving qualities ...

6. **Connect Yourself to the Rope of Life-Giving Qualities.**

   When you have a strong rope of eternal qualities in your timeline, take a moment and step into the present moment. Feel the rope flowing from your past, into the core of your being in the present moment, and then out into the future ...

7. **Identify the Inviolate Eternal Nature of these Timeless Qualities.**

   See this golden rope of life-giving qualities as a link throughout your life. As you are aware of these qualities in the present moment, take some time to appreciate that nothing that has occurred in your life, not your worst or the worst the world has done to you, has been able to extinguish this rope – it may have gotten frayed at times, but nothing has defeated it ...

8. **Assess the Impact of the Quality on Your Level of Hopefulness.**

   Use the 0-10 scale to assess how hopeful you are now about your future ... How has your sense of hopefulness changed? ...

The Temporal Expression of Eternal Qualities

Many of the qualities we value such as friendship or peace are timeless; they existed before we were born and will continue long after we are gone. In our lives these eternal qualities have been manifested in a specific temporal event or person. Another way to describe this is: everything we value comes to us in a vehicle. For example, a candle provides light, but the candle isn't the light, it is a vehicle for the light. Problems arise when we confuse the value with the vehicle.

Idolatry

When we confuse the eternal quality with the temporal vehicle by which we knew the quality we are likely to become trapped in idolatry. Clinging to the temporal vehicle rather than being enfolded in the eternal quality that the vehicle helped us to experience is the essence of idolatry.

A prayer book is a temporal thing that points to an eternal or timeless quality. The same is true of the Scriptures. The Bible is a temporal translation of words that point to the Word. Clinging to the words or an interpretation of the words is very different from beholding the Word. The first will be a frantic, fearful, clutching of words, the other will set you free. Clinging to a book of words, regardless of how sacred they are, is no different than clinging to a sacred statue. Being in the presence of the life-giving God that both book and statue point to will set you free.

There are many other ways that we can confuse the timeless quality or value with the temporal vehicle by which it has been manifested. For example, theological certainty is a form of idolatry. The person who puts their trust in the content of their theology rather than the Living Eternal One that the theology points to will be trapped in the temporal limitations of their own mind. When Galileo and others demonstrated that the world revolved around the sun and wasn't flat, some people lost their faith and their hope, whereas others with an open faith and an open mind were called into a deeper awareness and awe of the mystery and wonder of creation and its Creator.

Imaging Timeless Qualities

Certainty that there is only one way to experience an eternal quality is to deny the essential timeless nature of the things that are truly life-giving. When we image a timeless quality in the exercises, we need to be specific about the quality but open and flexible in the way we imagine experiencing it in the future.

Doubt grows with knowledge.
— Johann von Goethe

The atheist staring from his attic window is often nearer to God than the believer caught up in his own false image of God.
— Martin Buber

I do not feel obliged to believe that the same God who has endowed us with senses, reason, and intellect has intended us to forgo their use and by some other means to give us knowledge which we can attain by them.
— Galileo Galilei

Hope and Religion

From my experience as a priest and psychologist, I can clearly say that there are helpful religions and unhelpful religions. I have found this to be true of all religions – in fact I would say it is true of all human endeavors, as I have witnessed and experienced both helpful and unhelpful psychotherapies. We humans have an incredible capacity to take a blessing and turn it into a curse. The good news is that we also have an incredible capacity to take curses and turn them into opportunities to experience new life. When it comes to faith and hope we need to ensure that our faith helps to create a genuine sense of hope and not a false sense of hope based on delusion or fantasy.

Discerning Truth

Most faith traditions have mechanisms for discerning truth. Some Christian traditions use an alignment of "Scripture, Reason,and Tradition." Some add "Experience" to that list. Other traditions would say they rely solely on the Scriptures; however, such views fail to account for the outlook and subjectivity of the person reading and interpreting the Scriptures.

What is missing in many of these discernment strategies is "Outcome." What is the outcome of a person's truth discernment? What is the outcome of a person's faith?

History is full of the horrors of well-intentioned people using their Scripture, Reason and Tradition to perpetuate fear and injustice. A misuse of Scripture, Reason, and Tradition resulted in Jesus being crucified.

I am a pragmatist at heart. The proof of the pudding is always in the eating, not in the ingredients, nor in the preparation or cooking. As a gardener I have planted many bare-root fruit trees. I purchase them in the winter when they are nothing more than sticks. While I have to trust the label when I purchase the tree, the only way I can know for sure what tree I purchased is when it bears fruit.

Some pastors place great emphasis on having the "correct" beliefs and interpretations of Scripture. I don't care about the correctness of your beliefs, I want to know whether you can love and whether you are growing in love. As a psychologist and pastor I have seen many people who use the right religious words but who live fearful and hateful lives. What I want to know is this: Do your beliefs help you to grow in your capacity to share in love with yourself and others?

A positive attitude may not solve all your problems, but it will annoy enough people to make it worth the effort.
— Herm Albright

You will know them by their fruits. Are grapes gathered from thorns, or figs from thistles? In the same way, every good tree bears good fruit, but the bad tree bears bad fruit. A good tree cannot bear bad fruit, nor can a bad tree bear good fruit.
— Matthew 7:16-18

Faith, Doubt, and Certainty

The enemy of faith is certainty. The servant of faith is doubt. It creates humility. It is arrogant to think that we can completely understand God, the nature of the universe, and our place in it. Genuine faith requires that we use our God-given capacity to doubt and question what we believe, so that we can be open to discovering new possibilities and not stay trapped in self-confirmatory loops of believing and experiencing. This type of doubting is not a non-believing despair, but rather a holding lightly onto what we know to be true and remaining open to learning more of the mystery of God's love and purpose.

Because what we believe focuses our attention, and what we attend to becomes our reality, faith is self-confirmatory. We will find evidence in our daily life to affirm our faith and ignore evidence that would refute our faith. If you believe God is angry and punishing, you will take to heart Scriptural passages that support your belief, and you will see signs of God's punishment in human suffering and calamities such as earthquakes and hurricanes. At the same time, you will ignore Scriptural passages that tell of God's love. But if you believe that God is loving, you will find Scriptural evidence to confirm that view and ignore passages to the contrary. The way out of this dilemma is to focus on the fruit of your faith and continually refocus on those things that help you manifest the desired fruit.

Checking the Fruit of Your Faith

Here are some questions I use to discern whether people are on a helpful path when it comes to matters of faith:

- If what you believe makes you more loving and stretches your heart, then you are probably on the right track.

- If what you believe makes you take responsibility for your life and future, then you are probably on the right track.

- If what you believe is good for all your neighbors and not just for you and some of your neighbors, then you are probably on the right track.

- If what you believe leaves you in a place of awe and wonder at the Source of all things, then you are probably on the right track.

- And if it is always okay to change tracks, then you are definitely on the right track!

Certainty is making a judgment that you are smarter today than you will be tomorrow.
— Steve Andreas

I've learned that people will forget what you said, people will forget what you did, but people will never forget how you made them feel.
— Maya Angelou

Even if you are on the right track, you will get run over if you just stand there.
— Will Rogers

Faith and Hope

Since nothing about the future is certain, our hope can never be absolute. We may responsibly make plans, taking into account as many things as cross our minds, but then something unforeseen happens such as an earthquake, or we become ill, or someone dies. How can we have hope when we face such uncertainty?

The writer to the Hebrews describes faith as "the assurance of things hoped for" *(Hebrews 11:1)*. Faith is what covers the gap between what we hope for and the lack of certainty we have about the future. A genuine faith that supports a realistic hope has two elements:

- Belief that we can achieve the future we imagine.
- Belief that we will be "OK" and able to adapt if something happens and we don't achieve the future that we imagine.

Genuine faith is not denial, avoidance, or a fantasy. Rather, it is based on what we have experienced and found to be true in the past. The appreciative process of discovering and building on the best of our past is an effective strategy to build a genuine faith and a realistic hope.

Active Hope vs. Passive Wishing

Genuine hope is not passive; it inspires and requires our active engagement in making our preferred future a reality. One of my role models for hope is Martin Luther King, Jr. Inspired by his faith, he was hopeful – he had a dream of a better future. But he didn't passively sit around wishing for that dream to come true. He took responsibility for what he could do and joined with others to make that dream a reality.

"Things Got Better When I Gave Up Hope"

While a realistic hope can be an important part of living vitally in the present moment, a false hope built on denial, avoidance, or fantasy can be dangerous. When people say that they gave up hope and things got better, they are really saying that they gave up avoidance, denial, and fantasy. They may really be saying: "When I saw how bad things really were I knew *I* had to make changes rather than just hoping that *things* would change." Rather than living in a fantasy of the day when all the problems were gone, they began to take steps in the present to create the life they wanted.

Cancer patient research indicates that people who pressure themselves to stay optimistic and refuse to look at the possibility that they may die actually have poorer survival rates than those who have a more

---

*Stop acting
as if life is a rehearsal.
Live this day
as if it were your last.
The past is over and gone.
The future
is not guaranteed.*
— Wayne Dyer

*Most people stumble
over the truth,
now and then,
but they usually manage
to pick themselves up
and go on, anyway.*
— Winston Churchill

*The fruit of the Spirit is
love, joy, peace,
patience, kindness,
generosity, faithfulness.*
— Galatians 5:22

realistic and emotionally congruent appraisal of their circumstances[3]. Being authentic by being miserable when you are miserable, and continuing to engage in those things that are meaningful, is more helpful than a pressured optimism built on denial.

"I Will be Happy When ..."

One of the ways a false hope is manifested is in the statement: "I will be happy when ..." In this statement we are delaying happiness until some date when we have achieved or obtained what we think will provide happiness. A hope based on wanting is no hope at all.

Using this statement is a good way to stay miserable. Whatever we think will make us happy becomes an idol which we worship. Some of these idols can become terrible monsters. The path of happiness is found by giving up wanting, not by getting what you want. You can never be happy tomorrow; you can only be happy now! It is with happiness that you can pursue your desires.

Religious Faith as a Help to Hope

I cannot prove to you the existence of God, nor can you prove to me that God doesn't exist. Both believing and not believing are acts of faith rather than scientific proof. Since the issue of faith is a personal statement, the following is my personal reflection.

Personally, I cannot remember asking to be born. This means to me that I am someone else's idea? While it is possible to say that I am my parent's idea, whose idea were they? The point I want to make is that we – and in fact the whole of creation – are not the source of our own existence. That leaves me with two possibilities: either creation is a colossal accident or there is a creative principle behind it all. I take the second view. I call that Principle the Source of Life. This is the core of my faith.

You may call the Source of Life "God," or something else. For me the name is not that important, as it is merely a label for something beyond all labels. To the reader who doesn't believe in God, I will say that I have discovered that I probably don't believe in the gods you don't believe in either. When people say they don't believe in God, I have found it helpful to inquire into the nature of the god that is not being believed in. In just about every circumstance it has been an act of wisdom not to believe in what they think God is.

The second element of my faith is that this Source of Life has the nature of love and accepts us unconditionally. It rains on the just and

*Its time
for the children of God
to grow up and become
the adults of God
and take responsibility for
their actions and their lives.*
— Steve Bhaerman

*Love is life.
All, everything that I
understand, I understand
only because I love.
Everything is, everything
exists, only because I love.
Everything is united
by it alone.
Love is God,
and to die means that I,
a particle of love,
shall return to the general
and eternal source.*
— Leo Tolstoy

*Before you tell your life
what you intend
to do with it,
listen for what it
intends to do with you.*
— Parker Palmer

*Don't ask yourself what
the world needs.
Ask yourself what makes
you come alive, and go
do that, because what the
world needs is people who
have come alive.*
— Howard Thurman

*We were known by God
before we knew ourselves
and it is in God
that we have a
divine purpose
to manifest in
a human world.*

the unjust. It does not make distinctions. It is also irrepressible. Despite everything that happens, it keeps on giving life. I find it amazing that in the spring of 1946 grass began growing in Auschwitz and Buchenwald as it has down through the ages, despite the atrocities humanity inflicted upon itself there. I would think that Life would abandon places of such evil, but it doesn't. In the light of these reflections I believe that ultimately good will prevail against evil, and love will prevail against hate. It may come at the cost of great suffering, but they will prevail.

The third element of my faith is that the Source of Life created me with a purpose to manifest. It has also equipped me with the resources to manifest that purpose. Writing this book is part of my mission to help and bring healing as part of my manifesting the helpful, humorous, healing person I was created to be.

There are many other aspects to my faith: why I am a follower of Jesus, the mysteries of death and resurrection, and the like. However, each of these things point back to these three elements. I summarize these three elements in my basic faith proposition:

At the heart of the universe is a heart of love that embraces us and accepts us unconditionally. This heart of love is the source of our existence and life. This loving heart created us for a purpose and has given us every resource we need to fulfill that purpose.

Religious faith such as I have articulated can be a great resource to provide hope. Some of the elements of that hope are:

- Being connected to something greater than yourself. This provides a deep sense that we are not alone.

- Having a purpose and a mission and the opportunity to co-create the future with God. This gives life a meaningful focus.

- Humanity lives in the shadow of death. Most religions offer some "answer" to the mystery of life and death. Freed from the fear of death, we can live hopefully in this present moment.

- Having a sense that life is essentially good, and despite that which we perceive as bad, good will ultimately prevail.

- That God can bring good out of that which appears bad. This is the essence of resurrection, that new life can be found in death, light can be found in darkness. As well as in the deepest existential issues, this is also true in the temporal and seemingly mundane. I have seen people fired one day, and find a much better job the next – which they wouldn't have found if they hadn't been fired.

Each of these spiritual realities has a social parallel in religious community. Being part of a love-based community that shares a set of core beliefs and values can also provide resources to live a life of hope.

- Being part of a community with a purpose helps us be part of a social system that is bigger than ourselves.

- The community's purpose can strengthen and support our individual purpose.

- In community, we can find emotional and physical support to deal with the day-to-day issues that the death of a loved one can cause.

- In community, we can find support to challenge and overcome injustice and the consequences of natural calamities such as earthquakes or hurricanes.

- In community, we can find acceptance when we fail.

Religious Faith as a Hindrance to Hope

While faith can be a help to hope, it can also be a hindrance. When faith is really a wish for something, rather than a belief in something, it creates an "I am hoping like hell there is a heaven" mentality. This does not create peace of mind, nor a sense of assurance that enables the person to live fully in the present moment. Nor does it equip them to work resourcefully to create their preferred future.

The Easter resurrection message is a great source of hope. It means we can live each day fully without denying or worrying about the reality of death. Unfortunately, this message can also become a problem when people see life on Earth as something to be endured while waiting to get to the "better place" called Heaven.

The point of the resurrection is not that we can sit around and miserably wait to get to heaven. It is to free us from the fear of death so that we can create heaven here, in this world, now. Seeing faith as a way to ensure you get your ticket to the next life, is a radical waste of the life we are given today. Many of the clichés rolled out at funerals such as "he is in a better place" or "God wanted her to be with the angels" reek of this unhelpful form of faith. They create guilt and denial in the face of feelings of grief, rather than helping resolve the feelings and restoring a person to hope.

Faiths that offer acceptance as a future gift to be earned as a reward for good behavior are also unhelpful. Such faiths are based in fear – fear that we will be rejected if we don't produce sufficient good behavior. Helpful faith doesn't hope for acceptance. It is grounded in

None of us are as smart as all of us.
— Japanese Proverb

A fanatic is one who can't change his mind and won't change the subject.
— Winston Churchill

Everything works except when it doesn't.
— Bill O'Hanlon

acceptance. This is St. Paul's great conundrum when he describes that the harder he tries to do right the more he sins *(Romans 7:15-25)*. The solution was to give up the struggle and realize that the grace of God in Jesus was not dependent on his goodness, and that his sinfulness could not separate him from God. In releasing his egocentric ideas of right and wrong, he found the freedom and power to do right.

Religions that focus extensively on humanity's sinfulness often create the reality of "all the good I do is God, and all the bad I do is me." A slightly different variation is "all the bad I do is the devil." This makes humanity a battlefield in which God and the devil fight it out – clearly not a hopeful place or a pleasant place to live. This does not foster hope and can lead to passivity. While it may appear that such people are taking responsibility for their actions by regularly confessing their sins, they are only taking responsibility for a small part of their lives. They are not taking responsibility for the gifts and talents they have been given, nor are they taking responsibility for being co-creators with God of a better future for themselves and for their neighbors.

Witnessing miracles may also have a negative impact on hope, or foster an unhelpful hope. In my early years as a Christian I was part of a small prayer group that saw one of its members get up from her deathbed after suffering for many years with cancer. At the time she was in her seventies and was being provided palliative care. She subsequently lived well into her eighties. As I reflect on her attitude I am aware that she was profoundly contented with either outcome, living or dying. What she knew and what we prayed for was that she would be enfolded in love and that Love would "do its thing."

On the other hand, I have witnessed people and their families experience miserable deaths with prayers being said around the clock. But they were prayers of fear, not prayers of faith. They were prayed by people who could not accept the possibility of death. If they could find just the right "trick" or say just the right prayer, then God would heal. This is not faith, it is fear-based wishing. These people walked on the knife-edge of enormous fear and wishing it were not true.

Fear-based religious communities with punitive or tyrannical gods create cultures of judgement, "should" thinking, guilt, and shame. They do not create hope or empower people to live and love. They are places of alienation rather than acceptance. They reinforce patterns of fear and hatred of people who disagree with their world view. If there is any hope in these communities it is that a select few (the "elect") will make it to the next world. For the rest of us there is no hope at all.

It is sheer arrogance to believe that your capacity to sin is greater than God's capacity to forgive and transform.
— Adapted from Thomas Hora

The cross is the full satisfaction of every objection that you have to the Good News that God loves you unconditionally just as you are.

Forgiveness is not about the recipient, it is about the one who forgives. God's forgiveness of us is more a statement about God, and God's perception of us, than it is about us.

As I have mentioned before, I am a pragmatist and a realist. I want to know the fruit of the faith rather than the overt words of the faith. When dealing with religious people, I am interested in whether their faith helps or hinders their ability to live loving, creative, vibrant lives. Likewise, when I think of faith and hope, I ask: "Does the person's faith offer a realistic hope, or does it create fear and ungrounded wishes?" When faith is unhelpful, it's time to change the faith rather than becoming more committed to something that doesn't work.

Changing Faith — Change the Language and the Practice

When changing our faith we need to pay attention to the impact of language on what we experience. Certain words and practices can be conditioned to create an habituated response. Changing the words (regardless of how correct they may be) and behaviors will be necessary to change the habituated response.

People who have grown up with a punitive God will need to change their names for God. If the name "Jesus" was used as the one who would send you to hell if you were bad, you probably will need, at least for a significant period of time, to stop praying to Jesus. Likewise, if praying or reading your Bible causes anxiety and misery, change the way you are praying and stop reading the Bible. I have known people who have taken years to decontaminate themselves from unhelpful faith practices.

I know of a pastor who grew up with the childhood admonition that "Jesus would get him" for being naughty. This "Jesus" literally drove him to drink. It took fifteen years of sobriety, through a Higher Power and Alcoholics Anonymous, to decontaminate his image of Jesus, from the bony-finger-wagging guilt-monger of his childhood to the Loving Power that restored him to sanity.

Becoming an Atheist

If you find your image of God is tyrannical or unhelpful, don't analyze it, just get rid of it! In the Ten Commandments we are told not to make images of God – that includes images between our ears. The early Christians were often called atheists because they didn't carry their gods around with them. Become an atheist, by discarding any god that is tyrannical, demeaning, or an obstacle to you becoming a loving, caring, responsible human being.

On the following pages are some exercises to help you get rid of a problem god and then create a resource of unconditional love.

The gate to the Kingdom of God is narrow, but not because it requires a narrow mindset or viewpoint to enter; rather, it is narrow because so few are able to trust that God's love is so wide.

God is not the words we say about God, but we often confuse the two. People often love the words they use to describe God more than they love God. Consider how Christians argue about their words for God rather than sitting in the presence of the One their words point to.

Fearful people live in a scary world animated by a scary god. Hostile people live in a hostile world animated by a hostile god. Loving people live in a loving world animated by a loving god.

Instructions: In this exercise you will learn how to become or help someone become an atheist, by clearing your soul of any crazy and unhelpful gods. Here are some possible crazy gods.

Cosmic Cop: This is the god who rides around the universe waiting to catch and punish you for doing wrong. It's weird, but you are often unaware of him except when you look in the rearview mirror and there he is, with his lights flashing.

Cosmic Breast: This is the god that you latch onto for perpetual succour but who requires nothing from you. The problem is that if you climb aboard and suck, that is all you will do, and you will end up really "sucking" as a responsible human being.

Marquis de God: This god is vicious and capricious, inflicting pain and suffering on people just because he can. This god's followers strive to be just as vicious, or are beaten down as wimps.

Nationalistic God: This is the god who blesses your nation at the expense of others and calls upon you to convert or exterminate other nations. You know this god when you see your country's flag in his temple.

Cosmic Bellhop and/or Janitor: These gods are always available to bring whatever you need, whenever you need it, and will readily clean up every mess you make regardless of who was to blame. They say they don't require anything of you, but they really do like big tips.

The Master of Ceremonies God: This god is duty-bound to show up for baptisms, bar mitzvahs, weddings, and funerals, but has to leave people alone the rest of the time.

1. **Identify Your Crazy God.**
   Take some time to think of the god/gods you experience in your life that do not help you to become a loving, responsible person ...

2. **Identify What the Crazy God is Saying.**
   Take a moment and listen to what the crazy god has to say ...
   Whose voice does it speak to you with? ...
   Who introduced you to this god and whose god is it? ...
   Does the god have any wisdom for you? ...

3. **Separate Any Truth from Heresy.**
   Remember all heresies usually have some element of truth which has been distorted. Is there an element of truth or wisdom here that you want to keep? Separate that truth from the god, and imagine how you will experience that truth in the future when this god is not around ...

4. **Seek and Satisfy Any Objections to Saying Goodbye to the Crazy God.**
   Does any part of you object to saying goodbye to this god? ...
   If so, ask that part what it would need to satisfy that objection ...
   For example, a person may be afraid that they will become a really bad person if they get rid of the "cosmic cop." Ask them to find the part of them that does know right from wrong, and what they would need to trust this part rather than relying on this "external" enforcer.

5. **Send the God Away.**
   If the god belongs to someone else, send it back to its owner ...
   Don't fight with it, simply tell it to leave and let it go – because you don't need it anymore ...

Warning: The following exercise uses a metaphor based on taking your pulse. Pushed to its limits it will become absurd. It also may not be a helpful metaphor for someone with a history of heart disease. An alternative metaphor based on breathing will also be offered, which in turn may not be helpful to people with asthma or who have difficulty breathing.

Instructions: In this exercise you will create a metaphor of unconditional love or infinite loving kindness. Establishing this resource is recommended after you have let go of a "crazy god."

1. **Becoming Conscious of the Life that is Within You.**

   Take a moment to take your pulse ...

   As you feel your pulse, let your attention focus on the pulse sensation and begin to wonder: Why do I have a pulse? ...

   You may trace your pulse back to your heart ...

   Be aware of your heart beating and wonder: Why does my heart beat? ...

   Try to stop your heart from beating. What is it within you that overrides your act of will? ...

   Within each one of us is the Source of our life which gives us a heartbeat ...

   Focus your attention on the Source of life that is within you ...

   Whatever gives you life is within you. Others have their version of life that is within them, but your source of life is within you and goes wherever you go ...

   That which gives you life is not dependent on anyone else ...

   Others may die, but your life continues on ...

2. **Identify a Shaming Experience and Unconditional Acceptance**

   Now take a moment, and in the privacy of your own mind think of the worst thing you have ever done. I don't want you to tell me, I just want you to be aware of what you are ashamed of ...

   When you have in mind what you did that you are most ashamed of, ponder the following: Did that which is within you, that gives you life, come to you the day after you had messed up and say: "Yesterday you really messed up and I am leaving for two weeks!"? ...

   Did your heart stop beating? No! There is something within you that accepts you unconditionally. It is beyond your conscious mind, but you can be conscious of it ...

   Even when we really mess up it continually offers us life and invites us to join in living that life.. It doesn't even ask us to wait for an appropriate period of remorse ...

3. **Re-orienting from Shame to Unconditional Love**

   Let go of the shame, and focus your attention on that which accepts you unconditionally ...

   Does the source of your heartbeat have your best interests at heart? ...

   We can wonder what we want to do with our life or we can wonder what our life wants to do with us. Take a moment and wonder what your life wants to do with you ...

4. **Saying Yes! to the Life that is Within You.**

   Does any part of you object to saying Yes! to the life that is within you? ...

   Ask the part what would satisfy that objection ...

   If you feel afraid, don't analyze the fear, just ask yourself what you need to feel safe ...

   Allow yourself to rest in the presence of your life ...

Instructions: In this exercise you will create a metaphor of unconditional love or infinite loving kindness by using a breathing metaphor. Don't try this if you have breathing problems!

1. **Becoming Conscious of the Life that is Within You.**

    Take a moment and try to hold your breath …

    At some point you will gasp and begin breathing involuntarily. As you begin breathing again take a moment to wonder: What causes me to breathe? …

    Something inside of you keeps you breathing whether awake or asleep, or even unconscious, regardless of the rightness of your behavior …

    In the Acts of the Apostles (Chapter 17) Paul, speaking to the Athenians, says that "God gives life and breath to all mortals." This implies that if you can draw breath, God has not abandoned you and is continuing to give you life. And faith also tells us that God doesn't abandon us even after we cease drawing breath and our hearts stop beating.

    Focus your attention on the Source of life that is within you …

    Whatever gives you life is within you. Others have their version of life that is within them, but your source of life is within you and goes wherever you go …

    That which gives you life is not dependent on anyone else …

    Others may die, but your life continues on …

2. **Identify a Shaming Experience and Unconditional Acceptance**

    Now take a moment, and in the privacy of your own mind think of the worst thing you have ever done, that you are most ashamed of …

    When you have that thing in mind that you did that you are most ashamed of ponder the following: Did that which is within you, that gives you breath and life, come to you the day after you had messed up and say: "Yesterday you really messed up and I am leaving for two weeks!"? …

    Did you stop breathing? No! There is something within you that accepts you unconditionally. It is beyond your conscious mind, but you can be conscious of it …

    Even when we really mess up it continually offers us life and invites us to join in living that life.. It doesn't even ask us to wait for an appropriate period of remorse …

3. **Re-orienting from Shame to Unconditional Love**

    Now let go of the memory of what was shaming, and focus your attention on that which accepts you unconditionally …

    Does the source of your breath have your best interests at heart? …

    We can wonder what we want to do with our life or we can wonder what our life wants to do with us. Take a moment an wonder what your life wants to do with you …

4. **Saying Yes! to the Life that is Within You.**

    Does any part of you object to saying Yes! to the life that is within you? …

    Ask the part what would satisfy that objection …

    If you feel afraid, don't analyze the fear, just ask yourself what you need to feel safe …

    Allow yourself to rest in the presence of your life …

Instructions: In this exercise you will deepen the metaphor and create a resource of unconditional love. We will use this resource as a foundational resource for the forgiveness exercises.

1. **Being Aware of Unconditional Love and Acceptance.**

   Return to your awareness of the source of your life and its unconditional acceptance of you ... Imagine a large dining or banquet table where you can feel accepted. (If dining tables are not a safe resource for you imagine some other, perhaps secret, gathering place that is safe.) ... Invite all the parts of your self to the table, paying attention both to those things you value and those things you dislike about yourself. Invite them all to the table ...

   Notice that each has a pulse and breathes, each has life ...

   Be aware that all of you is welcomed to this table and given life ...

2. **Discovering the Name of Unconditional Love.**

   As you are conscious of that which accepts all of you, ask it what its name is ...

   When Moses stood at the burning bush he asked it what its name was. If it was okay for Moses to ask it will be okay for you to ask ...

   When it tells you its name, thank it and thank it for its love ...

3. **Deepening Your Awareness of Unconditional Love**

   Take note of what you experience when you recognize that you are loved unconditionally ...

   Allow yourself to remember other times when you have experienced these same feelings ...

   *If you remember people or events note **how** you remember, not just **what** you remember. Is the memory an image of a person, the sound of their voice, or the feelings you experienced? ...*

   Imagine these memories and experiences of unconditional love being kept in a "folder of love" in the filing cabinet of your consciousness. This is an infinitely expandable folder where you can store additional experiences and ideas of love as they occur ...

4. **Knowing Unconditional Love in the Future.**

   Take a moment to wonder how you will experience similar times of unconditional love in the future. Pay more attention to experiencing the timeless quality of love in the future and what that would be like, rather than focusing on specific people or events. Add these to the folder ...

5. **Adding Some Theology.** (Optional, this may or may not be helpful)

   Add to the folder any scriptures, readings, or hymns that remind you of unconditional love ...

   Pay attention to the fruit of your ideas during this step. If the ideas deepen your awareness of unconditional love, keep them; if not, return to your previous experience.

6. **Resolving any Should Thinking.**

   Check to see if there are any "shoulds" that you need to do in order to become lovable that linger around your awareness of unconditional love. If there are any "shoulds" consider the following: Is there anything you can do in the next 5 seconds to become lovable? If there is, then go do it! If there isn't, then spend the next 5 seconds being loved. And then repeat ...

7. **Storing the Folder of Love.**

   Return your awareness to your "folder of love." Behold how good it is and be grateful ...

   Let your inner wisdom decide how you want to store the folder. You may take it into yourself, perhaps in your heart, or you may want to walk into the folder and become one with it ...

Unconditional Love for Others

I don't think we are able, in and of ourselves, to love someone unconditionally. We are finite, and offering something infinite to another person is impossible. At some point our needs and wants will collide with the needs and wants of others, and we will place limits or conditions on our love. The good news is that we don't need to try and love people unconditionally.

Many people report that the feeling of "falling in love" is expansive and creatively opens them to new ideas and possibilities beyond that person. The experience of "being in love" is exactly that: we are "in" something. We transcend the "I love you" and "you love me" to become open to and part of the Love that is bigger than either of us.

As a parish priest, I discovered that one of my biggest motivations to love my parishioners was that I wanted **them** to love **me** because they saw me as a loving priest. The discovery process was a rather miserable experience of burnout and compassion fatigue. Thank God that I burned out, because the good news was that I discovered that when I gave up "trying" to love people I became one with a far greater Love.

Rather than trying to love people unconditionally, we can let go of our "little love" and become one with all the love in the universe. It is from this perspective that we can see others through the eyes of love that are free from our own ego wishes, wants, and needs.

The Good of God

I call this Love, "God." I also know it to be good. I find the Goodness of God[4] to be a helpful resource when relating to my loved ones, my enemies, and myself. In my life I have experienced not really knowing what would be good. I often thought I knew what would be good for me only to discover that it wasn't, or that there was something better. Likewise, as a priest and a therapist there were times when I thought I knew what would be good for parishioners and clients, only to discover I was ignorant.

Beholding people in the infinite goodness of God, without defining what that goodness is, is now my way of praying. I no longer tell God what I think would be good for them. I can wish God's goodness for those I love and for my worst enemy. I know God rains on the just and on the unjust. Our task is to learn how to catch the rain and share it.

Attachment, Grasping, and Clinging

I make a distinction between "attachment" and "grasping." The ability to freely connect and form attachments with others to share in life is essential to creating community. Without attachment we cannot become one.

Grasping and clinging, on the other hand, are unhelpful. Grasping onto others because we perceive them as the source of our life creates many problems. When we grasp and cling to others, we will strangle life from them rather than sharing in life with them. Possessiveness and jealousy are examples of this kind of grasping and clutching. When we grasp or cling we also experience fear: fear that we will lose what we perceive as the source of our life and happiness.

Resentment is another expression of grasping. We may cling to people who have hurt us. The irony is that we often hate these people and put great physical distance between us and them, but they still travel with us in our heads and in our hearts. We cling to what they did and didn't do and how they hurt us. We may cling to the hope that one day they will recognize how hurtful they were and make it right, or that some calamity will punish them for what they have done. In the section on forgiveness we will explore in more detail the dynamics of resentment, but for the present moment just be aware that resentment is a form of clinging to people or ideas.

Beyond people and things, we can also cling or be unhelpfully attached to ideas. Absolute certainty or unyielding belief in something is unhelpful. Hope based on this kind of certainty leaves a person vulnerable to disillusionment and hopelessness. At one point in time, humanity was certain that the world was flat. When people challenged that certainty, great unrest arose in people's minds. To prevent themselves from becoming overwhelmed by doubt, they clung more tenaciously to their ideas and banished or persecuted those who sought to disrupt their world view. Rather than clinging to our ideas, we need to hold them lightly and stay intellectually open and curious.

Since there are helpful and unhelpful forms of attachment, we need to know what to attach to and have a strategy to let go of attachments that are unhelpful. In the section on timeless qualities, we distinguished between temporal and timeless qualities. We need to be attached to the timeless quality and not its temporal manifestation. To prevent grasping or clinging to the timeless quality we can also

> *Resenting someone is a way of never leaving that person.*
> — Kare Anderson

> *Believe nothing just because a so-called wise person said it. Believe nothing just because a belief is generally held. Believe nothing just because it is said in ancient books. Believe nothing just because it is said to be of divine origin. Believe nothing just because someone else believes it. Believe only what you yourself test and judge to be true.*
> — Buddha

turn it "inside out" so that the eternal quality holds us. For example, we can cling to an image of love, or simply allow love to hold us.

Surrendering Others to the Goodness of God

When we become aware of the eternal goodness of God, we release our attachment to our ideas of how that goodness will be temporally manifested. We can use the same process to surrender others into the Goodness of God. We release our ideas of how that goodness must be manifested.

Wishing people well without defining that "well" is a way to express unconditional love to others. This becomes an important strategy and resource for dealing with people who have hurt us. Love and resentment are mutually exclusive. We cannot know love when we are in the midst of resentment. When people have hurt us our resentment keeps us attached to them and to our pain. We can release them into the Goodness of God, free from our clinging to ideas of who or what they are and what they have done. We can leave people in that goodness as we continue living our lives in this present moment.

On the following page is an exercise that will lead you through the process of being aware of the Goodness of God and how to surrender people into that Goodness free from our unhelpful attachments. We will use this resource later in the forgiveness process.

You will know that forgiveness has begun when you recall those who hurt you and feel the power to wish them well.
— Lewis B. Smedes

Instructions: This exercise is designed to help you perceive others through the eyes of love.

1. **Being Aware of Unconditional Love.**

   Recall your experience of unconditional love. Take a deep, calm breath or series of breaths and let yourself settle into the experience of being loved unconditionally ...

   Surrender yourself to Love: Let love "hold onto you" rather than you "holding onto love" ...

2. **The Goodness of God.**

   From the place of love be aware of how good it is ...

   Become aware of the timeless Goodness of God ...

   Remember times in the past when you have known this goodness ...

   Be aware of the goodness of being loved unconditionally right now ...

   Imagine experiencing goodness in the future, without defining the temporal way that this goodness will be manifested ....

   Know that it is good: good for you, good for others, good for everyone ...

   Imagine this goodness is an ocean that you can float on or sit in ...

3. **Extending Unconditional Love to Those You Love.**

   Think of someone you care about ...

   Surrender them into the Goodness of God ...

   Be aware of them surrounded by goodness ...

   Wish them well, without defining what that "well" should be ...

   Notice what it is like to see them through the eyes of love ...

   Using the image of the ocean of goodness, be aware of how you and this person are in the ocean of goodness together ...

4. **Extending Unconditional Love to Those You Find Difficult to Love.**

   Think of someone who annoys you, or who has hurt you, or you find difficult to love ...

   Imagine that you and they are in the ocean of goodness ...

   Notice where you have to place them in the ocean of goodness, in order for you to feel safe and still remain conscious of the goodness ...

   Sometimes they may have to be over the horizon ...

   Or perhaps at the edge of the horizon so you can just keep an eye on them because they haven't proven to be trustworthy ...

   If you need to, surrender any ideas that they don't deserve to be in the ocean ...

   It's not your ocean, it's the ocean formed from the rain that falls on the good and the bad ...

   You didn't earn it, neither did they ...

   Let go of any ideas of what the person did or didn't do ...

   Or how they should change, or how they should be punished ...

   Let them be in their place in the ocean of goodness ...

   Without defining how that goodness will be temporally manifested ...

   Just know that it will be good for them and it will be good for you ...

   When you have put them freely in the ocean of goodness without attachment, allow your attention to return to the goodness holding you and allow yourself to be held ...

Compassion as the Agent of Transformation

The Appreciative Way is designed to enable personal and social transformation. We are not simply interested in changing our external circumstances, but transforming how we fundamentally relate to ourselves, others, and the Source of our existence. We seek a life-giving way of being and living in the world that is just, sustainable, and transformational.

The Buddha taught that compassion is the agent of transformation. Jesus taught that love is the agent of transformation. We are taught to love our enemies, to love our neighbors, to love ourselves, and to love God. Because the word "love" is commonly used to describe feelings, actions, and/or attitudes that range from the very trivial to the most profound of human experiences, it is often inadequate to clearly describe a response to someone in distress. For this reason, I prefer to use the Buddhist understanding of "compassion" to describe a desired attitude and response to all people who I encounter. It is this understanding of compassion that describes Jesus' idea of loving one another. Compassion is the temporal manifestation of the eternal, infinite, loving kindness that permeates the universe.

The word *compassion* in the English language means "to feel with." Although it could mean to share in someone's joy, it is typically used to mean "to suffer with." Yet when we look at Jesus' engagement with others, we see him clearly doing more than "feeling or suffering with" them. As well as having empathy with others in his healing conversations with people, we can see him strategically working to bring an end to their suffering.

Simply suffering with people is likely to lead to compassion fatigue. It would also lead to a sense of hopelessness as the person would not be able to imagine a future without the suffering. We not only want to "feel with" people but to help them move beyond their suffering.

The Buddhist word that is translated as compassion is, *bodhicitta*. When translated directly, this word means "awakening mind." It is the altruistic intention of one who aspires to attain enlightenment for the benefit of all sentient beings. Compassion is the seeking of enlightenment to alleviate suffering. From this Buddhist perspective compassion is not simply to "suffer with" but to go beyond the suffering to alleviate it.

Psychologist and author Stephen Gilligan[5], a student of Milton Erickson, describes compassion as "suffering with while opening

> *If you want others to be happy, practice compassion. If you want to be happy, practice compassion.*
> — The Dalai Lama

> *I would rather make mistakes in kindness and compassion than work miracles in unkindness and hardness.*
> — Mother Teresa

> *Jesus never asked anyone how he or she got sick, only the Pharisees did... If your compassion level goes up when you know it wasn't someone's fault, then there is something wrong.*
> — Kay Warren

beyond so that the deepest consciousness is not in the suffering, but in the opening of the cracked heart to a deeper wholeness and shining spirit."

But were Jesus and the Buddha always compassionate in their response to others? Clearly there were times when they were caring of others in distress, but at other times they appeared angry or playful in their actions and conversations. If the Buddha and Jesus were always compassionate, then being compassionate is not simply a single, uniform response to people who are suffering. Gilligan also describes compassion as having three primal energies or faces: tenderness, fierceness, and mischievousness. Using this tri-fold understanding of compassion we can see how the great spiritual leaders were compassionate with those they encountered and how their actions resulted in transformation.

Compassion, Confusion, and Transformation

There are two ways people learn. The first is incremental learning, in which a person adds piece by piece to the learning they have already acquired. What they are doing is adding additional detail to their pre-existing map of reality. The second way of learning is transformation. The person may not have learned anything specifically, but their way of seeing has been transformed. They have a new map of reality, rather than simply adding to a pre-existing map. When transformation occurs nothing is changed but everything is different. Depending on the religious tradition, transformation may also be called enlightenment, being "born again," or awakening.

Transformation occurs when the old map of reality no longer portrays reality and a new map forms in consciousness. Confusion will exist between the time the old map no longer works and the new one takes shape. In some situations this may occur almost instantaneously, and in others confusion may prevail for several years. St. Paul on the Damascus road (Acts 9) is a vivid example of the transformation process. He has a map of reality which says "Christianity is bad" and he is on a mission to eradicate Christianity. On the road to fulfil his mission he has a profound experience of the risen Lord which shatters this map. He has no way to see or map this new reality and is blind. His sight returns when a new map which says "Christianity is good" forms in his consciousness and he begins a new mission to evangelize rather than eradicate Christianity. Unlike St. Paul's experience, some transformations are small and subtle and the confusion is momentary.

*Everybody can be great.
Because anybody
can serve.
You don't have to have a
college degree to serve.
You don't have to make
your subject and your verb
agree to serve ...
You don't have to know
the second theory of
thermodynamics in physics
to serve.
You only need
a heart full of grace.
A soul generated by love.*
— Martin Luther King, Jr.

*Compassion is
the love of God within us
in the giving of ourselves
to others.*

*I am not interested
in picking up
crumbs of compassion
thrown from the table of
someone who considers
himself my master.
I want the
full menu of rights.*
— Archbishop Desmond Tutu

I like nonsense.
It wakes up the brain cells.
— Dr. Seuss

I sit on a man's back,
choking him and making
him carry me,
and yet assure myself
and others that
I am very sorry for him
and wish to ease his lot
by all possible means
– except by getting
off his back.
— Leo Tolstoy

When transformation occurs
nothing is changed but
everything is different.

Minds are like parachutes:
they function best
when they are open.
— Unknown

John of the Cross describes this confusion process as the "dark night of the soul" when a person's understanding of God no longer works but the new understanding hasn't taken shape in consciousness. John of the Cross described this process as a "second conversion." The first conversion occurs when a person discovers the reality of God. The map of understanding of God at this time is likely to be heavily contaminated with projections, ego needs, fears, and desires. At some time in the person's life this understanding of God no longer works. Things that formerly made sense no longer make sense.

Touching the edge of what we think we know and entering into the realm of confusion can be quite disturbing for people. It can be very distressing when we are dealing with existential issues such as life and death, or heaven and hell. When people become afraid they are likely to revert and hold tighter to the old map. This is why some of the "crazy gods" can be held onto with such fierce conviction. Any challenges to that map are likely to be responded to with increasing rigidity and certainty. The challenge may offer the glimmer of heaven, but all that is truly known and responded to is the terror of going to hell.

The way of confusion preceding transformation is seen clearly in Jesus' ministry. His actions confuse people's understanding of the Messiah and how they are to live their lives. He doesn't fit in their map of understanding. When they become frightened by what they see, they kill him. Patterns of confusion are also seen in his followers. At times it appears they understand and then they get it all wrong and enter into a new state of confusion.

Jesus was also a master at deliberately using patterns of confusion in his transformational conversations with people. The woman at the well (*John 4:7-38*), the Canaanite woman whom he called a dog (*Matthew 15:21-28*), and Nicodemus, when he told him he needed to be born again (*John 3:1-21*), are all examples of Jesus intentionally inviting people into the land of confusion. In many of the healing narratives Jesus can be seen working at two levels. There is a physical healing on one level, and then there is a healing of alienation at the self-understanding level. For example, the Canaanite woman moves from an unworthy, "I am a dog," view of herself to one of a person of worth.

This process of confusion and dark night is not restricted to the spiritual and religious realms. It occurs in all fields of knowledge. Academia can become a vicious place when new discoveries challenge the ideas that people have built their lives on. I have witnessed it personally in the field of psychology. The strategies that I will present to resolve trauma and grief work rapidly, defying what many of us have been taught. I have helped clients sustainably resolve 20 years of re-lived trauma in about 45 minutes. It contradicts all I was taught in graduate school about treating trauma.

When demonstrating these strategies to therapists I have had several become very angry and disbelieving. What I had done clearly did not fit their map of understanding and, rather than pondering new possibilities, they reverted more vigorously to their prior understanding. They then gathered others to support their view and began to challenge everything I said and did. People often find it very difficult to give up their maps of reality that they have spent a lifetime, and thousands of educational dollars, to create. As I reflect on that experience, what I find fascinating is that not one therapist went and asked the client about the client's experience and outcome. It was much easier for them to cling to and protect their old map of reality.

Mastering the art of confusion will be essential if we are to be agents of transformation. For example, clergy who want to be transformational preachers need to become experts in evoking and managing confusion in their parishioners. Without confusion there will be no transformation. Information may be imparted about God but the hearers will not be transformed in God. On the other hand, too much confusion will overwhelm the hearer, and neither transformation nor incremental learning will take place.

As we explore the three facets of compassion, reflect on how tenderness, fierceness, and mischievousness evoke confusion by challenging a person's map of reality.

Tenderness

This is what we commonly associate with compassion: a sympathetic concern for someone in pain and a practical and immediate action to alleviate the suffering. Many of the healing stories in the Gospels show the tender side of compassion. In tender moments people are confronted with a challenge to their own self-understanding: "Am I unlovable or am I loved?" The tender touch deeply affirms that the person is undeniably loved, which transforms their perspective of themselves and the world in which they live.

If tenderness is the only response, people may experience compassion fatigue or burnout. There are times when tenderness is inappropriate. It is inappropriate to be tender in the face of evil. It is inappropriate to stand by and tenderly watch someone hurt another. When we think

*I know that you believe
you understand
what you think I said,
but I'm not sure
you realize
that what you heard
is not what I meant.*
— Robert McCloskey

*We will
bankrupt ourselves
in the vain search
for absolute security.*
— Dwight David Eisenhower

*I don't know what your
destiny will be,
but one thing I do know:
the only ones among you
who will be really happy
are those who have sought
and found how to serve.*
— Albert Schweitzer

of Jesus' and the Buddha's interactions with people, there were times when they were far from tender. If compassion is to be a useful way of transforming the world, we need something more than tenderness.

Fierceness

Anger gives us the energy or motivation to protect ourselves and overcome injustice. Yet it is clear that our human capacity for anger often creates injustice rather than overcoming injustice. When our capacity for anger is transformed from a self-seeking "just-us" attitude to social justice-seeking, we become fierce, with a single-minded, determined pursuit of the objective.

This quality of fierceness can be heard in the preaching of Dr. Martin Luther King, Jr.[6] His preaching was not simply an angry railing against a current evil or past atrocity, but the single-minded, passionate, determined longing for the day when equality for all will reign, and a fierce call to make that day a reality. It was his fierceness that caused him to pursue his dream of social transformation even in the face of threats and death.

Anger is about what has happened in the past. Fierceness is a single-minded pursuit of a just future. Resentment is an angry response to a past injury. Forgiveness sets us free to pursue the future.

Being fierce may be a necessary resource when we forgive people. Forgiving someone does not mean that we have to simply be tender with the person. We may let go of our anger over what has happened, but we may need to maintain a fierce attitude toward those who have shown they are predisposed to injuring us in the future. We may need to be fierce to put someone in jail, not as a means to punish them, but as a means to protect others from them.

There are clearly times when tenderness in the face of evil is inappropriate, yet fierceness in some of these circumstances also seems to aggravate the situation rather than leading to transformation. It is also clear from the great spiritual leaders that there were times when they were not simply being tender or fierce. We need another facet to our understanding of compassion.

Mischievousness

At first glance, mischievousness may seem inappropriate to our understanding of compassion. Webster's Dictionary describes mischievousness as "causing injury or harm," and "having a quality of malevolence." But the pursuit of justice is often seen as malevolent

Everybody can get angry,
that's easy.
But getting angry
at the right person,
with the right intensity,
at the right time,
for the right reason
and in the right way
– that's hard.
— Aristotle

I'm an angry person,
angrier than most people
would imagine,
I get flashes of anger.
What works for me is
working out when it's
useful to use that anger.
— Alan Alda

by those in power who live unjustly. There were those who found Jesus' Gospel so malevolent that they crucified him. Some of the hearers of Dr. King found his ideas very malevolent and were afraid that they would experience great harm if his dream of a day when little black children and little white children would go to school together became a reality – and so they killed him.

The other side of mischievousness is playfulness, manifested in a teasing curiosity that results in "out of the box" creativity. Buddhists call this form of compassion "crazy wisdom." Jesus and the Buddha were playful masters in their use of paradox, parables, koans and other indirect forms of communication.

Archbishop Desmond Tutu and Mahatma Gandhi also demonstrated the mischievous side of compassion. While fiercely determined for justice, they still maintained a lightness of spirit in response to the regimes imposing injustice.

Unlike tenderness and fierceness, which are overt, the mischievous way is covert. In many ways you are "playing" with people and they will not know what you are doing. This can lead to accusations of sarcasm and/or manipulation. To protect against a misuse of the mischievous way I encourage people to find a place of delight in the person they are working with prior to using a covert mischievous process. If I can not find a place of delight in the person then I will restrict myself to either tenderness or fierceness.

Using the Faces of Compassion

Most people feel comfortable with two of the three faces of compassion, yet being a compassionate presence in the world requires that we continue to develop all three faces. I am also aware that we need to continually transform our ability to use any human aspect. We can use our tenderness, fierceness, and mischievousness in self-serving manipulative ways, or we can allow them to be transformed into resources that we can use for the betterment of the world.

Growing in compassion requires knowing when to use each face. In general, be tender in the face of pain, be fierce in the face of injustice, and be mischievous in the face of resistance. In many situations we can also use a combination of the faces, such as being tender and fiercely determined to bring about an outcome, or being tender and mischievous at the same time. On the following pages is an exercise to develop your skills of tenderness, fierceness, and mischievousness.

Before you speak,
ask yourself:
Is it kind,
is it necessary,
is it true,
does it improve
on the silence?
— Shirdi Sai Baba

If an elephant steps on the tail of a mouse and you say that you want to remain neutral in the situation, the mouse will not appreciate your objectivity.
— Archbishop Desmond Tutu

Be tender
in the face of pain.
Be fierce
in the face of injustice.
Be mischievous
in the face of resistance.

Instructions: In this exercise you will explore your own experience of the three faces of compassion.

Tenderness: This is what we commonly associate with compassion: a sympathetic concern for someone in pain with a practical and immediate action to alleviate the suffering.

1. *Who is your role model for tenderness? ...*

2. *Take some time to reflect on examples of Jesus or your role model being tender ...*

3. *Notice how tenderness challenges and confuses a person's map of self-understanding ...*

4. *Remember times when you have been tender with someone when it challenged or confused their self-understanding and led to transformation. (Note that the transformation doesn't need to be radical, but may be a subtle shift in perspective.) ...*

5. *Where is your tenderness located in your body? As you remember being tender, be aware of where that tenderness seems to flow from within your body ...*

Fierceness: A single-minded determination to bring about a just future. It may be passionate with lots of emotion or it may be a quiet "steely" determined resolve.

1. *Who is your role model for fierceness? ...*

2. *Take some time to reflect on examples of Jesus or your role model being fierce ...*

3. *Notice how fierceness challenges and confuses a person's map of self-understanding ...*

4. *Remember times when you have been fierce with someone when it challenged or confused their self-understanding and led to transformation ...*

5. *Where is your fierceness located in your body? As you remember being fierce be aware of where that fierceness seems to flow from within your body ...*
   Notice the difference in location between your experience of tenderness and fierceness ...

Mischievousness: A playful, often covert way of engaging a person to challenge their perception of reality and create an opportunity for transformation. Some examples may include using paradox, parables, teasing, or strange behaviors, as in Jesus' spitting on the ground to make mud to put on blind man's eyes *(John 9:1-12)*.

1. *Who is your role model for mischievousness? ...*

2. *Take some time to reflect on examples of Jesus or your role model being mischievous ...*

3. *Notice how mischievousness challenges and confuses a person's map of-self understanding ...*

4. *Remember times when you have been mischievous with someone when it challenged or confused their self-understanding and led to transformation ...*

5. *Where is your mischievousness located in your body? As you remember being mischievous be aware of where that mischievousness seems to flow from within your body ...*
   Note the location within your body of your tenderness, fierceness, and mischievousness ...

Reflection: Notice how the masters of compassion move fluidly between the faces of compassion and often combine them, such as a tender and fierce response to achieve a desired outcome.

Instructions: In this exercise you will learn which face of compassion to use with people.

Growing in Compassion: Most of us can do two of the three faces of compassion relatively well.

Which is your strongest and most preferred face of compassion? ...
Which is your least preferred face of compassion? ...
What do you need to do to grow all three faces of compassion? ...

Calibrating Your Inner Wisdom: Experiencing your internal subjective sense of what is right.

1. *Clasp your hands together by interlacing your fingers. Notice which thumb is on the top.*

2. *Now unclasp your hands and re-clasp them together so that the other thumb is on the top and be aware of how that feels. Most people report that it feels weird or "just wrong."*

3. *Re-clasp your hands so that they feel "right." As we do the next exercise we will use this sense of "rightness" to discern what type of compassion to use.*

Using the Face of Tenderness.

1. *Think of a person who clearly needs your tenderness, and who you have no objection to being tender towards ...*

2. *Imagine that you have a Polaroid picture or snap-shot of that person ...*
Place that picture in the "tender" place that you identified in the initial part of the exercise and be aware of what you subjectively experience ...

3. People typically report feeling some of the following: peace, relief, warmth, heart enlarging etc.

   For many the sense of relief comes from getting the person "out of their mind" and "into their heart." This frees them from the mental effort that evokes worry and can leave them resourceful to carry on their daily tasks. For clergy, imagine what it is like to prepare a sermon when you have "someone on your mind."

Using the Faces of Compassion.

1. *Think of someone who really frustrates and annoys you ...*

2. *Imagine that you have a Polaroid picture of that person ...*
Take time to place the person in each of the tender, fierce, and mischievous places and see where it feels right that they belong ...

3. *Did you discover that what you are currently doing and what you need to do is different based on what you learned in this exercise? ...*
What can you do differently to still respond compassionately toward this person? ...

4. *What if the person didn't belong in any place? This is probably someone, to every extent possible, that you should have nothing to do with.*
Jesus said, "When you go to a town say 'peace' to the town. If the peace is not returned leave and shake the dust off your feet" (Matthew 10:12-14). Since you can't authentically offer compassion to this person, it would be better if you have nothing to do with them.
Use the exercise "Extending Unconditional Love to Others" on page 71 to leave them compassionately "in love" and "in love" continue on with your own life.

3: RESOLVING PAINFUL MEMORIES

When we remember painful events from our past we may find one of two different emotional responses: some past events evoke distress in the present moment when we remember them, while others, though painful at the time, no longer evoke distress when we recall them.

Painful Memory: We experience distress or pain in the present moment when we recall a past event. While the actual event is over, emotional distress continues in the present moment when the event is recalled. From an emotional or psychological perspective, we could say that the event is still not finished because we continue to experience distress in the present moment. The current distress gives a sense that we have not "gotten over" the event. The distress in the present also impacts our ability to function resourcefully in the present.

Resolved Memory: We experience minimal distress and impact in the present when we remember a past event that was painful at the time it occurred. We can recall that it was painful when it occurred, but it is now quite difficult to re-experience that pain in the present. The lack of distress in the present moment when we recall it gives us the sense that the event is "over" or "finished."

Avoided Memory: Some people may try to resolve a memory by avoiding recall of the memory. This does not resolve the memory. Avoiding distress is not the same thing as resolving distress.

Metaphor for Painful Memories

I can recall observing a young child painfully stubbing his toe. It was almost possible to see a scream travel from his toe, up his leg and chest to his mouth which had been opened to scream. He appeared to be in a form of suspended animation as the scream seemed to take forever to actually get to his already open mouth. This example is often used as a model to explain people's response to traumatic or painful events. Some people in the midst of a traumatic experience find the pain becomes so unbearable that they emotionally shut down and the scream never comes. They remain in that place of suspended animation and may never "wake up" to the fact that they survived.

Some schools of psychotherapy base their therapeutic approach on this understanding of painful memories and encourage their clients to "re-live" the experience and scream the unscreamed scream or cry the unshed tears. The cathartic experience is supposed to release the stored-up emotion and resolve the event. From my experience

The challenge of this life is not to stay alive. The challenge of this life is to stay in Love.
— *Chris Rankin-Williams*

Denial is a common strategy that substitutes deliberate ignorance for thoughtful knowing.
— *Adapted from Charles Tremper*

Sometimes I wish I were a little kid again. Skinned knees are easier to fix than broken hearts.
— *Unknown*

this may or may not be true. I have witnessed people experience significant relief from a cathartic experience, and I have seen others become more deeply awash in emotion that did not heal – in fact, it left the person in a worse place, as they seemed ensnared in an endless loop of reliving the trauma.

Memory Triggers and Levels of Distress

Painful memories result in varying levels of distress. There are two aspects to the distress: one is the intensity of the distress, and the other is the person's ability to control or influence the process of recalling. The most debilitating experience is to have high levels of distress combined with minimal ability to control the course of the recall. The sense of powerlessness over the memory will leave the person feeling additionally victimized by the memory as well as the initial experience.

In the most severe cases a traumatized person experiences flashbacks and intrusive memories with little conscious awareness of the current triggers that are causing them to relive the initial trauma. This can result in high levels of anxiety as the person is continually on guard against possible flashbacks. At this point the problem is not simply that the person had a traumatic experience in the past, but that they are now afraid or phobic in the present moment of having another flashback. The current phobia and high anxiety levels can cause severe disruption to their current functioning. This level of distress is called Post Traumatic Stress Disorder (PTSD).

Less severe episodes involve intrusive memories and distress in response to identifiable triggers in the environment. In these cases, the person may intentionally avoid places that parallel the original trauma and which may evoke a painful recall of the trauma. While the triggers may be identifiable, the person's present fear of being flooded with memories and pain remains a key feature of their current distress.

Milder, painful memories are those that arise, usually in response to an identifiable trigger, and result in emotional distress such as sadness or anger but are not accompanied with a fearful sense of reliving the trauma. While not afraid of having "a painful memory attack" the person may still be debilitated in the present moment by feelings of vulnerability, powerlessness, or sadness that limit their ability to experience pleasure and happiness in the present moment.

Goal for Resolving Painful Memories

We cannot change one iota of our past. The past is past and what was done cannot be changed. To try to change the past would actually be delusional. While we cannot change the past, we can change how we view the past. We can also change how we allow the past to inform or influence our present and future decisions and behavior.

Many years ago I badly tore up a finger with a chainsaw. When I went to the hospital the doctor looked at the finger and after x-raying it said that while I had not injured the bone there was no flesh left to stitch or repair. They applied a dressing which allowed a scab and finally scar tissue to form. Fortunately, I still have full use of the finger despite the significant scar tissue. I was also fortunate that the accident did not leave me afraid of working with chainsaws or woodworking, which is a hobby I continue to enjoy.

What I find interesting is that I remember that the injured finger hurt and throbbed for days – but I cannot experience or access that throbbing in the present moment. And I do not want to forget the experience, as I use it to help ensure I engage in safer woodworking practices. When I think of resolving painful emotional memories I look for the same kind of response. I want to be able to recall the event, when I choose, without accessing the pain or distress, and be able to use the event to inform my current and future behavior.

When resolving a painful memory we do not want to obliterate or erase the event from memory. It would actually be unwise to erase something from a person's memory. If I forget my chainsaw accident I am likely to continue in dangerous behavior and suffer additional injuries. People who forget their history are doomed to repeat their history. While that is a good thing if we have good history, repeating bad history is not a good idea. The critical goal is to help the person regain control over how and when they remember, and to be able to remember from a place of well-being and resourcefulness.

In summary there are three goals for helping a client resolve a painful memory:

- To be able to **recall** an event without **re-living** or reexperiencing the pain or distress of the event.

- To be in control of when and how the event is remembered.

- To be able to freely access and use what was learned from the event to inform present and future behavior.

We cannot change one iota of our past. We can however change how we view the past and how we allow the past to inform and influence our future.

We don't want to obliterate a painful event from our memory because then we would have to go and do it all over again to learn that it wasn't a smart thing to do in the first place.

We want people to be able to freely recall their past and not to painfully relive their past.

A Narrative Approach to Resolving Painful Memories

When someone has survived a trauma there are three perspectives from which their story can be told. There is a victim story, a survivor story, and a thriver story. These three stories represent three "truths" that need to be told if a person is to resolve the painful memory.

Whole Truth Telling: The Three Truths

1. The victim story: A bad thing happened.

This is the story of the negative event and the circumstances that gave rise to suffering, pain, fear, and anger. Unfortunately many helpers (and the public in general) often get voyeuristically attached to the trauma and are unable to help the person see beyond their horror to the life-giving realities that still exist. Some people, in a desire to "tell their truth," get trapped in this partial truth, telling the victim story endlessly and in ways that "re-member" them into a state of helplessness. The problem is no longer the trauma which occurred in the past, but that the person has lost their resourcefulness in the present moment.

There may also be considerable secondary gain by telling this victim story, as it elicits caring and assistance from others. The person may now be using the trauma to tap into the resourcefulness of others rather than rediscovering their own resourcefulness.

Victim stories are often typified by a focus on the emotional effect the trauma has had on the person, rather than the actual events. Also neglected in the victim story is any mention of what the victim was doing prior to, in the midst of, or just after, the trauma. Sometimes the deletion of the person's actions from the narrative are because the person experiences shame as they recall their vulnerability and powerlessness.

Others may neglect to report their actions because they had some part in their victimization. It is very rare for anyone to be a totally innocent victim of a painful event. In victim stories, unhelpful absolutes are often created. The victim is perceived as totally innocent and the perpetrator totally guilty. Trying to assign blame does nothing towards accomplishing resolution. Rather than pursuing ideas of blame we need to be able to recognize our own acts that contributed to our injury if we are also to be able to recognize what we did to survive the injury.

Never put a period where God has put a comma.
— Gracie Allen

You are the author of your own story. If you don't like the story so far, start rewriting.

Thou shalt not be a victim. Thou shalt not be a perpetrator. Above all, thou shalt not be a bystander.
— Holocaust Museum, Washington, DC

2. The survivor story: The person or group survived.

This second story is crucial because many people who have experienced trauma do not realize, from a psychological perspective, that they survived. They are trapped or frozen in the trauma and need to discover that they survived. While the person may have been rescued by others, the person needs to focus on what they themselves did during that time to ensure that they survived. Some of the survival strategies, such as avoidance or, in extreme situations, dissociation, may eventually become problematic. However, in listening to these stories we need to behold with wonder and awe the sheer creativity of the human psyche to respond to life-threatening situations. It is from this place of wonder, and not from judgment, that we can help them discover more effective strategies for living their lives.

Several years ago I was at a gathering of psychotherapists who were having a conversation about a man who had been injured in a national disaster. He had been triaged in the field and set aside to be "medi-vac'd" to a hospital. In the chaos he was overlooked and left abandoned for 8 hours before he was discovered and taken to the hospital. He was now suffering not only from his injuries but from the terror of having been abandoned in the midst of his suffering. The psychologists were talking about how terrible it was, who was to blame, and who should be sued and punished, especially for the traumatizing neglect that had compounded the man's suffering. All of these conversations were in collusion with the man's sense of victimization, and ultimately unhelpful to restore him to a place of resourcefulness. What I wanted to do was find the man, help him find the part of himself that had not abandoned him when all of humanity had, and take that part out for a beer so that we could celebrate and thank it for keeping him alive.

Most victim stories have a quality of powerlessness or things being beyond the victim's control. To counter these feelings, when telling the survivor story it is important to find the behaviors that the person actually did to assist in their survival. While a person may have been rescued from the roof of their house in the middle of a flood, the person needs to describe how they were able to get up on the roof and how they sustained themselves while they waited to be rescued.

It is in their stories of survival that people can see and regain their resourcefulness. In the telling of these stories of survival they are "remembered" into a state of resourcefulness. They can discover strengths

Don't become a victim of yourself. Forget about the thief waiting in the alley; what about the thief in your mind?
— Jim Rohn

Denial ain't just a river in Egypt.
— Mark Twain

The turning point in the process of growing up is when you discover the core of strength within you that survives all hurt.
— Max Lerner

where previously they only saw weakness and put these strengths to work, not in re-living their past, but creating their future.

Both the story of the bad thing that happened and the story of survival need to be told in relationship to each other. If we only tell the stories of the negative thing that happened, then we will foster victim consciousness and keep the person trapped in their past. If we only tell the positive stories of how they survived, we would minimize their suffering and foster denial. We need to tell both stories, because each only has meaning in relationship to the other. Only when both stories are told can we create the possibility of transformed living in the Life that is beyond the notion of positive and negative. This leads us to the third truth that needs to be told.

3. **The thriver story: Despite the trauma, there is a life-giving future to be lived.**

I have heard people who have gone through horrendous ordeals say: "While I wouldn't wish this on anyone, including myself, I know I am a better person for it and my life today is much richer for the experience." Somehow through the entire experience the person has come to a place of thriving. They are not feeling victimized, or feeling that they simply survived. Despite their experience, they are fully alive and find life rich and rewarding.

While it may be a trite oversimplification, if you have a pulse you are being given life, and no matter what difficulties you have experienced, these difficulties have not deprived you of your pulse and your life. How you may engage in life may have been changed radically, but life itself has not been taken from you. It may be more profitable to wonder what that life wants to do with you rather than try to figure out what you are going to do with it. Our human history has numerous stories of people who have been disabled and who subsequently focused, not on what they have lost, but on what pleasure they can find in the present and the future despite their limitations.

We can also rephrase the thriver story from a theological perspective:

God, the Source of Life and Love, is greater than humanity's capacity for evil.

Where is God in the midst of suffering? Where is God in the horrors of the Holocaust, or genocide, or when a pastor molests a child? Why did we survive when others didn't? These are common and profound existential questions which most religions seek to address

---

Show me your face before your mother was born.
— Buddhist Koan
or put another way:

Show me your God-given face before the world tore it apart.

We don't want to explain yesterday's world, what we want to do is articulate tomorrow's possibilities

---

What the caterpillar calls the end of the world, the master calls a butterfly.
— Richard Bach

---

in some form. Despite all the evil humanity has inflicted upon itself throughout history, life goes on and is continually offered to each one of us, despite our deeds and the deeds done to us. World history is full of atrocities that humanity has inflicted on itself. Yet despite all that horror, life irrepressibly goes on and is continually offered to the just and unjust.

If your god does not have an adequate response to suffering or cannot "handle" human evil, such as the Holocaust or molestation, then it is much too small and you need to find another god.

Theologically the thriver story is the story of redemption. The Scriptures are full of stories of God being able to bring something good out of bad. The story of the resurrection following humanity's crucifixion of Christ is the classic Biblical thriver story: life for all comes from the death of one man. Joseph sold by his brothers into slavery and subsequently rescuing his brothers from famine is another (Genesis 37:1-36, 45:10-25).

Healing and the Three Stories

When a person has a prevailing victim narrative it will contaminate their future functioning. Their powerlessness will often defeat their efforts to engage in a satisfying life. This will create cycles of ongoing effort to change and feeling victimized by the subsequent failure. Attempts to make changes in their life are unlikely to be successful as long as the victim narrative is their prevailing narrative. Helping the person tell the survivor story will disrupt the ongoing power of the victim story and allow the person to work on creating their thriver story.

These three truths represent three different stories that can be told about any traumatic event: a victim's story, a survivor's story, and a thriver's story – the redemption story of new life. Helping a person to tell each of these stories is essential if they are to truly resolve painful memories and locate these events in their past.

If your god does not have an adequate response to suffering or cannot "handle" human evil such as the Holocaust or molestation, then it is much too small and you need to find another god.

To create a better world we don't need better people; we just need to help the people we have discover and be their best.

A Structural Way to Resolve Painful Memories

In the previous section I described the experience of painful events and memories from a narrative perspective of the victim, the survivor, and the thriver. Even though a person may be able to tell all three stories, they may continue to be distressed by painful memories of the trauma. This is similar to the experience that many people have when they have great insight into the causes of their problem but they experience no relief from the distress.

In the narrative approach, the focus is on the content of the stories. While the specific content cannot be changed, additional content can be added which will change the way we view the event. This is in essence what we have done when we get the person to tell the story from the perspective of how they survived and then from the perspective of thriving. When we change the perspective from which the event is viewed we are likely to experience a difference in how we feel about the event. For example, we are likely to feel distressed and powerless if we view the event from the perspective of the victim. In contrast we are likely to feel relieved and resourceful when we view the event from the perspective of the survivor.

In addition to changing the perspective from which the event is viewed we could also change **how** the event is represented or structured in our minds when we recall the event. Since changing the perspective changes how we feel about the event, then changing how we represent the memory in consciousness will also change the associated feelings we experience when recalling the event.

The Structure of Painful Memories

To create a solution to painful memories we need to discover how people structure or represent a prior experience in consciousness. We also need to explore any substantial differences between the structure of a painful memory and a resolved memory.

The first step to discovering the structure of a painful event is to remember a painful event and, rather than focusing on the content of the memory, become aware of how you are remembering. On the following page is an exercise to help you explore how you represent or structure the painful experience in consciousness. We will then explore and contrast how you structure a resolved memory.

Nothing in the world is more dangerous than sincere ignorance and conscientious stupidity.
— Martin Luther King, Jr.

When we change the way we look at things, the things we look at change.
— Unknown

Blessed are we who can laugh at ourselves for we shall never cease to be amused.
— Unknown

Instructions: This exercise is designed to help you discover how you represent or structure in consciousness memories that you would like to resolve.

1. **Choose a Memory that You Would Like to Resolve.**

   Because this is a learning exercise, choose a memory that evokes some distress but does not overwhelm you.

2. **Discovering How You Remember the Painful Memory.**

   Recall the painful memory. Rather than focusing on the content of the event, observe how you are representing the experience in your mind ...

   Are you "seeing" the event – representing the event in your mind as a picture? ...

   If you are seeing the event, explore a little further and see whether you are seeing it as a series of still pictures or as a movie ...

   Are seeing it in color or in black and white? How bright are the colors? ...

   Do the pictures seem close or far away from you? ...

   Are you "hearing" the event – listening to the conversations and sounds of the event? ...

   If you are hearing the event, observe the quality of the sounds such as loudness, tone, pitch ...

   Do the sounds seem close or far away from you? ...

   Apart from emotions of hurt that you might be feeling, are you "feeling" or experiencing any physical sensations in your body associated to the memory as you recall the event? ...

   If you are, where in your body are the sensations located? ...

   Are you aware of any smells or tastes associated to the memory? ...

   If so, are you "smelling" or "tasting" them now as you recall the event? ...

   Observe whether one way of representing (seeing, hearing, feeling, smell, taste) dominates the representation, or how they are combined to give you a total sense of what happened ...

   "Shake off" the previous experience by stretching or changing your posture before doing the next exercise.

3. **Discovering How You Remember a Resolved Memory.**

   Recall a memory of an event that was painful at the time but is no longer distressing when you recall it now. Repeat the above process, observing how you represent this memory in your mind.

   Are you "seeing" the event? ... (movies, still pictures, color, size, clarity, closeness etc.)

   Are you "hearing" the event? ... (loudness, tone, pitch etc.)

   Are you "feeling," "smelling," or "tasting" anything associated to the memory? ...

   Observe whether any way of representing the experience dominates the memory ...

4. **Compare the Representations of the Unresolved and Resolved Memory.**

   Compare any differences between how you represent or structure the two experiences in your mind as you recall them ...

---

*It isn't our position
but our disposition which
makes us happy.*
— Unknown

*I started out with nothing.
I still have most of it.*
— Michael Davis

*"Cheshire Puss,"
asked Alice.
"Would you tell me,
please, which way I ought
to go from here?"
"That depends a good deal
on where you want to go,"
said the Cat.
"I don't much care where,"
said Alice.
"Then it doesn't matter
which way you go,"
said the Cat.*
— From "Alice's Adventures in
Wonderland" by Lewis Carroll

Reflections on the Structure of Memories Exercise

For most people, visualization is the dominant preference when recalling a memory. Even when the specific images are not well-developed most people can recall colors, shapes, or sizes of the various aspects of their memory of the event. This parallels our sensory development. Barring visual disability, most people have a highly developed visual system and are well-equipped to deal with complex pictures or montages. This enables the person to attend simultaneously to a variety of visual images. In contrast, our other representational systems, such as our hearing, are not as well developed. For example, it is very difficult for most of us to pay attention to two different conversations at the same time.

Because our visual processing is usually more developed than other forms of sensing, it is likely to provide a larger portion of how we represent the memory of an event. Because it is a well-developed sense we will also be more skilled at altering the visual representations when we develop a strategy to resolve painful memories.

In the previous exercise, when you compared your visual representations of painful and resolved memories it is likely that you noticed some significant differences. While each person's representations will be different, I have found that painful memories are more likely to be represented by pictures that are large, vivid, and in color. In contrast, resolved memories are likely to be represented by pictures that are smaller and often blurry, with less saturated colors or even in black and white.

People have also reported differences in their subjective sense of where the pictures are located. In general, resolved memories seem more distant from the person. In contrast, painful memories often seem very close to the person.

We can use these representational differences to help a client restructure their painful memory to match the structure of a resolved memory as part of an overall strategy to resolve a painful memory.

Painful Memories in Relation to Perceptions of Time

In the previous exercise, we explored the differences between the structure of a painful and a resolved memory. We can also explore differences in the way we relate our painful memories to our perception of time[1]. Take a moment and think of how you stated your goal for resolving the painful memory.

When I listen to clients describe what they want in relation to a painful memory they will often say things like:

"I want/need to get over this."
"I want/need to put this behind me."

In contrast, when someone reflects on a resolved memory, they are likely to say something like:

"It used to hurt but I got over it."
"It was painful at the time but I put it all behind me."

Where are we "standing" in relation to the event if we need to "get over it" or "put it behind us"? These statements suggest that when we are experiencing a painful memory we have somehow placed ourselves before the event and are looking toward the event. This indicates that painful memories represent a distortion or disruption to the person's perception of time. This gives rise to the sense that we are trapped in the past, or in the midst of the event, rather than being free to live in the present moment.

In contrast, when a person recalls a resolved memory they are putting themselves "after" the event and are looking back on the event. This suggests that one of the things we need to do to resolve a painful memory is to understand how the person experiences time and restructure any disruptions in their perception of time.

These differences are represented on the following graphic. The level of experienced distress depends on where the person is "standing" or positioning themselves with respect to their experience of time:

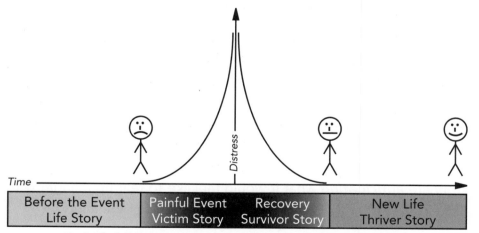

Painful Memories and Perception of Time

When a memory is very distressing there is likely to be an even more severe disruption to the person's experience of time. The person will continually stand just before the event, always anticipating the

> *You have to go and fetch the future. It's not coming towards you, it's running away.*
> — Zulu Proverb

> *When I was a boy of fourteen, my father was so ignorant I could hardly stand to have the old man around. But when I got to be twenty-one, I was astonished at how much the old man had learned in seven years.*
> — Mark Twain

> *You can't change the past, but you can ruin the present by worrying about the future.*
> — Unknown

experience erupting from their memory. From this perspective, the painful event is the next thing to be experienced in their future. Attempts to go forward into the future or imagine a future are likely to evoke a re-experiencing of the old experience. From this perspective the experience of a "flashback" is actually a "flash-forward" as the person is propelled into reliving the experience.

As we create a strategy to resolve painful memories, we will need to develop a process that includes correcting these distortions in perceived time. That will enable the person to view the event as past – as a concluded event from the perspective of present time.

Coming to Terms with the Past or the Future or Both

A common assumption in many therapeutic approaches is that people need to "come to terms with" their past. I find that assumption quite limiting as I think what we really need to "come to terms with" is our future since that is where we will spend the rest of our lives. From my experience, many approaches of "coming to terms with" the past involve seemingly endless conversations about the content of the past. This does not free people to live fully in the present moment as they work on creating the future they desire, but keeps them trapped in the past.

From an experiential perspective, painful memories from our past always seem to be hovering in our immediate future. Rather than coming to terms with the past we need to put the past *in* the past so that we can focus our attention on creating our preferred future.

Anticipated Pain and Actual Pain

Many of us have had the experience of anticipating a painful event, such as a root canal, be more distressing than the pain of the actual procedure. Previously, I mentioned injuring my finger with a chainsaw. When I tell the story as part of teaching on pain, I find that many people will flinch and experience distress at the thought of my finger being torn up. What I find interesting is that I look back on that event without distress, but the people who are experiencing distress when I tell the story are **anticipating** what it would feel like to tear up a finger with a chainsaw rather than **actually** feeling the pain of the injury.

As I have pointed out in the previous section, painful memories involve a distortion of perceived time. When a person is standing before an event, with respect to time, they are anticipating pain, not feeling the actual pain of the event. When we reflect on how we

> *If you come to a fork in the road, take it.*
> — Yogi Berra

> *It's not denial. I'm just selective about the reality I accept.*
> — Bill Watterson

> *If you keep telling the same sad small story, you will keep living the same sad small life.*
> — Jean Houston

experience a painful memory we are likely to find we engage in the following process:

- We will remember the event by playing a "movie" of it in our mind.

- Since we know the story we will begin to anticipate pain or distress as the movie begins to play.

- At some point the pain will get severe and we will stop watching the movie, long before we ever get to the part of how the experience was resolved. What we are actually playing is the movie of the victim story.

- Since the movie is stopped prior to resolution, we "slide" back in time to before the event began.

This suggests that a large component of a painful memory is a repetitive remembering of the beginning of the painful memory, the anticipation of pain, and then aborting the memory as the anticipated pain becomes severe. Because the memory is never completed the person "slides" back to the beginning of the memory. Repeated remembering of only the victim portion will reinforce the anticipation of pain rather than resolving the painful memory.

Creating a Strategy to Resolve Painful Memories

On the following pages is an exercise that focuses on how you represent painful and resolved memories and how to transform painful memories into resolved memories. Before completing this exercise I encourage you to repeat these exercises:

- Representing Time *(page 52)*
- Golden Thread of Life *(page 54)*

When done together these exercises are designed to integrate your understanding of the structure of painful memories and their relationship to time. In training programs I often lead people through these exercises before engaging in any of the preceding discussions. This is because the approach is novel and often outside of the typical paradigms for treating trauma. The experiential exercises create a more powerful learning experience than the intellectual presentation.

Do the exercises by listening to the audio recordings or have someone lead you through them in the order that they are presented to develop your experiential understanding of how to resolve painful memories.

*Not all bad things
cause painful memories.*

*Never be bullied
into silence.
Never allow yourself
to be made a victim.
Accept no one's definition
of your life;
define yourself.*
— Harvey Fierstein

*The idea is to rescue myself
from the role of a victim.
That I have a choice left.
Though I can't change
what has happened,
I can choose how to react.
And I don't want to spend
the rest of my life being
bitter and locked up.*
— Tori Amos

Instructions: For the purpose of learning about how you experience and can resolve traumatic memories, I invite you to think of some past experience that you still find moderately distressing and that you would like to resolve. Use the following criteria to choose the event you want to learn from:

- Choose an event with a moderate level of distress, so you can also attend to the learning process and not be overwhelmed by the experience.

- Choose an event that you would like to resolve, or that you have no substantial objections to resolving.

- Choose an event that is a discrete event from your past and is not part of an ongoing conflict with the people involved in the past event. These conflicts may contaminate your learning experience.

1. **Obtain a Baseline Measure of Your Distress.**
   On a 0-10 scale (10 being severe) assess your current level of distress as you recall the event ...

2. **Recall the Event as a Brief Movie.**
   Notice how you are experiencing the movie with respect to time ...
   If you are saying to yourself, "I need to get over this" you are standing before the event looking toward it rather than looking back on it.
   The distress you are experiencing is from anticipating the event rather than looking back.

3. **Add "Before and After" Movie Clips to the Event.**
   "Step back" from your experience so you can see the movie as part of your timeline ...
   From this vantage point add a brief movie clip to the beginning of your movie.
   The additional movie clip should be from a place of calm or well-being and be added to the beginning of the painful event. Run the combined movie ...

   Now "step back" from the movie so you can add a movie clip to the end of the movie ...
   The movie clip should be long enough to take you from the painful event to the first time you recall being calm or at ease after the event ...

   From this vantage point run the combined movie with the "before and after" clips ...

4. **View the Extended Movie as part of the Movie of Your Life.**
   Now "step back" from the short movie so you can see the event as one small part of the entire movie of your life. Play your life movie through very quickly in high fast forward and when you get to the present moment "step" into your present moment ...
   From the present moment look back on the event which is now in your distant past ...

5. **Assess Your Current Level of Distress.**
   In the present moment assess your level of distress on the 0-10 scale as you recall the event ...
   You will still be able to remember the event but most people will report a substantial reduction in current distress as they recall the previously distressing event.
   Notice how you are now standing after the event looking back on the event rather than standing before the event looking toward it occurring ...

6. **Adding Awareness of the Golden Thread of Life.**
   Stand in the present moment and be aware of what gives you life today ...
   Separate the life-giving quality from your temporal experience of the quality ...
   For example, see the quality of friendship as distinct from your specific friends ...

See this life-giving quality as a golden thread in the present flowing out into the future ...
Now look back and see the thread of life flowing up from your past before the event ...
Through the event ... into your present ... and into your future ...
Realize that this bad experience in the past was not able to stop that which gives you life ...
Check your level of distress as you recall the event now.

The Following Steps May be Helpful to Resolve any Residual Distress.

7. For Auditory Triggers.

Check to see if your distress is triggered by sounds of the event; if so, repeat the process of adding movie clips, but watch the movie as a silent movie ...
You could also try running the movie as a black and white movie ...
Check your level of distress as you recall the event now.

8. Compare and Modify Representation.

Look back on the time period of the distressing event and find another event that does not elicit any significant emotion ...
Note how you are representing that event. Is it in color or black and white, clear or fuzzy? ...
Note also the size of the neutral picture from that time period ...

Check the representation of the distressing image ...
Convert the distressing picture to the same size and qualities of the non-distressing picture ...

If you still have a movie of the distressing event, convert the movie to a poster like those used to advertise a movie, and then convert the poster to the same size and qualities as the non-distressing picture ...
Check your level of distress as you recall the event now.

9. Consider Whether There is Something to Learn from the Event.

If you are unable to transform the pictures to non-distressing images, ask the pictures: "What wisdom do you have to share before you will allow yourself to be transformed?"
Often our inner wisdom will not allow us to resolve a painful memory until we have learned its lesson. Allow the picture to teach you what to do differently in the future if you are confronted with a similar situation ...
Imagine doing the new behavior in the future ...
Now return to the past images and allow the distressing images to be transformed into the same form as the non-distressing images from that time frame ...
Check your level of distress as you recall the event now.

10. Check For and Satisfy any Objections.

Does any part of you object to completely letting go of the distress? If there is an objection ask that part what the objection is and what would satisfy the objection ...
Satisfy these objections rather than overcoming them ...
Check your level of distress as you recall the event now.

11. Final Step — Assess the Outcome.

When you have the current distress down to between 0 and 1, repeat step 6.
Now recall the event and try to feel the old level of distress.

The Appreciative Way

Integrating the Narrative and Structural Approaches

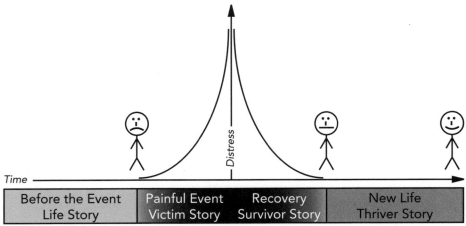

Integrating the Narrative and Structural Approach

The small abbreviated movie of the event is the victim story. When a person gets caught in the victim story, repeatedly telling the story only reinforces the distress rather than alleviating it. Each retelling evokes the anticipation of distress, which is then aborted, thus returning the person to the beginning of the story.

The additional clip of what happened afterward is the survivor story. It completes the story. Now a retelling of the enlarged story will allow the person to enter a non-distressed state.

Awareness of life in all its fullness in the present moment is the foundation of the thriver story. This story firmly places us in the present moment from which we can look back and see the event as one aspect of our past. As one person, reported the event becomes "one speck in the spectrum of my life."

Using the Process to Resolve Memories

The preceding exercises can be used to help a client resolve a painful memory. The scripts will need to be adapted to the particular needs of the individual you are working with. Here are some additional guidelines for using the process with a client:

- You will not need to lead the client through an "educational event" or teach them about the process. Simply lead them through:
  - the Representing Time exercise *(page 52)*
  - the Golden Thread of Life exercise *(page 54)*
  - steps 1-6 of the Resolving Painful Memories exercise *(page 94)* and if necessary any of steps 7-10 *(page 95)*

- I have used the process successfully without the Golden Thread step, and I have also found the Golden Thread exercise helpful in resolving residual distress.

- When using the process with a client, you yourself will not need to know the content of the memory. This is one of the remarkable aspects of this healing process. It defies much of what we have been taught!

- Some clients may feel more comfortable if you listen to the essential details of the memory. However, while offering empathy to facilitate acceptance, it is important not to get so immersed in the re-telling of the story that the victim narrative is simply reinforced. If the client does tell you about the event, pay attention to the way they are representing the event in consciousness and not just the content of the event.

Satisfying Objections to Resolving Painful Memories

Because the previous exercise was an educational demonstration, it was based on the premise that you wanted to resolve the memory that you chose. When working with a client, you may have to be more specific about seeking and satisfying any objections to resolving the painful memory. This is especially true if the client is unable to experience a reduction in their distress or there is some degree of residual distress.

When an objection is discovered it is important to "welcome" the objection as part of the client's internal wisdom rather than judging it and fighting with it as though it is a delinquent or resistant part of the client. Often people will be ashamed that part of them objects to finding healing and ignore the potential wisdom that is in the objection. Satisfying the objection, rather than overcoming the objection, is profoundly respectful of the part that is objecting and is a way to access its wisdom.

When I Wouldn't Use the Process

I would not use this process when the client has a high level of anxiety or distress that makes it difficult for them to stay safely engaged in the healing process. Examples of these would include sustained abuse or trauma that resulted in symptoms of PTSD such as flashbacks. These symptoms often include severe anxiety or a phobic response toward situations that trigger the intrusive memories and reactions. In the next section I will describe a process that can be used to resolve these types of severe traumatic memories.

The last thing I want to be known as is 'The Girl Who Got Raped'. The big turn around you make in your head is from victim to survivor.
— Tori Amos

Jesus did.
I was hopping along, when suddenly he comes and cures me. One minute I'm a leper with a trade, next moment me livelihood's gone. Not so much as a by your leave. Look, I'm not saying that being a leper was a bowl of cherries. But it was a living. I mean, you try waving muscular suntanned limbs in people's faces demanding compassion. It's a bloody disaster.
— Monty Python

Resolving Traumatic Memories

Traumatic memories are an extreme example of painful memories. They are characterized by intrusive flashbacks of the traumatic event. They are often associated with high levels of anxiety and arousal. The person is likely to avoid situations that may evoke the flashbacks.

In addition to high levels of anxiety, traumatic memories are also associated with a significant distortion in perceived time. One woman who had experienced over 20 years of traumatic memories reported that her picture of the trauma was just up to the right of her face. It was literally the next thing on her timeline that she had to experience. Every waking moment of her life she was faced by this traumatic experience. In these situations all of life will be "seen" through and colored by this experience.

Creating a Strategy to Resolve Traumatic Memories[2]

One of the first steps is to pay attention to the specific nature of the current problem. When a traumatic thing has happened there several things we can focus our attention on:

- The actual event. Since the actual event is over it is never the current problem. Talking about the past event will not help unless it impacts some or all of the following:

- How the event is being remembered or re-represented in consciousness.

- How the client responds to the re-representation, such as panicking, "freaking out," or engaging in safety behaviors such as "hitting the deck" to avoid imagined gunfire.

- How they feel about their response to the re-representation, such as embarrassment or shame.

- What they do to deal with these feelings such as avoiding public places where the shame may occur.

Paying attention to the exact nature of the current problem is important. A person may be avoiding public places not because they are afraid that the sound of a car backfiring will cause a flashback of a traumatic war event, but because they are afraid of "freaking out" in public. What needs to be "treated" is the fear of freaking out and not simply the traumatic memory that initiated the freaking out. Just "treating" the traumatic event will not help resolve the fear of freaking out, which is the actual current problem and point of distress.

Creating Safety

High levels of anxiety indicate the client is not feeling safe. If the coach develops a strategy to respond to the trauma that evokes these levels of anxiety, then the resolution process is likely to be disrupted, which will leave the client even more deeply associated with the anxiety and their distress. As Bill O'Hanlon says, we need to "heal the trauma without the drama." One of the essential parts of the strategy is to create a safe place for the client to view the experience and its resolution. We want them to be able to view the event from a place of personal assurance and resourcefulness rather than a place of victimized powerlessness.

Your presence as a coach offering acceptance through each stage of the process will help provide a sense of safety. However, beyond external resources we need to help the client develop internal resources of safety from which to view the anxiety-producing experience. When we think of dangerous situations, one thing that provides safety is distance from the danger. In the coaching process we will help the client create emotional distance between themselves and the troubling experience. This parallels the sense we have of things that we have resolved being in the distant past.

One way to create emotional distance from an event is to observe ourselves in the event. We can put even more distance between ourselves and the event by viewing our selves as we view ourselves in the event. We could also add additional distance by "stepping back" even further to view ourselves viewing ourselves as we view ourselves in an event (though too many "steps back" become unhelpful, as we are likely to become confused as to who is watching what).

Another way to create safety is to make sure the place we watch from is safe. We could watch the scene through bullet-proof glass, or in the company of a friend. It is common in some Christian circles to view painful events with Jesus and in his presence find healing. This can be a very powerful technique, but it is often then viewed as a testimony to Jesus being the "true" healing agent in the process. There is no spiritual healing magic to Jesus' presence in these processes. The person could also view the scene in the company of Buddha, a favorite saint, or the Easter bunny for that matter, or simply on their own, and find the same healing. What Jesus or any other "preferred companion" offers in these situations is an additional resource of safety to be able to view the scene. I have successfully used the process with and without such resources.

Our sorrows and wounds are healed only when we touch them with compassion.
— Buddha

Worry never robs tomorrow of its sorrow, it only saps today of its joy.
— Leo Buscaglia

Darkness cannot drive out darkness; only light can do that. Hate cannot drive out hate; only love can do that.
— Martin Luther King, Jr.

When working with a client, my questions are these:

- What does the client need to feel safe?
- What resources does the client have to provide that safety?

If Jesus is a resource of safety, I might use that. If we have established a resource of unconditional love, I might use that. Most of the time I don't use either because I find that people can experience sufficient safety by creating distance between themselves and the event and they do not require additional resources.

Watching the Event as a Movie

We will use the process of putting distance between the event and observing the event from a place of safety by inviting the client to imagine viewing the event from the projection room in a movie theater. To create emotional distance we will have the client not simply watch the movie, but watch themselves watching the movie. We will also have the movie run in black and white, and if necessary as a silent movie, to reduce the emotional intensity and impact of the movie. If necessary, we can also ensure that the projection room is a safe place to watch the movie by having the client access any internal resources they need in order to feel safe.

Viewing Heinous Events

In the process of healing the client is going to be invited to view the traumatic event. This raises the following questions:

- How should the person view the event?
- What does it mean to view the event from an emotionally safe or emotionally neutral place?
- Is that morally acceptable when a heinous thing has been done to them?

My answer to these questions is pragmatic. What way of viewing the event helps the client live fully today as they work on building a better tomorrow? Viewing the past with anger does not create a just tomorrow, it simply keeps us attached to the atrocity. Excusing or denying the fundamental wrongness of the behavior is also unhelpful because we will simply encourage that kind of behavior to continue. What we need to do is view the event from a place of emotional safety, and not from a place of emotional comfort. I don't think it is appropriate to be comfortable when we view something heinous.

*I hate war
as only a soldier
who has lived it can,
only as one who has seen
its brutality, its futility,
its stupidity.*
— Dwight David Eisenhower

*The most shocking
fact about war
is that its victims
and its instruments are
individual human beings,
and that these individual
beings are condemned by
the monstrous conventions
of politics to murder or be
murdered in quarrels
not their own.*
— Aldous Huxley

I think we need to help clients view events through the eyes of compassion. Viewing a past heinous act compassionately means to view the event from a place of emotional neutrality, while standing firm in the understanding that the behavior was wrong, and being fiercely determined to being part of co-creating a future in which those kinds of atrocities don't happen again. Viewing something compassionately means we are detached from our emotions related to what happened in the past and our emotions are attached to pursuing justice and peace in the future.

Caution! This May Mess Up Any Legal Claims

Sometimes there is a secondary gain to being the victim of a traumatic event. If a client has a legal claim for pain and suffering following a traumatic event, engaging in this exercise may radically mess that claim up, or the need to stay in pain to justify the claim may mess up the healing process.

Beyond financial rewards, there may be other secondary gains to being the victim of a traumatic event. A person may receive deferential treatment because of their victim status. Finding healing means we are no longer victims and will no longer be able to access these secondary gains. If the healing process seems to get blocked, these secondary gains can be explored and resolved using the seeking and satisfying objections strategy.

On the following pages are the steps to resolve traumatic memories. I have successfully used the process to resolve traumatic experiences on a variety of levels, from a panic reaction triggered by an adversarial performance appraisal to a person witnessing a death following a violent crime. While the process is essentially the same, each situation required some minor adaptation to meet the specific needs of the client's experience. In these situations it is important to continue to check the outcome of the interventions and seek complete resolution rather than settling for the initial major reduction in distress.

There is a wonderful almost mystical law of nature that says the three things we want most – happiness, freedom, and peace of mind – are always attained when we give them to others.
— Fran Power Judd

People are like stained-glass windows. They sparkle and shine when the sun is out, but when the darkness sets in, their beauty is revealed only if there is a light from within.
— Elisabeth Kubler-Ross

Instructions: The goal of the exercise is to be able to review the traumatic experience from a place of safety and well-being rather than re-living it from a place of distress. In the process the intense emotional reaction will be separated from the memory so that you will be able to recall the event without distress when you choose, and not re-live the memory with all of its emotional distress.

If you are leading a client through the exercise, tell them all the steps you are going to go through first, and then have them do it.

Note: The coach does not need to know anything about the precipitating event. This process can be done entirely content-free. However, in some situations it may be helpful from the perspective of establishing an atmosphere of acceptance for the client to know that the coach knows some aspects of the event. While being empathetic, we don't want to be voyeurs and become distracted from the task of bringing healing.

1. **Clarify the Nature of the Current Distress.**

   Is the problem the memories of the event or a subsequent response such as having a "freak out" or panic response in public? If the distress is related to a panic response, then make the panic response and not the initiating event, the traumatic event in the following process. If it is both, first start with the activating event and then repeat the exercise with the panic response if there are still significant levels of distress at the end of the exercise.

2. **Obtain a Baseline Measure of Distress.**

   On a 0-10 scale (10 being severe) assess your current level of distress as you recall the event ... If you have multiple episodes within the memory, choose the most distressing as an archetypal expression of all the other events.

3. **Briefly Describe the Steps to the Client.**

   I am going to lead you through the following process. I want to tell you the steps before you actually do them.

   I am going to get you to imagine sitting in a movie theater from about halfway back from the screen. Then I am going to get you to imagine floating up out of your body into the projection room so that you can watch yourself watching yourself view a movie.

   The movie playing on the screen will be a black and white movie of the traumatic event from its beginning all the way through until you are at a place of resolution or peace after the event. You will be in the projection room in safety watching yourself watch the movie, rather than actually watching the movie itself.

   When the movie is done I am going to get you to leave the projection room, gather yourself up from the theater, and climb up into the last scene on the screen. Then you will play the movie backwards in color at high speed with you in the movie, all the way to the beginning. Is that clear? I will guide you through the process so you don't have to remember the steps. I just want to be sure you understand the steps ...

4. **Creating a Place of Safety.**

   Imagine being in a movie theater, about halfway back from the screen ...
   As you sit in the theater feel the chair against your back and buttocks ...
   When you are able to fully imagine being in the theater, float up out of your body into

the projection room so that you can look down from the projection room and see yourself watching the screen ...

5. **Watching Yourself Watch the Movie.**
Watch yourself watching yourself in a movie of the event ...
Pay attention to yourself watching the screen rather than what is on the screen ...
The movie is in black and white and will end when you have gone through the event to a place of resolution. Let me know when the movie has ended ...

6. **Reunite With Yourself.**
Now leave the projection room and reunite with your body in the movie theater. Climb up into yourself on the screen in the final scene where you are at a place of resolution ...

7. **Play the Movie Backwards.**
From within the movie, play the movie backwards, in color, very fast, until you are back before the event in a place of calm. You may find it helpful to make a swooshing sound as the movie goes backward very fast ...

8. **Assess the Outcome.**
Recall the event and use the 0-10 scale to assess your level of distress. You will be able to recall the event but you should be able to do so without any significant distress ...

Many clients will report that the level of distress is down to a 3 or 4, from perhaps an 8 or 9. While significant, we want to get the level down to below a 1 to ensure the resolution is sustainable. Below are some additional steps or adaptations that may be necessary to achieve a final resolution. If you need to, do the additional step(s) before the final step #9.

9. **Rehearse Scenarios that Used to Evoke Distress.**
Now that you have this new resourceful state I invite you to visit in your imagination any scenes that activated the old flashbacks, and rehearse being in those situations with this new state of safety and resourcefulness ...

Additional Steps and Adaptations.

If there is residual distress consider some of the following possibilities. After completing any of the following steps invite the client to remember the traumatic event and assess their level of distress. Keep working until you get the level down to a 1 or less and then return to step 9.

- **If the Process Seems Hesitant.**
  If the process seemed very stop-start use the first attempt as a practice and repeat the process in one continuous fluid process. Some clients have felt the need to do each step several times to ensure they are doing it right. Rather than repeating individual steps, have them do all the steps once from beginning to end.

- **If the Client is Worried that the Flashbacks Will Return.**
  When it works, clients will not need to repeat or practice the process at home.
  Some clients who have suffered for a long time may believe that they need to continue to practice watching the movie as homework to ward off a return of the distress. Reassure them that this is not so, and that in fact reviewing the movie may reactivate the distress.

- **Difficulty Achieving a State of Safety.**
  When the client is unable to achieve a state of safety to view themselves watching the movie:

  Reinforce that the task is not to watch the screen from the projection room, it is to watch themselves watching the screen.
  The goal is to have the client experience the event the way a video recorder would record it, with sight and/or sound. Video recorders do not record emotion.

  It may be necessary to add an extra step of distance between the client and the event.
  Invite the client to imagine floating out of their body and sitting in the back of the movie theater, watching themselves watching the movie, and then inviting them into the projection room so that they can watch themselves in the back of the movie theater, watching themselves in the middle of the movie theater, watching a movie of themselves.

  Invite the client to imagine a sheet of glass in front of them that they have to peer through.
  It may be helpful to have them put their hands up and "on the glass" as they peer through it.

  Ask if there is anything that the client needs with them to help them stay safe as they watch the movie ...
  Invite them to imagine having that resource with them in the projection room ...
  When the client is able to feel safe, repeat the steps 4-9.

- **Unresolved Triggers.**
  Check for any distressing stimuli in the event, such as sounds that the person is associating to.
  For sounds repeat the process but watch the movie as a "silent movie."

- **Is the Client Still Seeing the Event as a Movie?**
  Representing events as movies in consciousness often elicits more emotion that a still picture does. Check to see if the client is still recalling the event as a movie. If they are still seeing a movie then use the following process to transform the movie into neutral pictures:

  Take a moment and find an emotionally neutral event from that period of time – it may have been something painful at the time but no longer evokes any distress, or it may just be an emotionally neutral event...
  Observe the qualities of how you view that picture: its size, color, intensity, etc. ...
  Turn the movie into an archetypal poster, such as those found in cinemas ...
  Convert the poster into a picture like the other emotionally neutral pictures from that time ...
  Relocate this picture to be amongst other pictures from this time frame ...

  Assess the outcome and complete step 9.

- **Seek and Satisfy any Objections to Letting Go of the Distress.**
  Check to see if the client has any objections to letting go of the distress and living fully in the present moment. Ask the part that objects what would satisfy the objections. Satisfy the objections and then repeat steps 4-9 of the process.

Resolving Organizational Memories

Organizations such as a congregation can also be affected by traumatic or painful events, such as clergy misconduct or conflict among members. When a congregation's members have collectively experienced an event such as clerical sexual misconduct, a complex entanglement of pain and emotion arise that will require compassion and specialized skill on the part of those entrusted with the congregation's ongoing care. While the members may not have personally been subject to the abuse, many will feel significant distress at the violation of their values and the injury inflicted on those they know and care about.

Within the congregation there may be multiple views of the misconduct and its consequences. Many of these views will become polarized and conflicted. Some parishioners may be in denial, unable to believe that their beloved pastor did the things of which they are accused, and they may minimize the pain of others and/or become hostile toward the victims and their advocates. Others will have totally vilified the pastor and only want revenge. For them, to move beyond the trauma would be to minimize its reality and to deny justice.

Conversations about forgiveness can make the situation worse as some will use a rush to forgiveness as a way to minimize or "sweep under the rug" what has been done. While some may rush to forgive, others may never forgive and years later still remain trapped in their pain and resentment. They will not only resent what was done, but resent those who have forgiven and moved on with their lives.

Rather than minimizing suffering, true forgiveness requires a deep awareness of what needs to be forgiven. This requires the hard work of listening to the stories and moving beyond the victim stories to the survivor and thriver narratives.

While it is possible to see the resulting problems belonging to each individual, there are also synergistic effects among the members of the congregational system. These can either reinforce the negative effects of the trauma or be used to provide resources for healing.

Communities of people such as congregations create and maintain their sense of identity by virtue of the stories they formally and informally tell about themselves. When people get together and simply share the story of being victimized, they create and maintain a victim identity which will result in a sense of powerlessness that will flow into all aspects of their life and ministry.

Congregations need to come to terms with their future rather than spending time dwelling in their past.

I still say a church steeple with a lightning rod on top shows a lack of confidence. — Doug McLeod

Unless someone like you cares a whole awful lot, nothing is going to get better. It's not. — Dr. Seuss

Some of the results of repeatedly telling victim stories include:

- Demotivation of people to engage in ministry.

- Loss of trust and willingness to engage with others.

- Lifeless worship.

- Conflict, often over trivial issues unrelated to the trauma.

- Conflict between people who have moved on and those who haven't. Some are accused of not forgiving while others are accused of forgiving too easily.

- Members using threats of withholding resources such as pledges to influence outcomes. In the midst of powerlessness people may use fear to terrorize others as a way to gain influence.

- Loss of membership and the inability to attract new members.

- Loss of financial resources.

- A sense of hopelessness, that there is nothing they can do change their lives or their world.

(It is important to note that having any or a combination of these experiences in a congregation is not an indication that they have been traumatized.)

Attempts to deal directly with any of these issues will be unsuccessful as long as the underlying victim narrative remains the congregation's predominant narrative. The sense of powerlessness that emanates from the victim narrative will often defeat, in self-fulfilling ways, attempts to confront and deal with these issues.

Consultants and denominational leaders may add to the problem by applying diagnostic and pejorative labels (such as "resistant" or "pathological") to the congregation. These labels reinforce the victim consciousness and create ongoing negative spirals of enfeeblement. When the trauma is a past event, it is never the problem. The problem is the way the trauma is kept alive in the present moment through the labels, which are shorthand anchors to the underlying narrative.

Since congregations often lose their clergy as part of the traumatic experience, transitional clergy have to be skilled in helping them transform their narrative. The transformed narrative needs to be communicated beyond the congregation to the denominational leaders and the new clergy as well. I have known really effective transitional clergy work with congregations to transform these narratives only for denominational leaders and the newly-arrived clergy to continue to see the congregation through the old lens of victim, or the pejorative

I like long walks, especially when they are taken by people who annoy me.
— Fred Allen

Love is the total absence of fear. Love asks no questions. Its natural state is one of extension and expansion, not comparison and measurement.
— Gerald Jampolsky

Avoidance and denial are forms of negative focus. They just keep the avoided thing as the focus of unspoken, mind-gripping attention.

labels of dysfunction. Within days the old narrative was reactivated and the drama of conflict, blame, and incompetence re-initiated.

Transforming the Underlying Narrative

Since the victim narrative is maintained by storytelling, it can also be transformed by storytelling. Appreciative Inquiry processes that engage a congregation in shared storytelling of their best experiences of the congregation will help the members tell and establish their thriver story. These stories are elicited by the use of predetermined questions that focus parishioners on the life-giving qualities of their congregation. When dealing with a congregation that has gone through a difficult time, the congregation also needs to focus their attention on how they survived as well as their best experiences.

For example, I once worked with a congregation that had gone through a major upheaval and lost over half of their members. When we began our work together, they could only talk about the bad thing that had happened. After listening to their victim story I asked them: "I am curious, what is here that is so valuable to you that you stayed, rather than leaving like the others?" As they began talking what was valuable and life-giving, they began sharing their survivor narratives, and spontaneously began to call themselves "the faithful remnant."

The "faithful remnant" is a huge Biblical narrative, and these people could see their small narrative as part of this greater narrative. It was from the joining of their narrative to God's narrative that they could begin to plan a thriver narrative because, despite what had happened, God was still present and offering them life. This process of embedding a smaller narrative in a larger narrative is at the heart of the Biblical way and will be used at the end of this section in a meditation that can be done with a congregation.

Here are some Appreciative Inquiry questions that can be used to transform a congregation's narrative. How you create and ask the questions is the key to the appreciative approach. The goal is to deeply engage the congregation in shared storytelling about what they value and find life-giving in their congregation.

- Tell me the story of your best experience as a parishioner at your church. Recall a time when you felt most alive, most involved, spiritually touched, or most excited about your involvement.

- Recall a time when you or people from your church reached out and cared for people in the wider community that left you feeling proud to be a member of your congregation.

Those who do not have power over the stories that dominate their lives, power to retell them, rethink them, deconstruct them, joke about them, and change them as times change, truly are powerless because they cannot think new thoughts.
— Salman Rushdie

Nobody gets to live life backwards. Look ahead – that's where your future lies.
— Ann Landers

The most serious mistakes are not being made as a result of wrong answers. The truly dangerous thing is asking the wrong question.
— Peter Drucker

- What do you deeply value about your church? Tell me a story about a time when you experienced what you value.
- If God gave you three wishes for your church, what would they be?

After people have shared their best experiences, values, and wishes, life-giving commonalties can be discerned. These core values and life-giving realities are then used to discern a shared vision for the future. Living into this vision creates the new thriver narrative for the congregation. Often, engaging in an Appreciative Inquiry process and envisioning a preferred future will restore a congregation to a place of hope without having to directly engage the victim narrative or its negative consequences.

The use of positive storytelling is not done to deny the past or the problems that have arisen from the past events. Every one of us has good stories and bad stories. The question is this: Which stories help us create our preferred future? We cannot create a future on the foundation of having "less bad" stories. We need to bring our best to the task of creating the future. And so we tell stories of the times when we were at our best, and within these stories discover our resources that we can use to create the future.

Creating a congregation-wide Appreciative Inquiry process to transform a congregation's narrative, to rebuild trust and restore them to a place of hopefulness, is beyond the scope of this book. Additional Appreciative Inquiry resources can be found at the Clergy Leadership Institute web site: www.appreciativeway.com.

The Loss of Trust

Probably the most lasting impact of abuse in a congregation is that the fabric of trust is violated and torn. The lack of trust may be found in a variety of relationships. Parishioners may no longer trust clergy, and act in ways that cause clergy not to trust them. Anger may be displaced onto the victims, or onto the bishop or adjudicatory leaders, for causing their beloved pastor to be removed. Parishioners may no longer trust one another, as some may have known of the abuse and done little to confront the pastor. Others may feel the situation was dealt with inappropriately. Some may have "moved on" while others remain fixated on the abuse.

While the cause of the broken trust may be in the past, the concern is for how the lack of trust is being manifested in the present. Without trust, people are unable to establish a community that can work together to change the world they live in. Without a sense of trusting

Without knowing their God-given purpose and grounding their goals in this purpose, change processes are likely to be random, life-sapping distractions that mire the congregation in mindless mediocrity.

If we fall, we don't need self-recrimination or blame or anger – we need a reawakening of our intention and a willingness to recommit, to be whole-hearted once again.
— Sharon Salzberg

community, apathy and pessimism will prevail.

In the following list of signs of a lack of trust, notice how they are all occurring in the present. While these signs may be associated with a history of abuse, their presence does not imply abuse has occurred. A subtle erosion of trust can occur in any congregation and may be reinforced through story-telling and gossip to become the prevailing culture.

Regardless of the causes in the past, the following signs of a lack of trust are always in the present:

- Some congregations may find it difficult to have open conversations about any significant concern.

- Meetings may be brief and tense with significant conversations being had in the parking lot between smaller groups.

- Power may be localized in a small group that makes decisions in secret.

- There may be little transparency with respect to finances.

- Parishioners may be uninspired and unwilling to engage with others in ministry to the community.

- An atmosphere of fear may pervade the congregation rather than an atmosphere of love and joy.

- Parishioners may intentionally avoid one another.

- Church meetings may be tense arguments over minor issues while larger issues are ignored.

- The diocese or other external agencies may be held in contempt, with the congregation acting as though they are under siege.

When we look over a list of signs of a lack of trust we can see that there is a common underlying element: it is no longer safe for people to come and be themselves. There is only alienation where there needs to be acceptance.

Rebuilding Trust: Truth and Reconciliation

Rebuilding trust requires that we have a clear idea of what trust is and what it is not. I define trust as "the ability to make vulnerable to another person's actions what you value, knowing that what you value will be kept safe."

We can destroy ourselves by cynicism and disillusion, just as effectively as by bombs.
— Kenneth Clark

Have you ever been hurt and the place tries to heal a bit, and you just pull the scar off of it over and over again?
— Rosa Parks

I'm not upset that you lied to me, I'm upset that from now on I can't believe you.
— Friedrich Nietzsche

One big mistake people make in regard to trust is that they make trust an "either/or" concept rather than seeing trust as being on a continuum. The task in life is not simply to trust or not trust, but to know "who to trust with what." It is foolish to trust people who have demonstrated that they are not trustworthy. This becomes important in the forgiveness process as many people think that forgiving someone means that you have to trust them. You may need to forgive the fox that kills your chickens, but that doesn't mean that you have to trust the fox and make the rest of chickens vulnerable to the fox's carnivorous actions. This false understanding of trust does not restore safety.

To rebuild trust, we need to first rebuild safety. Without making it safe, forcing people to talk when there is no trust will only make things worse. When people are unwilling to engage in conversation with one another we need to first ask: "What do you need to make it safe enough to have this conversation?"

One strategy to create safety is to focus on what people need **today** to feel safe, rather than on the origins of their lack of safety. People can be invited to remember times when they have felt safe in the past and explore what made them feel safe. Using this remembered experience and knowledge, they can then reflect on how they can offer these qualities, attitudes, or behaviors of safety to others.

Since trust is based on the ability to make vulnerable what we value, having conversations in a safe environment about what we value will help rebuild trust. The appreciative process of shared storytelling around what we value will often create a foundation for rebuilding trust without having to directly explore the lack of trust.

The South African Truth and Reconciliation Commission process was designed to make it safe enough for people to share the injustices that had been perpetrated by people on both sides of the conflict. In dealing with a past injustice, it is important to stay focused on the goal of reconciliation, which is about how we will live and work together in the future. The outcome of the healing process must be greater acceptance rather than increased alienation. The process is not truth and punishment, nor is it denial and reconciliation.

Just talking about the past will not help, unless it leads to changes in the present. Forgiveness is an essential part of the process. From my experience, many in the church do not know how to forgive. We will return to the issue of forgiveness in the section on forgiveness.

Farming looks mighty easy when your plow is a pencil and you're a thousand miles from the corn field.
— Dwight David Eisenhower

Too many decisions about changes are made by people untouched by the change process.
— Peter Block

And the day came when the risk to remain tight in a bud was more painful than the risk it took to blossom.
— Anaïs Nin

Conducting a History Day

Another approach that is used to transform a congregation's narrative is to conduct a "history day" where people can come and tell the stories of the congregation's past. From these stories the life-giving qualities of the congregation can be discerned and used as the foundation for imagining and building the congregation's future. Here are some things to help prepare for and lead a history day.

- Advertise the day well in advance so that people can include the day in their schedule.

- Prepare a room with blank newsprint on a wall. Create a timeline of the congregation's history, including a portion for the future. Divide the timeline into periods of time that make sense to the congregation, such as a senior pastor's tenure, or by decades.

- Invite people to bring photos and memorabilia of the different times to add to the timeline.

- At the history day, invite people to tell their story by writing notes on the newsprint. One strategy is to invite the people who joined the church during a particular timeframe to begin the history-telling, and then inviting others to share their experiences.

- Remind everyone that there are multiple perspectives or versions of the history, especially the history of a time that was conflicted. Rather than arguing over whose view of history is correct, simply allow people to put their multiple versions on the timeline.

- If a period in the life of the church was traumatic or distressing, ensure that the people include on the timeline the things they did to survive, and how they have survived the problems.

- After the stories are told, invite the congregation to discuss and discover the life-giving qualities of each period. Pay particular attention to any specific life-giving qualities that have been manifested consistently across periods of time.

- Engage the congregation in imagining the future by seeing the life-giving qualities going out into the future. Have the congregation imagine they have been really successful over the next 5 or 10 years, and write down what they would have achieved and would be doing. Add these to the future on the timeline.

- On the following page is a mediation that can be used at the end of the history day to help the congregation integrate their personal experience into the community's experience and also resolve any painful memories in the church's history.

The larger the island of knowledge, the longer the shoreline of wonder.
— Ralph W. Sockman

*History will be
kind to me
for I intend to write it.*
— Winston Churchill

*And God is able
to provide you with every
blessing in abundance,
so that by always having
enough of everything,
you may share
abundantly in
every good work.*
— 2 Corinthians 9:8

Instructions: The purpose of this exercise is to synthesize and integrate the members' shared histories into one congregational history. If there has been a difficult period in the congregation's history that still causes members to experience distress, the purpose is to help the members integrate the "victim narrative" with their "survivor narrative" and lay a foundation to create a "thriver narrative" if they have not already begun to do so. The overall goal of the exercise is to leave the congregation in a resourceful state as it considers its future.

- The exercise will take about 20 minutes. Depending on the time of the day and the previous activities it may be appropriate to take a brief personal refreshment break before doing this exercise.

- Inform the people that you will be leading them on a guided imagery meditation. Although you will be referring to "imagery" it is not a guided visualization. Some people have difficulty visualizing, but all can imagine. Proof of the ability to imagine is in the universal ability to worry, for worry is pure imagination.

- For those unfamiliar with leading a guided imagery exercise, we encourage you to practice with a couple of people before the session. For most people the key thing is to slow down and allow the participants to actually take the time to remember and to imagine.

- Invite the people to remove items from their laps, get comfortable, and relax.

- It is preferable for them to be able to see the history day timeline.

1. **Integrating Their Personal Story.**
   Remember the story of your first day in the congregation ...
   Remember what you valued and how you felt ...
   Remember what interested you and brought you back ...
   Now remember the highlights of your time as a member of the congregation ...
   Identify what has been life-giving and valuable to you ...
   Distinguish the life-giving quality from your temporal experience of it ...
   See this life-giving quality as golden thread running through your time and out into the future ...
   See this life-giving quality flowing back before you arrived ...

2. **When There Has Been a Distressing Event.**
   Play the distressing event through in your mind as a video ...
   Now in your mind "take a step back" from the event so that you can see it all as a set of still photos or events on the timeline ...
   Now "step back" so you can see what came before the event and add those pictures to the set of pictures of the event ...
   Now "step back" so you can see what happened after the event and how you have survived ...
   See what you did and what resources you relied on to survive ...
   Now "step back" so you can see the difficult time as a part of your entire time in the congregation ...
   Step into the present moment and see the life-giving quality flow back through the event ...

3. **Integrating The Personal Story With the Congregation's Story.**
   In your mind "step back" from your story so that you can see your story as part of your entire congregation's story ...

See the life-giving threads running through the congregation's story and through you ...
If your church is part of a denomination: In your mind "step back" from the congregation's story so you can see your congregation's story as part of your denomination's story ...

4. **Integrating the Congregation's Story With the Story of Christendom.**

   In your mind "step back" so you can see your church (and denomination) as part of Christ's church, the ongoing expression of Christ's ministry in the New Testament ...
   In the communion of Saints we are one with all who have followed Jesus ...
   See the life-giving threads weave through the church's history through your church and out into the future ...
   Notice how, even though they may get frayed, new forms and ways of experiencing these life-giving qualities occur ...
   We can remember St. Paul's words: "For I am convinced that neither death, nor life, nor angels, nor rulers, nor things present, nor things to come, nor powers, nor height, nor depth, nor anything else in all creation, will be able to separate us from the love of God in Christ Jesus our Lord." ...
   Notice how nothing has been able to destroy or overcome these life-giving threads ...

5. **Integrating Christendom into God's Story.**

   In your mind "step back" so you can see the church as part of God's entire story.
   From the beginning of time when God gave life to all things ...
   Through the Old Testament ...
   Through the New Testament ...
   Through the entire church history ...
   Through your church's history ...
   Through your history ...
   Be aware that God's power to bring new life is greater than any darkness ...
   That there is nowhere that is beyond the reach of God's love ...
   That time and again humanity has turned from God's love only to be loved back into Love ...

6. **Imagining the Future.**

   Now stand in the present moment and look into the future ...
   See those life-giving qualities flowing from God through the course of history, through you and others, out into the future to make a new history ...
   Be curious about how you and those who follow you will experience these life-giving qualities...
   Take a moment to look forward to the day when you can look back and behold with wonder the great things you and God have co-created ...
   Go to that place in the future and look back and see what you and others have accomplished as you have journeyed with God ...

7. **Return to the Present Moment.**

   And now allow your attention to return to this room, bringing your awareness that God's Spirit is within you and your community, and that in God's Spirit you are fully equipped to love and be loved, and to fulfill God's purpose ...

4: Resolving Grief

Grief is the psychological experience we have when we lose something we value. While we typically associate grief with the death of a loved one, we may experience grief in response to any life change that results in a sense of loss. This would include losing a job, a friend moving to another town, the destruction or loss of property such as a house, or anything that deprives us of something we value.

From our **A ⇨ B** change model we would say that we will experience grief when any change results in the final **State B** being less valuable than the initial **State A**. The experience of grief is manifested in a variety of ways; sadness, anger, and numbness are just some of the many different responses to loss.

The Complexity and Intensity of Grief

The intensity and complexity of a grief experience is portrayed vividly in Psalm 137. The people of Israel have been exiled from Jerusalem to Babylon and are grieving the destruction of their temple and the loss of their homeland. In their pain and distress they cry:

By the waters of Babylon we sat down and wept, when we remembered you, O Zion.

As for our harps, we hung them up on the trees in the midst of that land.

For those who led us away captive asked us for a song, and our oppressors called for mirth: "Sing us one of the songs of Zion."

How shall we sing the Lord's song upon an alien soil?

If I forget you, O Jerusalem, let my right hand forget its skill.

Let my tongue cleave to the roof of my mouth if I do not remember you, if I do not set Jerusalem above my highest joy.

Remember the day of Jerusalem, O Lord, against the people of Edom, who said, "Down with it! down with it! even to the ground!"

O Daughter of Babylon, doomed to destruction, happy the one who pays you back for what you have done to us!

Happy shall he be who takes your little ones, and dashes them against the rock!

The psalm shows that grief is not a solitary feeling but a complex array of intertwined emotions and ideas. The people can remember Jerusalem with fondness and sadness, and then be filled with rage

In the night of death, hope sees a star, and listening love can hear the rustle of a wing.
— Robert Ingersoll

Only those who avoid love can avoid grief. The point is to learn from grief and remain vulnerable to love.
— John Brantner

Even if happiness forgets you a little bit, never completely forget about it.
— Jacques Prévert

directed at the people they blame for their loss. The strength of their anger is shown in the delight that they would experience if someone violently killed the children of their oppressors. In the midst of these powerful emotions, they think about their future. They are terrified that they will forget Jerusalem, and wonder whether they will be able to experience the reality of God's presence in this strange land.

Can We Ever Be Happy Again?

When responding to the death of a loved one the verse: *"How can we sing the Lord's song in a strange land?"* could be rephrased:

"How can I be happy now that my beloved is gone?"

This question can also be interpreted in at least two ways. First, the person may think that it would be wrong or a betrayal of their loved one if they were to find happiness again. Alternatively, the person may be thinking that they won't be able to be happy because the source of their happiness is now gone. In the midst of their grief they have lost all hope of having a happy future.

This raises the question of what it really means to resolve grief. Is it possible to restore someone to a state of happiness following the loss of a loved one?

Responding to People in Grief: Tormenting or Helping?

In Psalm 137 the Babylonians tormented the people by wanting them to sing the Lord's song even though they were in the midst of great distress. As a pastor, I have seen modern tormentors in the guise of people trying to cheer up a grief–stricken person. They are often prevalent at funerals and the reception afterward, offering platitudes that encourage the person to deny their sadness. Here are two platitudes that I find very offensive and unhelpful:

"He is in a better place."
"God wanted her to be with him in heaven."

Even if the statements are true, they are being used to "guilt" someone into denying their current sense of loss. Implying that someone should be happy when they are sad is a way of forcing them into the land of inauthenticity. Being inauthentic does not lead to healing or wholeness rather it leads to denial and blocks the person's way forward into a fulfilling future.

Later, the torment may be inflicted by others' unwillingness to mention the deceased's name for fear that it will evoke tears and distress on the part of the bereaved. As one widow said, "It's as though my Henry

To spare oneself from grief at all cost can be achieved only at the price of total detachment, which excludes the ability to experience happiness.
— Erich Fromm

You needn't be trying to comfort me, I tell you my dolly is dead! There's no use in saying she isn't, with a crack like that in her head.
— Margaret Janvier

never lived – no one will even mention his name." Far from helping, this just delays the resolution of the grief.

One of the first steps to helping anyone, including those who are grieving, is to join the person where they are and be present with them in the midst of their misery. We cannot stand in the land of our happiness and beckon people to join us. Rather, we need to enter into and join the person in their world by listening to their story. Talking about the deceased, and especially what the person loved and valued about their beloved, is both a great way to join a grieving person and an essential step in the path of resolving their grief.

Therapeutic Tormentors

The psychological community has on occasion also served as tormentors to those who grieve. From my experience, the "experts" on grief base their experience on the people who they see clinically. These clients have not been able to resolve their grief. The experts who treat them subsequently create models of grief and its resolution based on what hasn't worked.

These clinical experiences often result in the expectation that resolving grief following a major loss, such as the death of a spouse, takes lots of hard, painful work and time to resolve. From this clinical perspective, people who rapidly resolve their grief are really in denial, and deep feelings of loss, unless expressed, will return at some time to haunt the person, possibly as a physical ailment.

There is a vast difference between resolving grief and denying the experience of loss and grief. I am not advocating denial; rather, I am advocating that we study people who rapidly resolve grief. We can use their strategies to help grieving people resolve their grief and return them to creating their preferred future. In my experience, I have seen people achieve that result without putting in long, hard months, if not years, of distress.

Many counselors and therapists use Elisabeth Kubler-Ross' stages of dying[1] – denial, anger, bargaining, depression, and acceptance – as the stages of grief. However, these states are based on what many people go through as they anticipate their own death, and are not necessarily what people go through after they have suffered the loss of a loved one. Many of the books on grief provide great descriptions of these aspects of grief, but have limited advice on how to help people resolve each state.

While grief is fresh, every attempt to divert only irritates. You must wait till it be digested, and then amusement will dissipate the remains of it.
— Samuel Johnson

Show me a sane man and I will cure him for you.
— Carl Jung

If you want to be really helpful to grieving people, don't teach them about grief, because they are already experts at grieving. What we need to do is lead them through their grief to the place where they can imagine a future with qualities they value.

The Helpfulness and Limitation of Descriptive Responses to Grief

Imagine the situation of a person losing their spouse. As part of their grief they experience episodes of intense anger toward their spouse for "dying on them" and leaving them to face life on their own. As they experience their anger toward their spouse, they also become angry with themselves for hating the one that they love. This self-hatred is self-alienating and will often be more problematic than the anger toward their spouse and their grief over their loss.

Teaching the person that anger is often common in people who are grieving will normalize the experience and alleviate the self-rejection. This will result in considerable relief as the person is able to accept that they are angry without the self-rejection. However, while they find considerable relief, they are still angry and grieving the loss of their spouse. To be truly helpful we need to help them resolve their underlying grief.

There are other ways that the descriptive educational models of teaching grieving people about grief helps create an attitude of self-acceptance in the midst of their distress. When people are told that it will take time to resolve their grief, they are able to create a place of acceptance for what they are going through. While this may provide some comfort, a much better solution would be to resolve the grief rather than make it tolerable.

Religiously-oriented people may find their faith either helps or hinders their grief. Some religiously-oriented people will feel that grieving is a sign of a lack of faith. They may believe that if they really had faith, they would know their beloved was in a better place and that God would take care of them and their beloved. In these situations, faith is being used to deny their grief, which leads to inauthentic rather than faithful living. Genuine faith gives people the courage to be honest with their feelings. Helping people caught in this false understanding of faith to see in the Scriptures the great psalms of grief may help counter the falsehood that the people of God do not grieve. Again, it needs to be pointed out that this normalizing of the grief experience will lead to self-acceptance. It does not resolve the underlying grief which is our objective.

The future is uncertain, because love changes everything.
— Unknown

Teaching people about grief may help them feel better about being miserable, but they will still be miserable.

Life is not a journey to the grave with the intention of arriving safely in a pretty and well preserved body, but rather to skid in broadside, thoroughly used up, totally worn out, and loudly proclaiming: "Wow! – What a ride!"
— Erma Bombeck

How Shall We Remember?

Resolving grief is not about forgetting the person who has died. It is about the way we remember them, and how we use our memories of them to inform our future. We want to be able to remember our loved ones with positive emotion, not with distressing emotion, and to use these remembered relationships as resources for building our future.

At the Last Supper, Jesus shared bread and wine with his disciples and told them to continue to do this "to remember me." To re-member means to "put back together" and in the case of remembering a person, it means we put the person back together in our consciousness. For Jesus and his disciples, this way of remembering was based on their experience of the Passover meal. When people remembered the Passover, all the benefits and blessings of the original Passover were made available to the people in their present moment. When we remember Jesus in the Eucharist, all the healing blessings of Jesus are made available to us in the present moment to set us free and equip us to co-create with God our preferred future.

When we resolve grief, we want people to have that same ability to "re-member" their loved one – to remember them with gratitude and not misery, and to know that they can still access the blessing that their beloved was in this present moment. This kind of remembering provides a foundation for the person to begin moving into their future.

The Fear of Forgetting

One of the common experiences people have when they lose a loved one is a fear of forgetting. Staying in grief is a way to ensure that they never forget them. This fear of forgetting is illustrated by the Israelites exiled to Babylon after the destruction of the Temple. In their terror of forgetting Jerusalem they cry out:

> *"If I forget you, O Jerusalem, let my right hand forget its skill. Let my tongue cleave to the roof of my mouth if I do not remember you, if I do not set Jerusalem above my highest joy." (Psalm 137:5-6).*

In relieving this fear it may be helpful to reassure the grieving person that they will never forget, but the real question is: "How do you want to remember?" Do they want to remember with sadness and grief, or with love and gratitude for the life they shared? Never forgetting by remembering with love and gratitude opens the person to the future, in contrast to the future-limiting strategy of not forgetting by continuing to stay miserable.

Of course that is not the whole story, but that is the way with stories; we make them what we will. It's a way of explaining the universe while leaving the universe unexplained, it's a way of keeping it all alive, not boxing it into time.
— Jeanette Winterson

How shall you remember? Do you want to not forget them with misery and sadness or would you like to remember them with love and gratitude?

Death leaves a heartache no one can heal, love leaves a memory no one can steal.
— From an Irish headstone

Goals for Resolving Grief

As I work with people who are grieving, I have in mind the following goals and thoughts about what it means to resolve grief. While these goals are framed from the perspective of grieving a loved one's death, they can be adapted to any other loss.

- **To be able to freely access our memories of people we have lost with a sense of gratitude and love for the life we shared without having these memories elicit sadness or distress.**

  Resolving grief is not about forgetting someone or avoiding the reality of someone's death. Resolving grief is about having the emotional freedom and comfort to remember, when and how we choose, the people we have loved and lost.

- **To continue to be able to build a preferred future, not weighed down or hindered by sadness but to be able to access our memories as resources for building our preferred future.**

  Our preferred future needs to be reality-based. While our first preference is probably to have the person back, that preference is not possible. Though that preference is not possible we will still live our life in the future. Resolving grief helps us to resourcefully return to the task of creating the kind of future that we desire despite the current loss.

- **To clarify what was lost and what was not lost.**

  Our loved ones shared with us their temporal doing, and their eternal being which contains timeless qualities. In death we lose their temporal doing, but we do not lose their eternal being and timeless qualities. Despite their death, we can still access those timeless qualities as we go forward into the future.

- **To miss with fondness and delight rather than sadness and a longing to return to former times.**

  One of the things I shared with my dad was working with him on our dairy farm. He taught me many things, from plumbing to digging holes to building fences. Even today, some 40 years since he died, each time I find myself using one of these tips I smile in warm recognition of the time I first learned it from my dad. I miss those times but have no sadness or longing to return to them.

- **To lay to rest those things in the relationship that are not helpful to building our preferred future.**

In war as in life, it is often necessary when some cherished scheme has failed, to take up the best alternative open, and if so, it is folly not to work for it with all your might.
— Winston Churchill

For I am convinced that neither death, nor life, nor angels, nor rulers, nor things present, nor things to come, nor powers, nor height, nor depth, nor anything else in all creation, will be able to separate us from the love of God in Christ Jesus our Lord.
— Romans 8:38-39

Just as I have warm memories of my father, I also have other memories of times of pain. I can choose what I want to keep and use to inform my future. Forgiveness and healing distressing memories may also be part of resolving grief. Then we can go forward not weighed down by experiences that lead to resentment or a longing for a life that never existed.

- **To be restored to a state of happiness, assuming that the person was happy prior to their loved one's death.**

If the preceding goals are achieved, the person will be restored to a state of happiness. I do not mean that the person will be **happy** their beloved is dead, but that the person knows that the essential ingredients of happiness have not been taken from them.

They can celebrate that they shared in happiness with their beloved, but neither they nor the deceased was the true Source of happiness for the other. When people resolve their grief, they find happiness in their memories. They have also found other ways to share in happiness in their new circumstances, and can imagine being happy in the future. They can answer affirmatively: "Yes, I can be happy in this strange land."

It is foolish to tear one's hair in grief, as though sorrow would be made less by baldness.
— Marcus Tullius Cicero

Understanding the Dynamics of Grief

Rather than using Kubler-Ross' model of the stages of death and dying, we will use the **A** ⇨ **B** change model to create a healing response to a person's experience of grief.

The first step is to understand what people are experiencing when they are grieving. What is **State A** when someone is grieving?

When we listen to people who are in the midst of the early stages of grieving they will often say things like:

"I can't imagine going on without him."

"I don't know how I will cope."

"We are going to miss her."

When we examine these statements, we note that they are all about the future, not the past. The people have lost hope in their ability to cope with or have an enjoyable future. To have hope, a person has to be able to imagine a future that they would like to live in. When they are not able to imagine that future, they will experience great pain and a sense of loss. This pain may be expressed in sadness, rage, anxiety, or a mixture of these and other emotions. But the pain of loss is not simply a loss of something in the past: what has been lost is the ability to imagine a happy future.

Even after the grief has persisted for a period of time, people will say things like:

"I still really miss him."

"I'm not doing very well without her."

These are statements about not feeling resourceful in the present. It is very difficult for a person to feel that the future will be happy when they are not feeling resourceful in the present.

Here is an illustration of this grief experience in relationship to people's perception of time:

I was meeting with a family of 5 adult children and their mother to prepare a funeral for their dad and husband. We were gathered around the kitchen table, and the children were telling stories about their dad. There was much laughter as they remembered their dad climbing into a peach tree to prune a branch when the branch broke and dad came tumbling out of the tree. In the middle of telling the stories one of the siblings began to weep quite deeply. That person

We must welcome the future, remembering that soon it will be the past; and we must respect the past remembering that once it was all that was humanly possible.
— George Santayana

Misery is a communicable disease.
— Martha Graham

Looking back with happiness isn't a problem. Its the inability to look forward with happiness that is the problem.

had moved from looking back to an experience of their dad in the past, which was a pleasurable experience, to looking into the future in which their beloved dad was not. They could see the peach tree, but their dad wasn't part of the picture anymore, and they became distressed. The pain associated with loss comes from the inability to imagine what or who we will love in the future.

From this reflection we would define the experience of grief as:

Grief is the inability to imagine a tomorrow that you would enjoy or find life-giving.

Grief is not about being trapped in the past, it is about being unable to imagine an enjoyable future. Grieving people can look back with laughter and gladness; what they can't do is look forward with laughter and gladness. Without a future to look forward to, they will stay trapped in their memories of the past and will be unable to experience happiness in the present moment.

Appreciative Grieving: Inventing a Response to Grief

What is **State B**, or the goal, if we are helping someone to resolve grief? What would the person be doing if they weren't grieving? They would be enjoying life and looking forward to doing enjoyable things. Since the grief response occurs because people cannot imagine a preferred future, the "cure" for grief is to help the person imagine a future that they can look forward to. We might ask them:

- What made your life enjoyable?
- What do you need to be able to look forward to tomorrow?

While the specifics of what makes life enjoyable differs for each one of us, the essence of what makes life enjoyable is that it includes things we value and find life-giving. People grieve when they look into the future and cannot see what they value. Grief is resolved when the person is able to explore what was valuable about a past relationship, and then is able to imagine new ways of experiencing that value in the future, despite the loss of their loved one.

From an appreciative perspective, creating images of a preferred future is not about fantasizing, or naïve positive thinking, or living in denial. The imaging process begins by exploring what was good in the past. The image of the future is based on this foundation of things they have experienced in the past and therefore realistically **know** to be attainable. It is not based on what they naïvely fantasize **might** come true.

What we have
once enjoyed
we can never lose;
All that we love deeply,
becomes a part of us.
— Helen Keller

If you don't like something
change it;
if you can't change it,
change the way
you think about it.
— Mary Engelbreit

As for the future,
your task
is not to foresee it,
but to enable it.
— Antoine de Saint-Exupéry

Distinguishing an Eternal Value from a Temporal Vehicle

Things we value come to us in a form, or a "vehicle." But the vehicle is not the value, nor is the value the vehicle. This vehicle is a temporal manifestation of the eternal quality that we value. For example, the value may be "love" and the vehicle through which we experience love is the person who loves us. In assisting people to grieve, we need to help them distinguish the value from the vehicle. While the temporal vehicle may be lost and unattainable, the timeless value hasn't been lost. This may require "drilling down" or "mining" into the value in order to find the deeper value that is eternal, and not simply restricted to the temporal vehicle. Here is an example of mining a value in a person who is grieving their former pastor:

Parishioner: I just really miss Pastor Bob.

Pastor: You really miss your pastor ...

I'm curious, tell me, what do you really miss about him?

Parishioner: I really miss his preaching.

Pastor: You really loved his preaching ...

What was it about his preaching that you really value?

Parishioner: When he would preach I just had that wonderful sense of God's presence, and I knew everything was going to be OK.

Pastor: That's really wonderful, that sense of God's presence ... Take a moment and let yourself remember that sense of God's presence right now ...

It's really amazing, isn't it, that you can sense that right now ...

(in most cases people will move into that remembering, in the very Biblical understanding of re-membering, or making a past reality real in the present moment.)

What is really special is that the gift Pastor Bob gave you, that sense of God's presence – you still have that, it hasn't been taken from you ...

I wonder where you hold that presence within you?

Parishioner: It's in my heart and all around me.

Pastor: Holding it in your heart makes sense to me because wherever you go it will be there ... with you ...

I wonder, as you are aware of that feeling of God's presence right now, where else have you experienced that sense of God's presence? ...

If ever there is tomorrow when we're not together, there is something you must always remember. You are braver than you believe, stronger than you seem, and smarter than you think. but the most important thing is, even if we're apart, I'll always be with you.
— Winnie the Pooh (A. A. Milne)

Love is something eternal; the aspect may change, but not the essence.
— Vincent van Gogh

Take a moment and let your mind think of other places where you have experienced God's presence ...

Parishioner: You know we have a beach house and I often get this same sense of God's assurance when we sit on the porch and watch the sun go down.

Pastor: Take a moment and think of other times and places that you feel God's presence and assurance ...

Let your mind wander back and forward through these experiences as your remember them and hold them in your heart ...

Now take a moment and think of some places in the future where you would like to experience that sense of God's presence and assurance, and allow your imagination to bring God's presence from your heart into those places.

In this process we have separated an eternal value – God's presence – from its temporal vehicle – Pastor Bob – and made the value available in the present moment and in the future.

Helping the person to remember and associate other experiences of God's presence with their collective experience of God's presence challenges and breaks up their certainty that they can only experience God's presence through Pastor Bob's preaching. When they can imagine experiencing God's presence and assurance in the future, they will not be able to grieve the loss of their pastor's preaching.

What we are doing in this process is discovering a past value and grounding the person in their memory of that value, so that they are "re-membered" in that value. When re-membered the value is in the present, a present which doesn't include the temporal vehicle by which the person originally knew or received the value. Through this exercise, they learn that they still have what was really valuable. From the perspective of having the value in the present, they can begin realistically imagining having it in the future. Once they are able to imagine that value in the future, they will literally not be able to grieve.

There are some subtleties to this appreciative approach. For example, after we find the deeper value of God's presence, we would not ask the person a yes/no type of question, such as "Have you experienced God's presence since Pastor Bob left?" If we did ask that question they probably would say no, and we would have reinforced their loss and compounded their grief.

So our human life
but dies down to its root,
and still puts forth its
green blade to eternity.
— Henry David Thoreau

Keep a green tree
in your heart
and perhaps
a singing bird will come.
— Chinese Proverb

The moment you
have in your heart this
extraordinary thing
called love
and feel the depth,
the delight,
the ecstasy of it,
you will discover
that for you the
world is transformed.
— Jiddu Krishnamurti

Rather than asking a yes/no question, we invite the person to remember by reliving an experience, so that they can experience the value in the present moment. We can then ask a leading question such as: "I am curious, where else have you experienced that same feeling?" At that point the person is likely to explore their memory and begin making connections, perhaps where connections did not previously exist. They may not have recognized that the experience of the sunset was also about God's presence. As they gather these experiences, they will feel more resourceful and hopeful about their future.

Here is another example of mining into a value following the death of a loved one.

Parishioner: I really miss my dad.

Pastor: You really miss your dad ...

Tell me, what about your dad do you really miss?

Parishioner: He used to give great hugs. Whenever I was having a bad day I could just go in and get a hug. Now I can't do that any more.

Pastor: His hugs were really special ...

As you remember his hugs I wonder what you experienced when he hugged you.

Parishioner: He just really believed in me, and when he hugged me I would somehow get my confidence back.

Pastor: Your strength and confidence were restored.

Parishioner: Yeah.

Pastor: That's pretty neat ... Why don't you take a moment and remember that belief in you that you and your dad would share at those times ...

And be aware of the feeling of confidence that it gives you ... Gives you even now ...

Once the person is experiencing, in the present, this value that they thought was lost, you can help them to move into imagining having it in their future, especially if they carry it in a place like their own heart. This example demonstrates the need to mine into the value to find the timeless value. Obviously the person can no longer go and get a hug, but they can still access this internal and eternal quality that even death cannot destroy.

Death is Both a Robber and a Liar

Death can and does break into our lives and steal a loved one's physical presence from us, but it lies when it says it can take their love from us. Everything a deceased loved one has ever given you, you still have, unless you have given it away or someone steals it from you. You can choose what you want to keep and what you let go of. Having that power to choose gives you more power than death.

My dad was a very quiet, reserved, man who rarely expressed praise or affirmation. He died when I was 18 years old, just months after I graduated high school with the highest academic and character awards the school offered. Nothing, not his death nor the intervening 40 years, has taken from me the grin on his face and the quiet, bottomless pride he has in me. Everything he ever gave me I still have, except for some hand tools that were stolen out of my truck. We do not stop loving people when they die and our faith says they don't stop loving us either, for love is an eternal reality that does not know the bounds of time. I can tap into that love any time I choose.

The Eternal Nature of Love

In his letter to the Romans, St. Paul describes the eternal nature of God's love in Christ Jesus that not even death can overcome:

> For I am convinced that neither death, nor life, nor angels, nor rulers, nor things present, nor things to come, nor powers, nor height, nor depth, nor anything else in all creation, will be able to separate us from the love of God in Christ Jesus our Lord. (Romans 8:38-39)

My own theology says that all love comes from God, and the experience of being loved by another person is not simply one person loving another, but two people together entering into a temporal experience of God's timeless love. In our temporal lives, we give form to that love and make tangible that eternal quality. But the death or the loss of the tangible does not mean the eternal is lost. I would personalize and paraphrase St. Paul by saying: "For I am convinced that neither death nor life can separate us from the love we have known and shared."

Temporal Losses

While we have focused on reclaiming the eternal or timeless values embedded in our temporal experience, we do need to be realistic about temporal losses. If the deceased performed a physical or

*Death is not
the greatest loss in life.
The greatest loss
is what dies inside us
while we live.*
— Norman Cousins

*The things which are seen
are temporal;
but the things which
are not seen
are eternal.*
— II Corinthians 4:1-18

*To speak gratitude is
courteous and pleasant,
to enact gratitude is
generous and noble,
but to live gratitude
is to touch Heaven.*
— Johannes A. Gaertner

temporal function, such as taking out the trash, baby-sitting, or managing the finances, the person will grieve these specific temporal losses until an alternative way of taking care of these activities is found.

Complications to the Grieving Process

The circumstances of a person's death may complicate the grieving process. When someone has watched a loved one die a painful death, their memories of the person will be filled with memories of their loved one in pain. These memories may overwhelm the bereaved's ability to access pleasant memories. These painful memories will need to be resolved before the person is able to resolve their grief.

A traumatic death may also evoke additional feelings, such as guilt, that need to be resolved. After watching their beloved suffer for a long time the person may have just wanted their beloved to die – to be set free from their pain. These feelings of guilt may be exacerbated by the person also wanting an end to their own personal suffering related to having to helplessly watch their beloved in pain.

Feelings of guilt indicate that the person is experiencing self-alienation. Part of the self is hating another part of the self for their thoughts of wanting the person to die. To resolve this internal conflict, both parts of the self need to be invited into consciousness, and each part needs to discover and appreciate the positive intention underlying the other's behavior. "Wanting someone to die" is actually "wanting an end to suffering." Wanting someone's or our own suffering to end is an honorable desire and is part of a compassionate response to suffering. Not wanting to lose a loved one is also compassionate. Both parts need to be held in a deeper compassion that can integrate these conflicted and paradoxical responses. From this place of deeper acceptance, the person can be invited to engage first in the resolution of their painful memories, and then in the resolution of their grief response.

So live that after the minister has ended his remarks, those present will not think they have attended the wrong funeral.
— Unknown

How far you go in life depends on your being tender with the young, compassionate with the aged, sympathetic with the striving, and tolerant of the weak and strong. Because some day in life you will have been all of these.
— George Washington Carver

The Qualities of an Effective Funeral

The model of resolving grief by remembering the past, discovering what is valuable, and imagining a future containing that value often forms the basis of effective funeral homilies and services. In the eulogy time, people are invited to remember the person through the telling of stories that extol the virtues or values of the deceased. Then, in the homily, the preacher invites the mourners to use the person as a role model for those values and to continue those values in their lives as they go into the future. In a real sense the preacher is "sprinkling" the mourners' future with the things they valued about the deceased.

Sifting the Relationship for the Gold

While the previous approach of eulogizing the deceased may be helpful with a person who has lived an esteemable life, it becomes difficult when the deceased has done little to be admired and has done much to be detested. It is inauthentic and unhelpful to evoke empty platitudes in these circumstances. In these situations, the grief may be experienced upon the realization that now that the person is dead they will never be able to get that love or praise that they desired.

I once was asked to conduct a funeral for a man who had been very abusive to his family. His adult children felt quite relieved that he was dead and could no longer physically intimidate them. As we talked about the funeral service, they looked forward to the possibility of putting him in the ground and jumping on his grave to compact the dirt. At the funeral service, which was fairly small and limited to family and close friends, the homily went something like this:

> As you are aware, Harry was a difficult person to live with and was often abusive.
>
> (There were many head nods in the congregation at this point in the homily.)
>
> And I know that no one is totally bad nor totally good, and so I invite you to remember your dad and sift your memories for those things that he did do that you value ...
>
> I want you to hold onto these little nuggets of gold because in a few minutes we are going to go to the graveside and bury the sand, the things that you don't want to take into your future, but I don't want to bury the gold.

You should always go to other people's funerals; otherwise,
they won't come to yours.
— Yogi Berra

Memory is a way
of holding onto
the things you love,
the things you are,
the things you
never want to lose.
— The Wonder Years
   Television Program

The reason so many people turned up at his funeral is that they wanted to make sure he was dead.
— Samuel Goldwyn

> I'm always relieved when someone is delivering a eulogy and I realize I'm listening to it.
> — George Carlin

Before we bury the sand I want you to take a moment and think of the ways your dad hurt you and think about how you wanted to be treated by him ...

How would you have preferred to be treated by your father ...

And now take a moment and think of your own children and families and how you treat them. Notice how it's not all that helpful to say, "I will never treat my kids that way." It's actually more helpful to see yourself treating your children in the way you would have preferred to have been treated as a child.

Take some time to see yourself treating your children the way you would have preferred to be treated ...

And holding onto these nuggets of gold let us go bury the sand ...

Satisfying Objections to Resolving Grief

When working with clients in the midst of grief, and especially with people who are "stuck" in their grief, we may find contradictory desires:

- Part of the person wants to move on with their life – or at least find some way not to be so miserable.

- Another part of the person objects to moving on and wants to hold onto the misery, perhaps as a way to "hold on to" their loved one.

To ensure that the client is able to resolve their grief and sustain that resolution, these objections need to be satisfied rather than overcome. When an objection is simply overcome, the person will experience a sense of violation and is likely to resist the change. The resistance may be an overt determination not to change, or a covert sabotage of any change efforts despite appearing to be agreeing to the change. A non-active response to overcome an objection is for the person to passively resign themselves to the change. Unfortunately, this passivity is likely to leak out into other areas of their life and make it impossible for them to truly move on and live life to its fullest.

Rather than simply denying or overcoming the objection, we need to compassionately invite the part of the person that is objecting into consciousness. We can then discover the nature of the objection and the positive intention behind the objection. Once this objection is discovered, we then need to find a way to satisfy that objection and achieve the positive intention.

The first strategy to satisfy an objection is to inquire of the part that is objecting as to what would satisfy its concerns. In my experience, when helping people in grief, the part that is objecting to resolving the grief is unlikely to be able to express what would satisfy the objection. Not having this solution in mind is part of why people stay "stuck" in their grief. What has been helpful to people at this point is to discover the positive intention behind the objection and then to inquire how effective the strategy of staying miserable is in achieving that intention.

When a person becomes aware that the strategy of being miserable is a costly and ineffective way of achieving a goal, they have two choices: to try harder by becoming even more miserable, or to give

You can clutch the past so tightly to your chest that it leaves your arms too full to embrace the present.
— *Jan Glidewell*

If you chase two rabbits both will escape.
—*Russian Proverb*

There are things that we don't want to happen but have to accept, things we don't want to know but have to learn, and people we can't live without but have to let go.
— *Unknown*

up misery and find an alternative strategy to achieve the goal. In my experience, when presented with these two options, people will let go of the objection and opt for finding an alternative path. The following are some of the objections to resolving grief that I have encountered.

The Fear of Forgetting

We have already noted the fear of forgetting as one of the objections people may have to letting go of their misery. They may find that their memory of the person is fading and their sense of misery is one way to keep the person in consciousness. The fear of forgetting may be compounded by the experience of going out with friends and enjoying an activity during which time they never thought about the person they have lost. To prevent this type of forgetting, they may studiously avoid any pleasurable activity that distracts them from their loss.

One of the things we may need to help the client access is their confidence in their memory and ability to recall people when they choose. The client can be invited to remember times when the person was alive and the client would go out with other people and have a good time without the deceased being present or even consciously remembered during that time. But that good time didn't create forgetting. When they re-encountered their loved one they weren't encountering a stranger, it was someone they knew and still remembered. Likewise, just because someone has died and we have had a good time with other people, that good time will not erase our memory of our loved one.

Another strategy to resolve the fear of forgetting is to explore how the client thinks the person would like to be remembered. The coach could say something like:

> *"You have told me all these great stories of times that you shared with the person, and as you think of this person, I wonder whether they would like to be not forgotten through you being miserable."*

Another way of phrasing the question that has proven effective is:

> *"I am wondering whether you would like to not forget the person by being miserable, or whether you would like to remember them with love and gratitude?"*

To help a client remember with love and gratitude, we can invite them to remember those times in the past for which they are grateful. We can then invite them to imagine in the future doing or seeing something similar that brings a smile of familiarity and gratitude to the client.

Carve a tunnel of hope through the dark mountain of disappointment.
— Martin Luther King Jr.

We need to stop trying to earn God's love and just start spending it.
— Steve Bhaerman

Let no one weep for me, or celebrate my funeral with mourning; for I still live, as I pass to and fro through the mouths of men.
— Quintus Ennius

Betraying Their Loved One

For some people, the idea that they can go out and enjoy themselves after their spouse has died seems wrong or disloyal. Some may feel that they need to spend an "appropriate" amount of time feeling miserable before they will allow themselves to be happy. Part of their thinking may be that if their grief is resolved too quickly, then perhaps they never really cared for the deceased. Their current distress is evidence that they did really love them.

To avoid a sense of disloyalty, the grieving person may refuse to engage in a special activity that they were introduced to by the deceased. Rather than being disloyal, engaging in the activity can be viewed as a way to be grateful and to celebrate the person's life and the life they shared.

Societal Objections

Some of the objections to resolving grief may be societal. For many people it would be unseemly for someone to quickly get back into their life and begin dating or meeting new people. Other family members may feel this is disloyal to the person that they are still grieving. Only after a "suitable" period of mourning is the person allowed to re-enter the fullness of life.

Some of these objections may be well-founded on the experience of people in the midst of grief entering into new relationships that turned disastrous. In the midst of misery, it is difficult for people to make wise decisions. On the other hand, some people are able to rapidly resolve their grief and move on. Societal rules based on the norms of society may be helpful to some, but very unhelpful to others, because norms never allow for the distinct individuality of each person.

Objections to Distinguishing the Value and Vehicle

Some clients may object to making the distinction between an eternal value and the temporal vehicle by which it was known, because they feel it is a betrayal of the person or their memory of their loved one. What they miss is not the value but the very being of the person! And to talk about the person as a "vehicle" is simply to insult the essential dignity of another person. Obviously the word "vehicle" is a metaphor, and pushed to its extreme it could be perceived as disrespectful. On the other hand, the fact that the person can talk of their beloved's essential dignity is a helpful resource because this essential dignity is a timeless quality that not

*Do not shed tears
when I have gone
but smile instead
because I have lived.*

*Do not shut your eyes
and pray to God
that I'll come back
but open your eyes
and see all that
I have left behind.*

*I know your heart
will be empty because
you cannot see me
but still I want you to be
full of the love we shared.*

*You can turn
your back on tomorrow
and live only for yesterday
or you can be happy
for tomorrow because of
what happened between
us yesterday.*

*You can remember me
and grieve that I have gone
or you can cherish my
memory and let it live on.*

*You can cry
and lose yourself,
become distraught
and turn your back
on the world
or you can do
what I want –
smile, wipe away the tears,
learn to love again
and go on.*
— David Harkins

even death can destroy. Helping the client to access their beloved's timeless dignity will help resolve their grief.

Grieving for What They Never Had

From my experience as a pastor, the easiest people to grieve for are those with whom we have had a deep, satisfying relationship. We mutually shared what we wanted with each other and we don't look back with any regrets.

On the other hand, grief becomes very complicated when we have had a conflicted relationship with someone. We may love them and be angry and resentful that we didn't get the love we truly wanted from them. Now that they are dead, we are confronted with the reality that we will never get their love. We may resentfully keep them alive in our minds in a forlorn attempt to hold onto the hope that one day they will love us and give us what we want. A client in this situation may object to resolving their grief because they sense that if they "let go" of the deceased they will never be able to get what they wanted from the person. The client will need to engage in the forgiveness process before they are able to resolve their grief.

Survivor Guilt

When a person survives an accident or battle in which others were killed, the survivor may experience guilt over their survival. This survivor guilt may complicate a person's grieving by creating internal objections to moving on with their life. The survivor may find it difficult to happily move on with their life knowing that a friend or loved one has died. Finding internal permission to let go of the misery will be necessary to resolve their grief. This permission may be discovered by inviting the client to engage in a dialogue in their mind with the deceased to help the client move on with their life.

When engaging in a dialogue with a deceased person to resolve an issue or access permission to embark on a project, it is important to deal with them as they currently are and not how they were. This is especially true if the deceased was often mean-spirited. Psychologist Dannie Beaulieu[2] frames such conservations this way:

> I want you to take a moment and think of [the deceased] after they have spent time studying intensely with God since they died. How do you think studying intensely with God has changed them? ... Let's have the conversation with them now after they have spent so much time studying intensely with God ...

Life has taught us that love does not consist in gazing at each other but in looking outward together in the same direction.
— Antoine de Saint-Exupéry

Guilt: the gift that keeps on giving.
— Erma Bombeck

The guilty one is not he who commits the sin, but the one who causes the darkness.
— Victor Hugo

Living and Loving: Finding a Way Forward

My sister Marilyn, her husband Don, and their daughter Brie are my heros when it comes to grieving. Marilyn and Don's son, Zaan, died when he was 8 years old after he had lived with a brain tumor that was first diagnosed when he was 18 months old. Zaan was an amazing person who somehow seemed to know his life on this earth was short and that he needed to seize each day and take from it everything it had to offer. He had no time for the petty trivialities that distract both children and adults alike from the richness life has to offer in this present moment.

In the following story my brother-in-law Don describes how he not only received his son Zaan's permission, but his admonition, to get on with his life when Zaan died.

It was several weeks after Zaan died and I was locked in an intense grief and almost physical pain wondering how I was ever going to survive. It was here that I asked myself two questions that both were entwined with the other.

The first question was: 'What would Zaan want me to do, how would he like me to live the rest of my life?' I had a mental picture of passing over, having stayed in the frame of mind I was currently in, and being greeted by a very angry son who was yelling at me, 'Dad! Why did you waste the rest of your life! You know life is for the living, I surely showed you that by my example.'

The second question was: 'If Zaan is right (and I had no doubt that he was right, because the mental picture was very vivid) how do I progress forward from this overwhelming grief and hurt?' I decided that the grief would always be there. No matter what I did it was never going to go away. Having accepted that, I then decided I would surround and envelop that grief in love. Love for Zaan, love for Brie, love for Marilyn, love for myself and most importantly Zaan's love for all of us. I would wrap it very carefully and allow myself to visit it whenever I felt like it and to whatever intensity I needed at the time.

Having done that I then decided that I would construct a new life around that love and grief with it being the center of my being, my strength, my integrity, my love for my family, my love for life. I would slowly build a new life in layers, a bit like laminating layers of plywood together. I would take my time and make it strong. I told Marilyn and Brie my thoughts and they adopted the same

If you lose hope, somehow you lose the vitality that keeps life moving, you lose that courage to be, that quality that helps you go on in spite of it all. And so today I still have a dream.
— Martin Luther King, Jr.

You must not lose faith in humanity. Humanity is an ocean; if a few drops of the ocean are dirty, the ocean does not become dirty.
— Mohandas K. Gandhi

pattern, even though I suspect Marilyn had already subconsciously been there before me. It enabled us all to function again. It was the beginning of the way forward.

We all still live from that beginning, each in our own way going back to visit that 'love/grief centre' whenever we need to. Nine years on, it is now mostly love in that center, and it still gives us our strength. It still feels like Zaan is part of our living family and we wouldn't want it any other way. It is probably a strange way of coming to terms with the death of a child, but for us it has worked. It has allowed us to survive and thrive and to honor, love, and cherish our son and brother."

Grieving and Resolving Grief is a Process

As Don's story shows, grief is resolved by what we do and not simply by what we understand about the nature of grief. The strategies of resolving grief I have presented are very different from many psycho-educational approaches where the intervention focuses most of its time teaching the person about grief to normalize feelings of loss, anger, or sadness. Educational processes may be somewhat helpful in reducing the self-alienation that follows their self-judgments about being angry or sad and not coping well, but they rarely help the person move from their sense of loss to a place of hope.

To truly help someone move from grief to hope we need to walk with them **through** the process, not teach them **about** the process. We would never teach or tell them that they are miserable because they can't imagine their future and that what they need to do to feel better is imagine a happy future. Rather, we invite them to share stories about what they miss and what they valued, and then help them to discover that these essential values are still accessible.

In the next section I will describe advanced strategies that can be used to speed the healing process and ensure that the hope-filled response is sustainable.

There are souls in this world which have the gift of finding joy everywhere and of leaving it behind them when they go.
— Frederick Faber

Death is a challenge. It tells us not to waste time ... It tells us to tell each other right now that we love each other.
— Leo F. Buscaglia

Structural Strategy To Resolve Grief

In the previous section, we used a narrative approach to understand the dynamics of grief and to describe the process of helping a client resolve their grief. This narrative approach relies heavily on reframing the content of the client's grief experience. We can combine this understanding with the way we structure the content of our experience in consciousness to create a process to help clients rapidly and sustainably resolve their grief[3].

The Nature of the Distress: Is it Grief?

When people lose family members they often experience intense emotional responses that get "lumped" under the title of grief. However, in some situations the feelings that need to be resolved are not simply grief. In the section on complications to the grief process I discussed several scenarios such as unresolved resentments, or being traumatized, that complicate the experience of grief. Before engaging in the grief resolution process, we need to ensure that we are dealing specifically with grief. If there are complications such as resentment or trauma, then these complications will need to be resolved prior to resolving the grief. See the chapter on forgiveness to resolve resentments or the chapter on resolving painful memories to resolve the feelings related to a traumatic death before engaging in the grief process.

The Structure of the Grief State

Discovering the way the client structures their grief experience in consciousness is often the hardest part of this strategy. What we need to discover is **how** the client experiences their memories of the person they have lost. In many situations I have found that this is the most difficult step of the process. Once this discovery has been made, the rest of the process is relatively straightforward.

Death creates a physical separation between people. That separation is expressed in the language of "gone" or "lost." People also experience a sense of separation at an emotional level that is often expressed in spatial contrasts such as: "We used to be so close, now he seems so far away." When we inquire more deeply into how they are structuring their experience in consciousness, we find that their representations of the deceased also parallel the language people are using to describe physical loss. For example, when someone describes an individual as "lost" they may have difficulty creating a clear picture of that person. Their picture of that person is also likely

*Love cures people –
both the ones
who give it
and the ones
who receive it.*
— Dr. Karl Menninger

*Spread love
everywhere you go:
first of all
in your own house.
Give love to your children,
to your wife or husband,
to a next door neighbor ...
Let no one ever come to
you without leaving better
and happier.
Be the living expression of
God's kindness;
kindness in your face,
kindness in your eyes,
kindness in your smile,
kindness in your
warm greeting.*
— Mother Theresa

to be distant from them, as though they are viewing the picture from far away.

To discover the structure of their grief experience, invite the client to recall the person they have lost. When they are recalling the person, ask them to describe how they are remembering them. In particular, we want to discover how the client is imaging the person in their mind. In most cases, clients will have some "picture" of the person. Some will not initially have a picture, but will have a "felt sense" of the person. Inviting the client to dwell on this felt sense and asking "visual" questions such as "What color shirt are they wearing?" or "What do you see them doing?" will help them re-create a visual memory of the person.

Once the client has a picture of the person, we need to discover how they structure the image in their mind. Because the felt sense of grief involves representations of separation, we want to be especially aware of the location of the picture with respect to the client's sense of themselves. Here is the language from the Representing the Past exercise on page 48 that I often use to help the client discover how they are representing the person in consciousness.

> "This is going to sound a little strange but I want you to try something. As you are remembering the person, close your eyes and be aware of where in your space is your sense or picture of the person. For example, are they out to the left, or to the right, or in front, or behind you? ... When you are aware of where that picture or your sense of the person is located point to where that is ..."

In many cases this initial request will be met with confusion, or the client will respond with a statement that describes the location involved in the memory such as "we are down at the beach walking on the sand." In this case I will respond:

> "No, that's not what I mean. Let's try something else to help you understand what I am looking for. Think of two people that you know fairly well ... As you remember them let yourself see in your mind's eye two individual pictures of them ... Now as you look at the two pictures at the same time, tell me which one is on the left and which is on the right ... In fact you can point to the two different people ... (I model pointing to where the person has the two different pictures) ... Now as you look at these two pictures tell me how far away they are out from you

Whether you believe or not believe is not important. But to destroy someone's hope is an evil thing.
— Winston Churchill

Hope is like a road in the country; there was never a road, but when many people walk on it, the road comes into existence.
— Lin Yutang

... Are they two feet away? six feet away? How far away are the pictures from you? ..."

Once the client is able to make these distinctions and describe how they are locating the images in their perceptual realm, then they can return to identifying the structure and location of the person they are grieving.

Discovering the Resolved Grief Resource State

One of the basic assumptions in the **A** ⇨ **B** model of change is that if a person can create a goal **B**, then they must have experienced something of that goal in their past. Without that prior experience they would not have been able to create in consciousness the new goal. When someone says that they would like to resolve their grief then they must have resolved a grief in their past.

This prior experience of resolving grief can be used as a resource they can use to resolve their current grief. This resolved grief does not need to have been as intense or significant as their current grief. Just as we learn the process of running by building on the resources of walking and maintaining balance, the client can use a previously resolved grief as a resource for resolving their current grief.

What we need to discover is how they structure this resolved grief in their consciousness. Here's a sample script:

> *"Take a moment and think about someone in the past that you have lost and at the time you grieved for, but for whom, as you sit here today, you no longer have those intense feelings of grief that you had back when you lost them.*
>
> *And as you remember them, close your eyes and point to where your sense of that person is located."*

In most cases, clients who have identified the location of the person they are grieving in the previous step will have little difficulty locating their image or felt sense of the person remembered in this step. What I continually find to be fascinating is that these locations are quite different; typically, the resolved grief location is much closer to the person than the grief state image.

Once we have identified the resolved grief resource, we will transform the grief response to the resolved response. Before we make the transformation we need to seek and satisfy any objections to making the changes to ensure that the change is sustainable.

When I am working on a problem I never think about beauty. I only think about how to solve the problem. But when I have finished, if the solution is not beautiful, I know it is wrong.
— Buckminster Fuller

I would rather have a mind opened by wonder than one closed by belief.
— Gerry Spence

Our dreams must be stronger than our memories. We must be pulled by our dreams, rather than pushed by our memories.
— Jesse Jackson

Satisfying Objections To Transform the Images

Before we transform the image I ask the client:

> *"Check in with yourself. Is there any part of you that objects to moving the person from this location ... (I point to where they identified the image of the person they are grieving) ... to this location (I point to the location of the resolved grief) ...?"*

In addition to the objections previously discussed, clients may have an objection to moving the image of the person they are grieving to the location of the resolved grief. The first resource state may not be a resource state for the image of the current person they are grieving. For example, a person may say: "I really loved my Dad," (the person they are currently grieving) "and it doesn't feel right to put him with my Grandmother" (the person with whom they have resolved their grief). "She was a real witch and I never really liked her." In this situation we need to find an alternate resource state that matches the person's experience. I might say:

> *"That makes sense to me that you wouldn't want to move your Dad to be with your Grandmother. Let's find an alternative. Think back over your life and recall someone who you did care for and who you lost. They may not have died, but perhaps moved away, and at the time you were quite sad but as you reflect on them today you are not feeling the sadness ... Where is your image of that person?"*

In most cases the person will be able to identify an alternative image that can serve as a resource location for their current grief. On one occasion I worked with a person who had lost a child and, although she was able to identify several other people that she had lost, none of the locations felt right or appropriate for this special person in her life. In that situation I acknowledged the person's objection and then asked the person's inner wisdom to create a place:

> *"I can see that you had a very special relationship with your son and none of these places we have identified seem special enough to hold the memory of your son ... Take a moment and let your inner wisdom decide where you would like to hold these memories ..."*

The person decided to hold them in her heart, which she did by physically reaching out with her hands and then placing them over her heart. Transforming her sense of her son from a very distant and vague "lost" image into her heart enabled her to dramatically resolve the deep feelings of grief that she had been experiencing for several years following the death of her child. Later she reported that when her son had died it felt like her heart had left her body and had been searching the wilderness for her son who was lost. She now not only had her son back but she had her heart back in her body.

Transforming the Image

Once the objections are satisfied we can invite the client to move the image of the person they are grieving to the location of the resource state.

> "Now move the image of the person from here ... (point to the grief state location) ... to here ... (point to the resource location) ... and tell me when you have done that ..."

Note that I do not say, "see if you can move the image." That question simply asks whether or not they can move the image – what we want them to do is actually move the image, and then leave the image in this new location. The language needs to be invitational, rather than demanding, and with an underlying assumption that the client can move the image. If the client is unable to move the image, or the image does not stay in the resource location, then check for any additional objections:

> "Check in with yourself. Are there any other objections that need to be satisfied before the image will move to the resolved grief place?"

The phrasing of this request is based on the assumption that once these objections are satisfied the image will move. The language is also invitational rather than demanding, and assumes that the client will not have to force the image to move, but that it will naturally move. In my experience once these additional objections are satisfied the image will often automatically move without effort on the part of the client.

Restoring Hope

We have previously defined grief as the inability to imagine a tomorrow that the client would enjoy or find life-giving. Having transformed the image of the person the client is grieving to the resource state the next step is to help the client rebuild their image of the future. To have hope, the client needs to be able to see the things they value in their image of the future. To achieve this goal we need to discover the timeless qualities that the deceased shared

> Live with vision
> and purpose.
> Resilient people
> don't wait passively
> for the future
> to happen to them –
> they become the future
> by consciously creating it.
> — Joan Borysenko

> We all live
> under the same sky,
> but we don't all have the
> same horizon.
> — Konrad Adenauer

> I am only one;
> but still I am one.
> I cannot do everything,
> but still I can do something.
> I will not refuse to do the
> something I can do.
> — Helen Keller

with the client. As we explore with the client what they valued about the person, we need to ensure that the values are transformed into timeless qualities. I find it helpful to keep note of these qualities as the client discusses them.

We can invite the client to imagine these qualities written on cards, or the petals of flowers, autumn leaves, snowflakes, or some other item that the person can imagine being "cast" into and floating down over their future. My preference is to use a seasonal metaphor that appeals to the client, such as flower petals if the person enjoys gardening, or fall leaves. One Star Trek fan imagined the rapidly reproducing small furry creatures called Tribbles as metaphors that represented the specific qualities. I invite the client to hold multiple copies of these qualities in their hands and imagine that they multiply to the point that they are heaped up and flowing over.

Once the client has an overflowing sense of the qualities, I invite them to stand and cast them out into the future and watch them float down over their future. I also invite them to have an attitude of curiosity and wonder about how they will experience those qualities in the future. While we want to be quite specific about the qualities, we need to be open and curious about the form in which those qualities will be experienced.

I have not found it necessary to do a detailed inquiry into the location of the client's sense of their future that we looked at in the section on timelines. Rather, I note where the client looks when I mention their future and then point to that place when I invite the client to cast the qualities into the future.

If the relationship has been conflicted, it may be helpful to include in the future image qualities, such as affirmation, that the person wanted from the deceased but was never given. Memories of these qualities shared by other people can be used as resources to be included in the image of the preferred future. Similarly, undesired negative experiences, such as disrespect, can be transformed into their desired quality (respect) and added to the future qualities.

Special Activities or Family Events

On some occasions a client may report that they have been unable to engage in a pleasurable activity that they used to share with the person. Even the thought of going fishing or to a concert or some other shared activity elicits significant distress. These activities need to be addressed specifically to completely resolve the client's grief

> *All the great spiritual leaders in history were people of hope. Abraham, Moses, Ruth, Mary, Jesus, Rumi, Gandhi, and Dorothy Day all lived with a promise in their hearts that guided them toward the future without the need to know exactly what it would look like.*
> — Henri J. M. Nouwen

> *Everything is material for the seed of happiness, if you look into it with inquisitiveness and curiosity. The future is completely open, and we are writing it moment to moment. There always is the potential to create an environment of blame – or one that is conducive to loving-kindness.*
> — Pema Chodron

and restore their freedom to engage in any activity that they find pleasurable.

There are two aspects to restoring the client's freedom to engage in these activities. The first is to discover any timeless qualities that the client experienced when sharing in these activities. These qualities can be added to the images cast into the future. The second is to rehearse, in the client's imagination, their engaging in the activity in the future. This may evoke some objections that need to be satisfied. The client can be invited to imagine engaging in the activity in the future, with warm memories and gratitude for past experiences and their current engagement in the activity as an ongoing expression of gratitude for times past.

If it seems appropriate, the client can be invited to imagine sharing that activity with someone else as a way of honoring and being grateful for these past experiences. Sharing a timeless value with someone else is one of the best ways of keeping it.

Family events may also be the focus of a person's grief. On one occasion the focus of the client's grief for her deceased father was on her son's upcoming wedding. The client's father had blessed her on her wedding day and she grieved that he would not be there to bless her son at his wedding. I invited the client to remember the blessing she had received, and still had, and then to imagine some part of the wedding celebration, perhaps dancing with her son and whispering in his ear, "When I got married my dad blessed me and now I am passing that blessing on to you ..." When she was able to image that timeless blessing being present at her son's wedding the distress instantly disappeared and was replaced by a joyful smile.

Testing the Outcome

Once the steps have been completed we need to check that the grief response has been resolved. Invite the client to see if they can get the feelings of grief back. When they can't, invite them to try even harder to get the feelings back. This testing achieves two goals:

- To check that the process has been successful.

- To associate and reinforce a different emotional response to the memory of the person they have lost. The outcome testing becomes a practice exercise of the new response and reinforces in the client's mind that they can remember the person as they choose without having the intense emotional reaction.

Those who bring sunshine into the lives of others, cannot keep it from themselves.
— *James M. Barrie*

A gift that cannot be given away ceases to be a gift. The spirit of a gift is kept alive by its constant donation.
— *Lewis Hyde*

To live in hearts we leave behind is not to die.
— *Thomas Campbell*

*Joy and sorrow
are inseparable ...
together they come
and when one
sits alone with you ...
remember that
the other is
asleep upon your bed.*
— *Kahlil Gibran*

If the client is able to get the grief feelings back or there is still some level of distress, then we need to repeat the steps. Pay particular attention to any additional objections to resolving the grief that need to be satisfied. Also check to see whether there are still some other qualities from the person that the client needs to imagine in their future. After repeating the steps, check to ensure that the desired outcome has been achieved.

On the following pages is a complete protocol with scripts for assisting a client to resolve their grief. While the scripts are provided they need to be rephrased into your own language as you respond to the specific needs of the client. The process needs to be done **with** the client and not **to** or **on** the client.

Instructions: Adapt the language of the following process to meet the needs of your specific client. Where possible, use names of the deceased rather than the generic pronouns or "loved one." The goal is to have the client be able to remember the person when and how they want, without distress, and to be able to use the relationship as a resource for creating their preferred future.

1. **Clarify the Nature of the Distress. Is it Simply Grief?**

   Invite the client to remember who/what they have lost.

   Are there any specific aspects to the grief, such as anticipating an anniversary, or the inability to go to a movie or holiday resort, that have become a focus of the grief?

   Is the client's grief complicated by a traumatic death or by conflict in the relationship?

   If the client was traumatized, then engage in the Resolving Painful Memories process (exercise on page 94) before doing the grief process.

   When the relationship was conflicted, invite the client to do the forgiveness exercises (see 169 and 174) and then engage in the grief process.

   For conflicted situations, invite the client to recall a positive memory of the person since they may be "stuck" in a negative memory. Once recalled, this positive memory can be set aside.

2. **Identify the Structure of the Client's Grief.**

   Pay particular attention to the location of their felt sense of the person as they recall them. The following instruction to the client will help them discover the structure of their memory.

   This may sound a little strange, but as you remember your loved one, close your eyes and become aware of how you are remembering them. For example, are you seeing a picture of them or do you just have a sense of them? ...

   Now take a moment and be aware of where your sense of them is located in your mental space: For example, if you are "seeing" a picture of them in your mind, is the picture out in front of your or behind, or to one side? ...

   Likewise, if you just have a sense of them where is that sense located in your mental space? ...

   Just take your time and when you have a sense of them just point to where that is ...

   When the client points to a place ask them how far is it from them.

   When you have located the memory, confirm the location and then invite the client to set it aside for a moment.

3. **Discover the Structure of Their Resolved Grief Resource.**

   Identify a person who they have lost but no longer grieve. Identify the structure of this experience. Where is it "located" in the client's experience?

   Take a moment and think about someone in the past that you have lost and at the time you grieved for, but for whom as you sit here today you no longer have those intense feelings of grief that you had when you lost them ...

   Now close your eyes and point to where your sense of that person is located ...

   Make note of the two different locations. Usually the resolved grief resource will be closer and more accessible to the client.

4. *Seek and Satisfy Objections to Resolve the Grief.*

   Check in with yourself. Is there any part of you that objects to moving the person from this location ... (point to where they identified the image of the person they are grieving) ... to this location ... (point to the location of the resolved grief) ...?

   Satisfy any objections. Here are some possible objections and their satisfaction:

   Objections to moving the person to that location.

   The resource position may not be a desired location for the memory of the person they are currently grieving. For example, a client grieving a child may not want to "re-locate" their memory to the location of a deceased parent with whom they had a difficult relationship.

   Seek an alternative location, paying specific attention to the qualities of the relationship they had with the person they are grieving. For example, if the client describes being "really close" to the deceased find a resource position with a person they were "really close" to.

   That makes sense to me that you don't want to move them to be with that person. Take a moment and think of a someone that you were "really close to" and that you lost. You remember grieving for them, but as you remember them today you realize that you are no longer grieving. You remember them fondly and without distress ...
   Where is that person located in your mental space ...

   If the client is unable to remember a resource person.

   Think of a person who you are currently "really close" to ...
   Where is that person located in your mental space? ...
   Does any part of you object to relocating their memory of the deceased to that location? ...

   When all else fails and the client is unable to identify a satisfactory resource location.

   That's OK. Let's do this instead. Take a moment and let your Inner Wisdom decide the best place where you would like to hold these memories so that they are always accessible to you so you can keep this special person in your memory with a sense of love, gratitude and peace ...

   A special place where you have no objection to moving your memory of them to ...
   Take a moment and create that special place ...

   Satisfying objections to letting go of the feelings of grief.

   These may be expressed in the fear of forgetting, or some form of unresolved conflict or need. For the fear of forgetting ask:

   Do you want to not forget them by being miserable, or would you like to remember them with love and gratitude?

   Satisfy any other objections before moving to the next step.

5. **Transforming the Grief Response.**

   Relocate the image or felt sense of the lost person to the resource location of successful grief.

   Now that you have satisfied the objections, move the image of the person from here ... (point to the grief state location) ... to here ... (point to the resource location) ... and tell me when you have done that ...

6. **Restoring Hope: Re-imaging a New Preferred Future.**

Invite the client to review the relationship and recall all the person's qualities. When a temporal quality such as a hug is shared, inquire into the experience to discover the timeless quality.

Tell me about your loved one. What do you really value and love about them? ...

Now I want you to open and cup your hands together and imagine they are filled to overflowing with blossoms, or petals, or leaves, or snow flakes, with each "blossom" being a metaphor or image of these wonderful qualities of your loved one ...

And you can have lots of duplicates of the things you really valued because they probably shared them with you more than once ...

Now I want you to cast the images of these timeless qualities into your future. Watch the images float down over the future ...

Without being specific, wonder how you will experience these qualities as you watch them float over and down into your future ...

7. **Rehearse any Special Events or Activities.**

If the grief was focused on a special event or activity, invite the client to remember the activity, both the temporal and timeless qualities of the activity. Add the timeless qualities to the new preferred future by scattering those qualities in the future as you did in step 6.

Satisfy any objections to engaging in the temporal activity again.

Does any part of you object to doing the activity again? ...
If so, ask the part what would satisfy its objection ...

Now take some time to imagine engaging in the activity again in the future with warm memories and gratitude for the times in the past when you got to share it with your beloved ...

If it seems appropriate, invite them to imagine sharing that activity with someone else as a way to gratefully share what they had in the past with someone else in the future.

8. **Check the Outcome.**

Take a moment and remember your loved one and see if you can get the feeling of grief back ...

When they can't get the feelings back:
I want you to try really hard to get the feelings back ...

9. **If they Can Still Feel the Grief.**

If they do get the feelings back or there is still some distress, go back through the steps to find what aspect of the grief still remains. For example:

- Are there other objections to resolving the grief that need to be satisfied?

- Are there other qualities that they are still missing and need to be imaged into their future?

- After repeating the steps, check the outcome.

Organizational Grief

Most of the previous discussion was related to helping individuals with grief, but the same basic strategies can be used with a large group, such as a congregation who may be grieving the loss of a pastor. The same understanding of grief applies to the congregation; what is lost is not simply the pastor but the congregation's sense of their future and their ability to access what has been life-giving to the congregation. Similarly, people may grieve the loss of a building, or a service if it has been cancelled.

When working with the organization, the important task is to become aware of how the community, through its collective storytelling, is making meaning of the loss and how they are reinforcing a positive or negative view of the future. Intervention is required when the community narrative has a negative impact on their ability to engage meaningfully in the present to create their preferred future.

Confusing the Candle with the Light

Clergy are candles; they are light-bearers but they are not the Light. There is one Light and many candles. When people confuse the Light with a particular light-bearer they will experience a deep sense of grief if the light-bearer leaves. Like the people of Israel taken into exile, people will wonder if they can still access God's grace now that their pastor has departed. The same process of distinguishing an eternal quality from its temporal manifestation can be used to help people resolve their grief.

From a theological perspective, these grief strategies help people realize that even if clergy come and go, God and God's love have not left. The Source of all blessings and life is still present. When the people of Israel were exiled to Babylon, they were confronted with a great theological challenge that is captured in the words of Psalm 137:

"How can we sing the Lord's song in a foreign land?"

The people believed that God would only hear their prayers when they were offered on Israel's sacred soil. This belief would cause grief, and they did grieve, as the Psalmist reports. That grief persisted until they were able to discover that God's blessing was still available even in a foreign land. The exile story also suggests that many people were not really able to make that transition, and this is something to keep in mind. Not all members of a congregation will be able to resolve their grief in the same time or fashion, and the focus may need to shift between a congregational approach and an individual one.

We must be willing to get rid of the life we've planned, so as to have the life that is waiting for us.
— Joseph Campbell

Clergy may shine the light, but they are not the source of The Light. We grieve when we confuse the bulb by which we knew the light with The Light.

Thousands of candles can be lighted from a single candle, and the life of the candle will not be shortened. Happiness never decreases by being shared.
— Buddha

Congregational Grief is Rare

From my experience of working as an interim pastor and as a church consultant, I would say that congregational grief which significantly impairs organizational functioning is actually quite rare. While one or two parishioners may have had a close attachment to the pastor and experience substantial grief when the pastor leaves, most parishioners understand that clergy come and clergy go and life goes on. They value their clergy, appreciate what they have done, and can celebrate these accomplishments and bless the pastor as they move into other ministries. There may be some mild missing and sadness at the departure but after a brief period the people return to their previous functioning. These people are able to distinguish that though the pastor may help to shine the light, they are not the Light and the Light continues to shine even when the pastor has left.

One of the other reasons that congregations don't grieve is that many parishioners see the pastor's departure as an opportunity to experience a change in direction. With large numbers of congregations in decline, parishioners know that something has to change if the congregation is to grow, and a change in pastor creates that opportunity.

In many situations the desire for a new pastor is not malicious, but a natural desire for novelty and the opportunity for fresh ideas and ways of doing things. Just as a pastor may seek a new ministry to move out of habituated patterns that are no longer fulfilling, so congregations may want the opportunity for a fresh approach. If these natural desires for new possibilities are ignored, by either the pastor or the congregation, they may fester into outright dissatisfaction and conflict.

In the midst of dissatisfaction and conflict, people will not grieve the departing pastor. Their departure may actually lead to delight. When a ministry is ended in conflict, members of the congregation may also be conflicted with one another. Some may not have been dissatisfied with the pastor and grieve their loss, while others are delighted the pastor has left. Resolving grief and/or resentment at an individual level will be necessary before the congregation can be reconciled to itself and its future.

When a Pastor Dies in Office

One exception to the mild grief response is when a pastor dies while in office. The pastor's death compounds the organizational loss with the deep existential issues of life and death. Consequently,

The congregation will need to keep telling you what they valued about their former rector until they know that you know what they valued and currently miss.

The best way to predict your future is to create it.
— Alan Kay

May you live your life in such a way that when your feet hit the floor in the morning, Satan shudders and says, 'Oh shit – she's awake!'
— Megan McKenna

the organization and its members are dealing with the loss on multiple organizational and personal levels. A further complication in moving forward is determining how to respond pastorally to the pastor's family while responding to the needs of the congregation. The pastor's family may be living in a parsonage that they will need to vacate. The pastor's death means that they not only have lost a loved one but also their home. Parishioners may respond to the family's needs out of guilt and encumber the congregation's future functioning. The death of a pastor is not insurmountable. Moving to a new future requires pastoral sensitivity and integrated responses at both the individual and corporate level.

Preventing Congregational Grief

Some congregations don't grieve when their pastor leaves because their next minister is very similar to the former pastor. For example, if a congregation deeply valued the former pastor's strong social justice sermons, and the new pastor also preaches strong social justice sermons, then the congregation will not have lost what they value and consequently their grief will be minimal. Congregations may fondly remember and mildly miss a former pastor's quirks of personality but not distressingly miss them when they have not been deprived of the deeper life-giving values. However, if the congregation calls a pastor who does not preach strong social justice sermons then they may begin to grieve for the former pastor and reject or become conflicted with the new pastor.

The best way to prevent this type of grief reaction is to help the congregation, during the search process, to continually clarify and focus on what they truly value and find life-giving about their congregation. They then need to use these core values as their search criteria so that they call someone who shares these values and can join the congregation at its life-giving center. This does not mean that congregations needs to call someone "just like" the last pastor in terms of personality and other temporal characteristics such as age or gender. What the congregation needs to do is discern the core, life-giving values of the congregation, and call a pastor who also values these things. As long as the congregation calls someone who can help them grow what they value as a congregation, there will not be a deep sense of loss, and consequently only minimal grief, as the congregation transitions to new leadership.

In *Assessing Skills and Discerning Calls: A Comprehensive Guide for the Clergy Search Process,* my wife, Kim, and I describe Appreciative

They say such nice things about people at their funerals that it makes me sad to realize I'm going to miss mine by just a few days.
— Garrison Keillor

The best way to prevent congregational grief is to ensure that the search process results in the call of a pastor who respects what the congregation values, and can join the congregation in growing those values. The first step in this process is to help the congregation discover what it is they truly value.

Ask not what your pastor can do for you. Ask what your church can do for your community and then ask, "What do we need in a pastor to help us do that?"

Inquiry-based strategies for all aspects of the search process. Detailed strategies to facilitate an Appreciative Inquiry summit to clarify core values and establish a vision for the future are provided. From this vision, criteria for the search process can be created and candidates can be assessed with respect to the life-giving future the congregation desires.

The Appreciative Inquiry process of engaging in shared storytelling of their best experiences and what they value, followed by visioning a future based on these life-giving experiences and values, will naturally inoculate a congregation against grief, provided that the new leader joins in and grows that vision.

Inoculating a Congregation Against Grief

Understanding the nature of grief and how to resolve it can also be used by the departing minister to inoculate the congregation against potential grief when they leave. In the last weeks of their tenure people will begin saying their good-byes and say things like "we are going to miss you." Rather than just saying "thank you" or "I will miss you too," the departing minister can use the situation as an opportunity to explore what the people are going to miss. Just as in the grief process, the pastor can mine into these values to help distinguish between temporal and eternal qualities. Then the person can hold onto the eternal qualities when the minister leaves.

This process can be used intentionally with groups during the last few weeks of the pastor's time. People can be invited to reflect on what they have been grateful for during the Pastor's tenure. This process can be used both as a way to celebrate the pastor's ministry and to say farewell to them, and as a way to begin the conversation within the congregation about their core values.

The key questions to ask parishioners during this time are:

- What do they value about their church?
- Where have they seen God working?
- What did they do as a result?

The more the departing pastor invites the people to move their focus from the pastor to focusing on where they have seen God at work and how they can continue to engage with God in continuing these tasks, the less likely they will be to grieve the pastor's leaving. While the pastor may leave, God is not leaving, and the opportunity to experience God's blessing will remain rather than depart with the pastor.

> Don't worry about the world coming
> to an end today.
> It is already
> tomorrow in Australia.
> — Charles M. Schulz

> Gratitude unlocks the fullness of life. It turns what we have into enough, and more. It turns denial into acceptance, chaos to order, confusion to clarity. It can turn a meal into a feast, a house into a home, a stranger into a friend. Gratitude makes sense of our past, brings peace for today, and creates a vision for tomorrow.
> — Melody Beattie

When parishioners are imagining sharing what they value from their past with people in their future, they will not be grieving.

One of my preferred ways of inoculating a congregation against grief is to conduct the "Remembering a Pastor with Love and Gratitude" exercise on the following page.

In this process, parishioners dialogue about what they value about the pastor and then discern the eternal qualities the pastor has given to them. Parishioners are then invited to imagine sharing these values with others who would benefit from that blessing. When parishioners are imagining sharing what they value from their past with people in their future, they will not be grieving. Rather, they will be actively remembering and making available those blessings to others.

Instructions: This exercise is designed for a plenary gathering of all parishioners. It could be conducted at a Sunday Service in place of a sermon and intercessions, or as part of a farewell celebration. It may also be used as a way to conclude small group conversations that have occurred at multiple locations across the parish in the weeks or days before the gathering. This process assumes that the pastor is present and that they have had a satisfactory relationship with the congregation.

1. **Invite the Parishioners to Share What They Value About Their Church.**

   I would like you to turn to the person sitting beside you, in front of you, or behind you, and ask them what they value about your church. Take turns to share with each other what you each value about your church ...

2. **Widen the Sharing to Include All the Parishioners.**

   When the people have shared with their neighbor, invite them to share what they have heard with the wider congregation.

   Now what I would like you to do is share with me what you have heard that your fellow parishioners value about your church. When you tell me I will repeat it over the microphone and if you heard the same thing or you also share in that value, I want you to say "Amen!"

3. **Responding to Valuing the Pastor.**

   When someone says they value the pastor, inquire more deeply into what they specifically value. As the values are shared people can respond with "Amen!" The coach can also help the people discover the timeless qualities that have been shared by the pastor in a temporal act.

   Tell me what things specifically you value about your pastor...
   As you remember your pastor take a moment a replay the memories in your mind when you got to experience (slowly repeat the timeless qualities that the parishioners have valued) ...
   And be grateful for these blessings ...

4. **Owning the Timeless Qualities.**

   Now I know that when your pastor leaves they are not going to take these values with them. They have been freely given to you to keep ...

   When the pastor is present this idea can be reinforced by inquiring of the pastor whether they will leave these blessings with the people or pack them up and take them with them.

   And so I invite you to think about how you want to own and hold these blessings. Would you like to hold them in your heart so that you can access them anytime you want even after the pastor has left? ...
   Take a moment and be aware of these memories in your own heart ... and be grateful ...

5. **Imagining the Future.**

   Think of someone you know who needs this gift that your pastor shared with you and which is now in your heart ...
   Imagine sometime in the future sharing the gift that you were given with that person ...
   Now imagine others in the congregation sharing what they value with others ...
   And wonder, what will the church become as these values and all the things you value about your church are shared with others in your community? ...
   For you will only get to keep what you give away. Amen!

Congregational Grief or Failure of Leadership

As a consultant I often encounter situations in which clergy experience significant conflict within several years of their arriving in the parish. One of the common attributions for the cause of the conflict is that the congregation is still grieving their former pastor and hasn't been able to accept their new pastor. In many of these situations I find the problem is not grief in and of itself, but a failure of leadership that may have evoked a grief-like reaction.

When people cannot see a worthwhile future they will look back to "better times." This looking back is dramatically demonstrated by the people of Israel when they were led out of slavery in Egypt by Moses to the promised land. In the midst of the tough desert transition they lose sight of the promised land (their future), they forget the hardship of slavery and remember only the good things from that arduous time, and they cry out:

> *"If only we had meat to eat! We remember the fish we used to eat in Egypt for nothing, the cucumbers, the melons, the leeks, the onions, and the garlic; but now our strength is dried up, and there is nothing at all but this manna to look at." (Numbers 10:4-6)*

The problem is not looking backward – the real problem is the inability to look forward, because the people have lost their vision for the future. Looking backward is actually an attempted solution to the problem of not having a vision.

The first and primary function of leadership is to communicate a shared, life-giving vision of the future. In the absence of a vision of the future, the people will look back to the past for a time that was comfortable. From my experience as a church consultant, creating and communicating a shared vision of the future is the most pressing need of the majority of the congregations with whom I have worked. I find it is very rare for the typical church members that I work with to be able to tell me clearly and succinctly what the purpose of their church is. From my perspective, this is not their failure but a failure of leadership.

The second major leadership failing that may evoke grief-like symptoms is a failure to be incarnational. The church knows how to celebrate the incarnation at Christmas very well, yet one of its leaders' biggest failures is knowing how to "do" the incarnation and join a congregation at its life-giving core. When a new pastor comes and, rather than joining the congregation, imposes either a vision or

People will have more confidence journeying to the future when they get to carry what they value from the past with them.
— Fifth Assumption of Appreciative Inquiry

Where there is no vision, the people perish.
— Proverbs 29:18

We need to discover how to be incarnational and not just be good at celebrating the incarnation.

change on the people, resistance, resentment, and potentially open conflict will be evoked. Joining a congregation and communicating a shared, life-giving vision is very different from imposing a personal vision, regardless of how wonderful or theologically correct the personal vision is.

When a vision or a way of doing things is imposed on people, their access to what they value and find life-giving will be disrupted and conflict will erupt. It may appear that the people are grieving their previous pastor, when they are actually responding to a failure of incarnational, vision-based leadership in the present moment.

Strategies to Incarnationally Join a Congregation

The simplest and most effective strategy to join a congregation is to ask people what they value about their congregation and, within a mosaic of such responses, discern what the life-giving core of the congregation is. Decisions then need to be made that ensure these life-giving characteristics are sustained and enriched. Here is an example of what not to do[4]:

> A large electronics firm underwent a change in CEO. Prior to the new CEO's arrival, if you had asked employees what the life-giving core of their company was, they would have responded; "the creativity of the Research and Development department." The company was known for its innovations in the field and the creativity inspired the other departments such as manufacturing, marketing, and sales. When the new CEO arrived they looked at the financial bottom-line and saw that research and development was a significant cost for the company. On the other hand, production was a significant revenue generator. To save costs the CEO decided to outsource research and development. Several years later the company had gone through a severe decline and went from employing 40,000 people to 8,000. While the downturn could be blamed on changes in the electronics field, a more likely reason was that the company had outsourced and lost its essential life-giving core, and consequently was dying.

When leading change it is essential that people are helped to look beyond the temporal values to the life-giving qualities. Circumstances do change. Programs need to be stopped and started. However, these temporal changes need to be servants of enriching the eternal life-giving qualities of the organization.

The leaders who work most effectively, it seems to me, never say "I." And that's not because they have trained themselves not to say "I." They don't think "I." They think "we"; they think "team." They understand their job to be to make the team function. They accept responsibility and don't sidestep it, but "we" gets the credit. This is what creates trust, what enables you to get the task done.
— Peter Drucker

If you have come to help me, you are wasting your time. But if you have come because your liberation is bound up with mine, then stay and let us work together.
— Australian Aborigine Woman

You may be deceived if you trust too much, but you will live in torment if you don't trust enough.
— Frank Crane

When people have a shared, realistic image of the future that contains what they find valuable and life-giving, and the belief that they can create it, they will not be grieving.

Building Trust

One of the initial goals of joining any group is to establish trust among the members of the group and its leaders. Trust is the ability to make vulnerable to another person's actions what you value, knowing that the value will be protected. People will trust a leader when they know that the leader knows and respects what the people value. Similarly leaders will trust the people when the people know and respect what the leader values. Appreciative Inquiry-based approaches of shared storytelling about core values will naturally build trust within a group because the process enables people to hold what is valued in common.

Resolving Grief and Appreciative Inquiry Processes

The process of discovering what was valuable in the past and using it as the foundation for imagining a preferred future, that I have described as a way to resolve grief, is essentially the same process that occurs in Appreciative Inquiry summits and visioning processes. In the Appreciative Inquiry summit a community develops an image of their preferred future by discovering and building on what was valuable in the past. In many congregations the Appreciative Inquiry strategic visioning process will actually help resolve or prevent grief, without the grief being a specific focus of the work. When people have a shared, realistic image of the future that contains what they find valuable and life-giving, and the belief that they can create that future, they will not grieve. For resources and more information about Appreciative Inquiry-based strategic visioning for churches, please see the Clergy Leadership Institute web site at www.clergyleadership.com.

5: FORGIVENESS AND THE ART OF RESOLVING RESENTMENT

In the United States it appears that we, both as individuals and a society, know very little about forgiveness. This is somewhat surprising given that the country is supposedly founded on the Judeo-Christian ethos, which places a high value on forgiveness. This lack of understanding is manifested in a national obsession with retributive justice rather than restorative justice. And our "high moral ground" is maintained by having a greater percentage of our citizens in jail than any other nation[1]. While I am not advocating a mindless throwing open of our prisons our obsession with retribution rather than forgiveness indicates that we are trying to correct the past rather than building a better tomorrow.

Without forgiveness, people remain trapped in their past, obsessing over what has been done to them. This obsession leads the person to use their injury as a way to re-injure themselves and stay in a state of victimization. While they are looking back to the past, it is impossible to look forward and to experience hope. If we are resentful of things from our past, when we do glimpse the future, we are likely to see a repetition of these painful experiences continuing into the future. Rather than welcoming the future we are likely to spend considerable effort in taking self-protective measures.

Some people find it very easy to forgive, while others, often despite their best efforts, find it difficult to release their resentment and live fully in the present moment. My experience of helping people learn how to forgive indicates that there are two primary areas to focus on:

- The person's skill or ability to forgive
- The person's motivation to forgive.

When people "can't" forgive, it is either because they don't know how, or because some part of them objects to forgiving and this objection impairs their motivation to forgive.

The Skill of Forgiving

Despite forgiveness being one of the core elements of the Gospel, my experience of most churchgoers is that we are very unskilled at forgiving others. As Steve Andreas[2] has pointed out, Jesus talked a lot about forgiveness and seemed quite skilled at forgiving but he didn't teach his followers **how** to forgive. Either he or the writers of

> A multitude of executions
> discredits a king,
> as a multitude of funerals
> discredits a doctor.
> — Seneca

> Forgiveness is a gift
> you give yourself,
> when you are ready
> to stop hurting
> for what someone else did.
> — Edith Stauffer

> We must develop
> and maintain
> the capacity to forgive.
> He who is devoid
> of the power to forgive is
> devoid of the
> power to love.
> There is some good
> in the worst of us
> and some evil
> in the best of us.
> When we discover this,
> we are less prone
> to hate our enemies.
> — Martin Luther King, Jr.

the Gospels neglected to teach the nature of resentment and the process for forgiving others. Perhaps the people of Jesus' time knew how to forgive a debt and only needed motivation to apply these strategies to their neighbors and their enemies. Regardless of why it is not in the Gospels the good news is that by studying people who are able to rapidly resolve resentment we can learn how to use their strategies both to help us forgive and to teach others how to forgive.

When we don't know how to forgive, we have four options:

- We can stay resentful as a self-protective blanket to prevent further pain.
- We can numb out our pain and become passionless and disengaged.
- We can avoid the context, such as the church where the injury occurred.
- We can learn to forgive.

Forgiveness is a skill that we can practice and develop. To develop the skill of forgiving, we need to understand the nature of resentment and what forgiveness is — and what it is not.

The Dynamics of Resentment

Take a moment and think of someone you resent. Rather than trying to get rid of the resentment, or judging yourself for being resentful, allow yourself to be curious about the nature of your resentment. Keep your resentment in mind as you read through this section and see which aspects of resentment relate to your experience. Without thinking about the content of what the person did to you, focus on the thoughts underlying your resentment.

Notice how you are experiencing the feelings of resentment in the present moment about something that has happened in the past. When we examine the thought patterns underlying the resentment, we often find a thought like: "They shouldn't have done ..."

This suggests that resentment is a current demand that someone or something in the past should have been different. While the event that created our resentment may be in the past, the resentment is in the present and is manifested as a demand about the past. What we cannot do is change the past. It doesn't matter how bad or egregious the offending behavior was, nor how hard we insist in this present moment that they should not have done what they did, it is in the past and we cannot change the past. What we can do is change how we view the past and how we refocus from what happened to what we want to happen in the future. Forgiveness is something that we do in the present to let go of the demand that the past be different[3].

When we forgive we release our current demand that the past or the people in the past should have been different.

This understanding of forgiveness forms the basis of the forgiveness process that we will present at the end of this section.

Demanding or Preferring

Forgiveness isn't denial that something bad happened. One of the steps in the forgiveness process is transforming the demand we have about the past into a preference. We move from *demanding* that a person should have behaved differently in the past to *preferring* that they had behaved differently in the past. By transforming the demand to a preference, we are not denying that something bad happened; rather we are changing the way we relate to what happened.

Transforming a demand into a preference also enables us to affirm rather than negate or violate our values when we forgive. One of the reasons we resent is because someone has done something to hurt us. This hurt is experienced because the person has violated one of our values. If in an attempt to forgive someone we say "it didn't matter," we are likely to have negated the value that the person violated.

Sometimes people will cling tenaciously to a demand that a person shouldn't have done something in the past. In these situations we may need to help the person discover the ineffectiveness of demanding the past be different. Here is a strategy I have found it helpful to help someone transform a demand into a preference:

Coach: Yesterday it rained just as I was getting out of my car. It was really annoying and I got totally drenched and had to get a change of clothes. (*I choose a natural phenomenon beyond my ability to control.*) Here is what I want you to do with me. Let's take some time and demand that the rain didn't fall. Demand really hard ... (*wait a moment*) ... Has anything changed? Did demanding make it not have rained yesterday? ...

Client: Yes, but that's the rain! [Person's name] shouldn't have done what he did, he should have known better.

Coach: Yes you are right, he should have known better. Let's try something else together. I'll join you in demanding that he

Some leave trails of criticism and resignation; others trails of gratitude and hope. What kind of trails do you leave?
— W. A. Ward

Demanding that the past should have been different is a really good way to stay miserable.

One can be very happy without demanding that others agree with them.
— Ira Gershwin

didn't do what he did. Let's do it now, let's really demand he didn't do it ... *(After a period of time.)* Has anything changed?

Client: No, but he shouldn't have –

Coach: You're right he shouldn't have, but demanding doesn't change things. Turning the demand into a preference allows you to keep the value but doesn't tie you to the past ... Take a moment to identify the value behind your preference ...

Now that you are aware of the value, take a moment and consider whether you want to keep this value in the future ...

(If the person wants to keep the value in the future)
Take a moment and imagine yourself in the future, seeking people to relate to who also share this value ...
Imagine yourself offering that value to someone ...
And receiving the value from others ...

Converting demands into preferences is also an effective strategy for realistically imaging the future. Going through life demanding that things and people be or act a certain way is a really good way to experience disappointment and frustration. Demanding that the future be a certain way does not take into account that many things, including people, are beyond our control. Preferring and working to make things a certain way honors our values and gives us flexibility when things don't work out the way we prefer.

Forgiving and Remembering

One of the common, truly unhelpful understandings about forgiveness is that we need to forgive and forget. Firstly, it is actually impossible to completely forget things, especially when you try hard to forget, as the very act of trying to forget will hold the issue in consciousness and refresh your memory. It is also potentially dangerous to forget what has been done to you.

Imagine if you had tried to pet a tiger and your arm was mauled. As part of your healing from the trauma you would need to forgive the tiger. If you forgot that tigers maul arms, you might end up losing the other arm when you tried to pet one again. What we need to do is forgive – and remember that tigers have the potential to maul arms[4]. Likewise, we need to forgive a breach of trust while remembering that some people are not trustworthy.

Forgiving and remembering is very different from forgiving and reliving. In reliving an experience, we will be awash with all the same painful feelings we had when the experience first occurred. In forgiving, we need to be able to remember the incident, without the distressing feelings, so we can learn from the experience.

Forgiveness and Trust

Trust is the ability to make vulnerable what you value to the actions of another knowing that what you value will be protected or kept safe. Forgiving someone does not mean that you now will trust them. If the person is trustworthy, then you may rebuild a trusting relationship. On the other hand, when someone continues to manifest behaviors that violate your values, it would be foolhardy to trust that person.

Another mistake people make in the area of trust is to make it an "either/or" behavior. It is foolhardy to trust everyone. Even with respect to a specific person it may be appropriate to trust them with some aspects of your life but not others. The wise person knows "who to trust with what."

Forgiveness is Not Reconciliation

Forgiveness is something we do independent of the person who offended us. We forgive regardless of whether the person wants to be forgiven, or even knows they are forgiven. Forgiveness is about how we relate in this present moment to events and people in the past. Reconciliation is about how we will relate to someone in the future. Reconciliation requires the willing consent of at least two people.

Because reconciliation involves the actions of another person we may have to wait for (or possibly never be reconciled to) someone we want to be reconciled with. On the other hand, we do not need to wait for another person to change or desire to be forgiven before we forgive them. The person who injured us may be gone, dead, or totally unconcerned about whether we forgive them. If we waited for people to ask for our forgiveness, we may have a very long wait before we release the anger and resentment that we carry around. The primary beneficiary of forgiveness is the person doing the forgiving.

Reconciliation

Unlike forgiveness, which is independent of the person who offended you, reconciliation requires the mutual engagement of both parties. Reconciliation is a commitment between two people about how they will live and relate together in the future. It would be foolhardy to be

Forgiveness does not change the past, but it does enlarge the future.
— Paul Boese

The key is to get to know people and trust them to be who they are. Instead, we trust people to be who we want them to be –
and when they're not, we cry.
— Unknown

Only a fool would be reconciled to someone who does not share their personal values.

reconciled to someone who does not share your values – that would be like casting your pearls before swine.

Jesus taught us to love our enemies, and to stay in a state of forgiveness toward people who continually offend us, but he did not teach us to offer unconditional relationships to people. He allowed the rich young man to walk away. He told us to leave the towns where our peace was not returned. While forgiveness is mandated by Jesus in the Scriptures, and reconciliation is a desired goal, the Scriptures also acknowledge that sometimes reconciliation may not be achievable *(Matthew 18:15-20)*.

Reconciliation cannot be coerced by one party from the other. It is not uncommon for perpetrators to beg or manipulate others for forgiveness and reconciliation when they have shown no indication that they have amended their ways.

Only after you have forgiven someone, and only if you have an ongoing relationship with the person, would I suggest a reconciliation conversation. In this case, the focus of the conversation needs to be on your apology for your resentment, rather than getting the other person to confess to their wrongdoing. The more important part of the conversation needs to be on what shared values you have, and how you will work together in the future. I would also want you to pay attention to how safe it is for the two of you to have the conversation. In some situations it may be helpful to have a facilitator present to provide a resource of safety to have the conversation.

Forgiveness and Manipulation

Forgiveness is about setting someone free and not about manipulating their future behavior. Forgiveness, or at least a false sense of forgiveness, can be used to manipulate others in several ways:

- The forgiver can use forgiveness as a way to assume a "superior" moral position over the forgiven.

- The "guilty" person may request forgiveness as a way to avoid taking responsibility for their actions. One common form of manipulation is the request: "If you love me you would forgive me." In these situations the sorrowful person is more likely to be sorry they were caught than they are about the injury they caused someone.

To avoid the possibility of manipulation I do not recommend that clients contact the person they are forgiving. In.my experience, trying

To our most bitter opponents we say: "We shall match your capacity to inflict suffering by our capacity to endure suffering. We shall meet your physical force with soul force. Do to us what you will, and we shall continue to love you. We cannot in all good conscience obey your unjust laws because noncooperation with evil is as much a moral obligation as is cooperation with good. Throw us in jail and we shall still love you. Bomb our homes and threaten our children, and we shall still love you. Send your hooded perpetrators of violence into our community at the midnight hour and beat us and leave us half dead, and we shall still love you. But be ye assured that we will wear you down by our capacity to suffer. One day we shall win freedom but not only for ourselves. We shall so appeal to your heart and conscience that we shall win you in the process and our victory will be a double victory."
— Martin Luther King, Jr.

to talk about forgiveness with the person who has hurt you to help you achieve a state of forgiveness rarely leads to healing. More often than not, talking with the person simply leads to further injury as the conversations evoke blame, judgment, denial, and defensiveness. Often the hidden motivation in these conversations is that we want the person to confess how hurtful they had been. Such motivation is a clear indication that the demand nature of the resentment is alive, and that we are really trying to change the other person rather than changing ourselves.

Forgiveness and Victim Narratives

Forgiveness requires that we change our personal narrative. When we forgive, we let go of the injury as a means of defining who we are. Resentment is a victim narrative. It is a narrative that says we were deprived of life at some point, and that we are presently being deprived of life by that past action.

In the process of forgiving someone, we let go of the victim narrative and its impact on our life. In its place, we may put a survivor narrative that focuses not on the injury, but on how we survived the injury, and how we are experiencing life in this present moment.

Forgiveness and Future Rewards

Forgiveness also means that we let go of any hope of reward or benefit from the injury. When we forgive, we are giving up the right to compensation. Whatever debt that was incurred is forgiven. Such benefit is not limited simply to any financial consideration, but also to any status or power, such as being a victim or martyr, that we may have obtained through the injury.

When we forgive, we can no longer use the injury as a means to gain sympathy from, or to influence or apply leverage to, either the perpetrator or others who may know of the injury. To be able to let go of any secondary benefit from the injury, we need to be aware that life is offered to us in this present moment, and that this life that is offered is independent of the past injury.

Forgiveness and Lawsuits

Under what circumstances would it be appropriate to forgive someone and still bring a lawsuit against them? In these situations we need to clarify the motivation for the lawsuit. Is it to punish the person who injured you, or is reparative compensation being sought to pay for an ongoing cost of an injury? When we forgive we cancel a debt and

Forgiveness is giving yourself back what you had before.
— *Unknown*

Sincere forgiveness isn't colored with expectations that the other person apologize or change. Don't worry whether or not they finally understand you. Love them and release them. Life feeds back truth to people in its own way and time.
— *Sara Paddison*

Forgiveness is me giving up my right to hurt you for hurting me.
— *Unknown*

we can no longer seek to punish the person or seek reward for the injury. On the other hand, after we have forgiven we can request that the person contribute to any ongoing cost of the injury.

There are also pragmatic issues to consider. Lawsuits are often long and messy and are likely to keep the injury alive and reopen the resentment. Is the lawsuit worth it? In the cases where a lawsuit may be worthwhile the question will be: "How are you going to wait?" If you are saying to yourself, "I will be happy when the case is settled," then you may have to wait a very long time to be happy. What do you need to be able to "wait with happiness" until the case is resolved rather than waiting for happiness when the case is resolved in the future?

Forgiveness and Punishment

What helps us achieve the future we desire? How does punishing someone help you to have a better future? Punishment and the threat of punishment is a very primitive, and rarely effective, strategy to create a loving future.

Putting someone in jail to punish them for their crime is, from my perspective, a waste of time and tax payers' money. On the other hand, putting a person in prison to protect society from them because they have demonstrated a disregard for the well-being of others makes a lot of sense to me. In fact, I would say that we as a society have an obligation to protect one another from injustice and those who would inflict injury on another.

Jesus told us to visit the prisoners (Matthew 25:31-46). He did not question our right or responsibility to put people in prison. Forgiveness does not mean that we simply open all the prison doors and allow dangerous people to hurt others.

At the same time, I think we as a society need to think deeply about our obsession with ideas of punishment and ask how incarcerating people helps us achieve the future we seek. What does it say that the nation that calls itself the leader of the free world has more of its citizens in jail than other country? And what does it say that states with the death penalty have higher rates of murder than those that do not have the death penalty[5]? This is not simple cause and effect. What is at work is how we as a society live with images of violence, and how these images influence all of our behavior. As Martin Luther King Jr. taught, violence begets violence. Only the path of peace will lead to a peaceful future. When we focus on punishment, we are trapped by our past and not able to pursue our desired future.

When you forgive, you in no way change the past — but you sure do change the future.
— Bernard Meltzer

With Christ's prayer of forgiveness from the cross the universal religion of revenge is overcome and the universal law of retaliation is annulled.
— Jurgen Moltman

If a fox gets in the chicken coop we need to get the fox out and protect the chickens by remembering that foxes are foxes and aren't safe around chickens.

Forgiving God

It may sound strange, but some people carry huge resentment toward God, because in their minds God caused something bad to happen, or at least allowed something bad to happen. While the steps may be slightly different, releasing our demands that God should have done things differently, and satisfying our objections to forgiving, remain the essential ingredients to forgiving God.

When someone is resenting God it may also be a time to clarify which god is actually being resented, and whether this a god that the person really needs in their life. If your god is a capricious god who inflicts evil on people then it might be time to get a new god. Strategies to explore and clarify your understanding of God can be found on pages 64 and 65 in the section on crazy gods, becoming an atheist, and unconditional love.

My God, My God! Why have you forsaken me!
— Jesus from the Cross Matthew 27.46

Forgiving Yourself

The person most often in need of your forgiveness may be you. Many people find it easy to forgive others, but stay trapped in guilt and shame or endless "shoulds" and "oughts" about their thoughts or actions in the past. This is both debilitating and demeaning. Rather than struggling with perfectionistic demands to assuage guilt, people will find it more helpful to forgive themselves. Following this section on forgiving others I will provide strategies to forgive yourself.

Some pray over things they have done, and make them seem like double, Some straight away forgive themselves and save the Lord the trouble.
— John Gaynor Banks

To Resent is Human, To Forgive is Divine

The final step in forgiving someone is to see the person through the eyes of compassion: to see them the way God or Unconditional Love sees them. Trying to forgive some people seems a huge agonizing mountain to climb. The good news is that we don't need to forgive them on our own; rather, we can stop trying to forgive them ourselves, and become part of God's forgiveness for them. Forgiveness is not something we do, it is something we join or become "one with."

In the Core Processes and Resources section (page 37) we explored the resource of unconditional love and how to extend that to someone else. After we have released a person from our demands, we can surrender both ourselves and the other person into that unconditional love. It is in that love that we can let the person take responsibility for their lives free from our manipulations, expectations, and desires. It is also in that love that we can turn from the past injury and take responsibility for ourselves and creating our future in a manner that is consistent with our values.

To err is human; to forgive, divine.
— Alexander Pope

Satisfying Your Objections to Forgiving

In the previous section we looked at the nature of forgiveness, what it is and what it is not. In this section we will explore some of the objections that we have to forgiving. Unless these objections are discovered and satisfied we will be unmotivated to forgive.

Take a moment and go back to your resentment. Before you forgive the person, check to see if any part of you objects to forgiving them. Pay attention to any objection, regardless of how small or trivial your objection seems to you. If you find a part of you that objects to forgiving, ask it what would satisfy the objection.

Most of the time the objections to forgiving have to do with issues of safety and/or justice.

Safety Objections

Safety objections are typically in this form:

> "If I forgive them they will hurt me again."

In these situations the person is using their resentment to provide for their physical and emotional safety. Unfortunately, resentment is not a very effective strategy for providing safety. It also has some costly side effects such as creating tension, or possibly stomach distress or even ulcers. However, it would be unethical to take away the person's resentment without providing an alternative strategy for keeping them safe. From a place of respect, we need to acknowledge that the person is doing the best they can to stay safe, and then help them to a place of safety that does not require resentment. Only when we have satisfied their objection will they be free to release the resentment.

Within a congregation where there has been significant clergy misconduct, such as child abuse, parishioners may object to forgiving the pastor because they are using their resentment to protect future children from abuse. While the goal of protecting children is laudable and needs to be respected, using resentment is emotionally costly and rather ineffective. An alternative method of protecting the children would be to have clear procedures and policies about safeguarding God's children, and knowing that forgiveness does not mean that the pastor can go back to working with children. This is a time for forgiving and remembering, not forgiving and forgetting.

Forgiveness is the economy of the heart ... Forgiveness saves the expense of anger, the cost of hatred, and the waste of spirits.
— Hannah More

Ask yourself this: "How does resentment help me have a better future?" If it does, keep resenting. If it doesn't, try forgiving.

When a person is using resentment as a way to stay safe it would be unethical to take away the resentment without providing an alternative strategy for keeping them safe.

One of the satisfactions that I have found helpful when responding to abuse situations is to contemplate Jesus' admonition to "turn the other cheek." *(Matthew 5:36).* Rarely do I see people turn the **other** cheek; rather, they keep on presenting the **same** cheek. Presenting the same cheek continues the abuser-victim pattern. Turning the other cheek may mean leaving, literally turning away, and not presenting the same old cheek to be victimized again.

Justice Objections

Justice objections come in many forms:

> "They need to be punished for what they did."

> "If I forgive them, how will the world know they did a bad thing?"

> "If I forgive them it will be saying that what they did didn't matter."

> "If I forgive them they will do it again to someone else."

While the preferred strategy in seeking and satisfying objections is to have the part of the client that has the objection to state the satisfaction, I have rarely found that the part that has a justice objection can state what would satisfy its objection. One of the strategies I have found helpful in responding to justice objections is to explore how effective resentment is in achieving the goal of the objection such as punishing the person, or informing the world how bad they are. In most cases people will quickly realize how ineffective resentment is in achieving these goals, and that the objection has minimal validity. Further exploration will reveal that this ineffective strategy also comes with a huge personal cost, as the psychological and physical effects of internalizing those negative feelings takes its toll. One way to demonstrate the ineffectiveness of the resentment to achieve the goal is to mischievously offer a potentially absurd alternative strategy. For example:

Client: My objection to forgiving is that if I forgive him, the world won't know how miserable he is and how people should avoid him.

Coach: How long have you been resenting him? You have been doing this resentment for twenty years, you said?

Client: Yes.

Coach: And how is that working? How many people have you convinced to stay away from this person?

Client: *(Looks sheepish)* Not many.

*The weak
can never forgive.
Forgiveness is
the attribute of the strong.*
— *Mohandas K. Gandhi*

*It's not about whether they deserve to be forgiven.
It's about whether
you want to be
free of your resentment.*

*Forgiving someone won't make them nice;
it will, however,
make you nicer.*
— *Unknown*

> *Forgiving does not erase the bitter past. A healed memory is not a deleted memory. Instead, forgiving what we cannot forget creates a new way to remember. We change the memory of our past into a hope for our future.*
> *— Louis B. Smedes*

Coach: I have a better strategy. Why don't you take out a full-page ad in the New York Times saying how he is a miserable person and everyone should stay away from him, and then you can get on with your life ... Would that work for you?

Client: *(Begins laughing.)* I think it would be smarter if I just got on with the rest of my life and forgot about him.

Once the objections to forgiving have been satisfied or released, the client can begin the process of releasing the current demands about the past and reorienting themselves to working on their preferred future.

Goals for the Forgiveness Process

When helping someone achieve forgiveness I have several goals:

- To help the client remember the injury or offense without distress and not relive the experience and resent the person.

- To evaluate, clarify, and honor the client's values as ways they prefer to live in the world now and in the future.

- To help the client resourcefully behold and act compassionately toward others, including those who have offended or hurt them.

The first goal deals with the past. The second and third goals help the person to live compassionately and fully as they create their future. On the following page is narrative process to help a client forgive.

Instructions: This process is entirely independent of the person being forgiven. I do not suggest nor recommend that the client contact the person who offended or injured them as these conversations typically leads to more injury than healing. When leading someone through the process, you do not need to know who is being forgiven or what they did.

1. **Establish a Loving Foundation for Forgiving.** *(See exercises on page 65)*
   Take a moment and re-member yourself in the midst of unconditional love ...
   Remember that there is nothing you have done or will do, nor anything anyone has done or will do to you that can separate you from unconditional love. Rest for a moment in that love and from that foundation of love proceed with the following steps ...

2. **Identify the Current Demand in Your Resentment.**
   Recollect what happened that led to your resentment. Play the story over in your mind without dwelling on any aspect in particular. As you play the story back, identify the demand you have today about what the person should or should not have done in the past ...

3. **Transform the Demand Into a Preference.**
   What would you have preferred to have had happen? ...
   What can you learn from the event? ...
   What would you prefer to do in the future if confronted with a similar situation? ...
   Do you want to keep that preference in the future? Does your preference represent a value you want to keep? ...

4. **Seek and Satisfy Objections to Forgiving.**
   Does any part of you object to setting the person free from your preference and surrendering them into unconditional love to take responsibility for their life free from your demands and manipulations? ...
   Satisfy any objections ...

5. **In Your Imagination, Release the Person From Your Demand.**
   "(Person's Name) ... I would have preferred that you would have ... and now I release you from my demand that in the past you would have, or should have, or shouldn't have ..."
   Imagine yourself in the future seeking situations where you can live out your values as preferences ...

6. **Extending Unconditional Love.**
   Return to your awareness of unconditional love and allow that love to surround you ...
   Be aware that unconditional love extends out to and also surrounds the person you have forgiven ...
   Wish the person well, without defining what that "well" should be ...
   Return to your awareness of unconditional love and see it flowing out into your future ...

7. **Assess the Outcome.**
   Recall the person and see if you can feel the resentment you were feeling a few minutes ago ...

   If they can, check for any additional objections that need to be satisfied. If the client continues to feel the resentment, use the structural process on the following pages.

Structural Strategy to Achieve Forgiveness

Just as we used a structural process to rapidly resolve grief, we can use a similar structural process to resolve resentment[6]. When a client says they want to be able to forgive someone, or even "not resent" someone, we know they must have achieved that state in the past with someone else. We can discover how the client achieved that state and use that process to resolve their current resentment. Most of the time people are unaware of how they achieved the resolution of their resentment. Nor are they aware of the final structure of the resolved state.

In the forgiveness process, we identify the structure of the client's resentment and the structure of their resolved resentment. We then transform the resented experience into the same structure as the resolved state. As part of this process, we will also need to seek and satisfy any objections to making that change in the way the client structures their experience.

The most important structural component in the forgiveness process is the sense of location of the resented person and a forgiven person in the client's mental space. Here is the language I use to identify the structure of the resentment and the resolved resource state:

> *"This may sound a little strange, but I want you to try something. As you are remembering the person you resent, close your eyes and be aware of where in your space is your sense or picture of the person ...*
> *For example, are they out to the left, or to the right, or in front, or behind you? ...*
> *When you are aware of where that picture or your sense of the person is located, point to where that is ..."*

Once we have identified the location of the resented person, we can ask about a person they have forgiven:

> *"Take a moment and think about someone in the past that hurt you, who you resented at the time, but as you recall them today you realize that you must have forgiven them because you no longer feel the resentment. The feeling you now have is neutral or one of calm without any distress ..."*
> *You can remember resenting them in the past but your feeling towards them now is neutral and perhaps, despite what they have done, you can even wish them well in their future ...*
> *Point to where your sense of that person is ..."*

In most cases, simply changing the location will dramatically resolve the client's resentment. It is possible that if a client is resenting a person who belittles them and "looms large over them" that the client may need to reduce the size of the representation of the person before they relocate the person in their mental space.

Satisfying Objections To Transforming the Images

As well as seeking and satisfying objections to forgiving, we need to seek and satisfy any objections to transforming the images from a place of resentment to a place of resolution. Before I invite the client to transform the image, I ask the client:

"Check in with yourself. Is there any part of you that objects to moving the person from this location ... (I point to where they identified the image of the person they are resenting) ... to this location ... (I point to the location of the forgiven person) ...?"

Clients may have an objection to moving the image of the person they are resenting to the resource location because it doesn't exactly match the nature of the person they are resenting. For example:

Coach: As you think of this person take a moment and get an image of them. Where is that image located?

Client: *(Points straight ahead about 2 feet from them.)*

Coach: Take a moment and think about someone in the past that hurt you. At the time you resented them, but as you recall them today you realize that you must have forgiven them because you no longer feel the resentment ...

           Now point to where the image of that person is.

Client: In my heart. *(Points to her chest.)*

Coach: Does any part of you object to moving this person *(coach points to the resented person)* to this place? *(coach points to the client's heart.)*

Client: Yes! I trust this person. *(Pointing to her heart.)* I don't trust this person. *(Points to the person she is resenting.)*

Coach: Ah! that makes sense to me. Take a moment and remember someone else who hurt you, who you resented at the time, but towards whom you no longer feel the resentment – though you still don't trust them, because they haven't demonstrated any trustworthy behavior ...

For my part I believe in the forgiveness of sin and the redemption of ignorance.
— Adlai Stevenson

The impossible can always be broken down into possibilities.
— Unknown

He who cannot forgive breaks the bridge over which he himself must pass.
— George Herbert

Where is that person located? ...

Client: *(Points to a place behind her.)*

Coach: Does any part of you object to moving this person *(coach points to the location of the person she is resenting)* to this place behind you? *(coach points to the location of the person she has forgiven but does not trust.)*

Client: No that would be OK.

In this case the coach needed to match the important characteristic of a person the client had forgiven but still did not trust. Other relationships and types of injury may require these kinds of "fine tuning."

Forgiving And Ongoing Relationships

Forgiving someone who has hurt you in the past and who is now gone from your life is relatively easy. It becomes more complicated when you have an ongoing relationship with the person because they are family or a boss or co-worker.

When a client has an ongoing relationship with a person who has proven to be untrustworthy, it would be unwise for the client to put the person behind them with others whom they have forgiven and no longer have a relationship. In several different situations I have had clients move the person from a dominant "in your face" location to a place that was off to one side but still in front of them so they could "keep an eye on them."

What I find fascinating in working with clients is that their inner wisdom, manifested in their objections, will not allow them to be put in a vulnerable position. Prudently keeping an eye on untrustworthy people is simply smart; just as Jesus taught people not to cast their pearls before swine. Such prudence without resentment or animosity is lovingly wise rather than naïvely gullible, and more effective than trying to protect oneself with resentment.

In other situations, the client may have a significant objection to forgiving as they think forgiving someone may make them vulnerable to further injury. In these situations, where people are using their resentment to create a sense of safety, it may be necessary to interrupt the forgiveness process and help the client create sufficient safety resources so they can both forgive and stay safe.

One of the basic resources that clients may find helpful is the idea that compassion includes fierceness and mischievousness, and is not simply

You cannot prevent the birds of sorrow from flying over your head, but you can prevent them from building nests in your hair.
— Chinese Proverb

There are two types of people — those who come into a room and say, "Well, here I am!" and those who come in and say, "Ah, there you are."
— Frederick L. Collins

a tender response to other people. I have found this understanding of compassion helpful as it allows the client to maintain their value of being a compassionate presence in the world while also fiercely protecting themselves from further injustice at the hands of someone who continually violates their personal space and integrity.

Strategies for creating resources to confidently relate to a difficult person are provided in the next section, after the forgiveness exercises. If a client has an ongoing relationship with the person who has hurt them, the forgiveness steps can be expanded to include the development of these self-protective resources. Once these resources are established, the client can return to the forgiveness process.

Forgiveness Exercise

In the forgiveness process on the next two pages I have incorporated the structural process into the narrative approach. When using the following process I have found that great results can be achieved using the structural steps 5, 6, 7, 8, and then concluding with step 10.

The step of transforming demands into preferences, while not always necessary, does help some people understand the nature of resentment and forgiveness that can be generalized to other relationships and ways of daily living. It is also helpful for those who think that forgiveness requires them to surrender or invalidate their values. Forgiveness isn't about saying "what happened didn't matter." What happened does matter, and the forgiveness process needs to honor a client's values.

Wrapping the whole process in unconditional love is also not essential but I have found it a helpful resource for people who are religiously or spiritually oriented. The exercises beginning on page 65 and offering unconditional love to others on page 71 provide resources to create the foundation of unconditional love. Because many of the clients I work with already have an awareness of unconditional love I typically take a couple of minutes to establish the awareness of unconditional love and do not do the entire process on pages 65-67.

I have also found "surrendering a person into unconditional love" a helpful strategy for clients who are enmeshed with people and need to create a state of differentiation where the other person is not subject to the client's manipulations. Surrendering a person into unconditional love is a way to wish them well without having to define what that "well" is or should be.

Never does the human soul appear so strong as when it foregoes revenge, and dares forgive an injury.
— E. H. Chapin

To forgive is to set a prisoner free and discover that the prisoner was you.
— Lewis B. Smedes

Father, forgive them, for they don't know what they are doing.
— Jesus from the Cross
  Luke 23:34

Instructions: This process is entirely independent of the person being forgiven. I do not suggest nor recommend that the client contact the person who offended or injured them. In my experience entering into such conversations typically leads to more injury than healing.

When leading someone through the process you do not need to know who is being forgiven or what they did. As the coach, you can simply ask the client when they have completed each step. The process may not be linear, nor sequential, but iterative, especially when satisfying objections.

1. **Establish a Loving Foundation for Forgiving.** *(See exercises on page 65)*
   Take a moment and remember yourself in the midst of unconditional love. Remember that there is nothing you have done or will do, nor anything anyone has done or will do to you that can separate you from unconditional love. Rest for a moment in that love and from that foundation of love proceed with the following steps ...

2. **Identify the Current Demand in Your Resentment.**
   Recollect what happened that led to your resentment ...
   Play the story over in your mind without dwelling on any aspect in particular ...
   As you play the story back, identify the demand you have today about what the person should or should not have done in the past ...

3. **Transform the Demand into a Preference.**
   What would you have preferred to have had happen? ...
   What can you learn from the event? ...
   What would prefer to do in the future if confronted with a similar situation? ...
   Do you want to keep that preference in the future? ...
   Does your preference represent a value you want to keep? ...

4. **In Your imagination, Release the Person from Your Demand.**
   "(Person's Name) ... I would have preferred that you would have ... and now I release you from my demand that in the past you would have, or should have, or shouldn't have ..."

   Imagine yourself relating to people who honor your values doing what you would prefer if a similar situation were to arise in the future ...

5. **Identify the Structure of the Client's Resentment.**
   Pay particular attention to the location of their felt sense of the person as they recall them. The following instruction to the client will help them discover the structure of their memory.

   This may sound a little strange, but as you are recalling the person you are resenting, close your eyes and become aware of how you are remembering them.
   For example, are you seeing a picture of them or do you just have a sense of them? ...
   Now take a moment and be aware of where in your mental space is your sense of them is.
   For example, if you are 'seeing' a picture of them in your mind, is the picture out in front of your or behind, or to one side? ...
   Likewise if you just have a sense of them where is that sense located? ...
   Just take your time and when you have a sense of them just point to where that is ...

   When the person points to a place clarify distance and direction to accurately establish the location.

When you have located the memory, confirm the location and then invite the person to set it aside for a moment.

6. **Discover the Structure of People They Have Forgiven.**

   Identify a person whom the client has forgiven. Identify the structure of this experience. Where is it "located" in the person's mental space?

   Take a moment and think about someone in the past that hurt you, who you resented at the time, but as you recall them today you realize that you must have forgiven them because you no longer feel the resentment. The feeling is neutral or one of calm without any distress ...

   And as you remember them, close your eyes and point to where your sense of that person is located in your mental space ...

7. **Seek and Satisfy Objections to Forgiving.**

   Check to see if there is any part of you that objects to moving the person from where they are ... (point to the location) ... to this place ... (point to the resource location) ... and having that neutral or peaceful feeling? ...

   Ask that part what would satisfy its objection. If necessary find an alternative resource location that "feels right" and satisfies any objection.

   If vulnerability or safety is a major concern with someone they still have to continue to relate to then switch to the Dealing With a Difficult Person exercise on page 179 and then return.

8. **Transform the Image.**

   When all objections are satisfied, invite the client to move the person's image to the resource location.

   Move the person from where they are ... (point to the location) ... to this place ... (point to the resource location) ...

9. **Return to Your Awareness of Unconditional Love.**

   Take a moment to remember being surrounded by unconditional love ...
   Put yourself in that love ...
   Imagine it flowing over and through you ...
   See that love flowing over and through the person you have forgiven and surrender them into that love ...

10. **Check the Outcome.**

    Recall the person and see if you can feel the resentment you were feeling a few minutes ago ...

    When the client can't get the feelings back invite them to try harder to get the feelings back. If they are still able to feel the resentment go back through the steps to find what aspect of the resentment still remains. Are there are additional objections to satisfy, demands to release, or things to learn? Remember that it is entirely appropriate to forgive someone and not trust them. We can wisely and compassionately not trust someone rather than resentfully not trust someone.

    Repeat the process until the person or incident can be remembered without the resentment.

Dealing with a Difficult Person

In the previous section we looked at forgiving someone who has injured us in the past. Achieving a state of forgiveness toward someone who we will continue to encounter is often more difficult, especially if the person continues to act in hurtful ways toward us. In these situations we need to create additional resources so we can both forgive and stay safe as we continue to relate to them.

When coaching clients who are struggling with a difficult person such as a boss or family member, the danger is that the focus of the work with the client will be on what they can do to get the difficult person to change. From a coaching perspective, it is impossible to coach a person who is not present. Focusing on the difficult person who is not present will waste the opportunity to work with the client who is present.

Changing other people is a very difficult (if not an impossible) task, especially when the person is unaware of their need to change or is unwilling to change. A better strategy is to change ourselves in a way that meets our needs and lets us pursue our future regardless of what the other person does.

When a client is dealing with a difficult person we can use the **A ⇨ B** change model to develop four questions to focus the work:

1. How are you around the person? (State A)

2. How do you want to be around the person? (State B)

3. When have you been that preferred state in your past? (Resource State)

4. What do you need to be in this preferred state when you are around the person? (Accessing Resources)

Here is a coaching vignette that portrays these questions:

Coach: Tell me how you are around this person.

Client: Sometimes I get angry but mostly I feel afraid and withdraw.

Coach: Being afraid tells me that you don't feel resourceful to deal with the person.

Client: (nods head)

Coach: Let's just assume for the moment that they are not going to change. Tell me how you would like to be around this person.

We who lived in concentration camps can remember the men who walked through the huts comforting others, giving away their last piece of bread. They may have been few in number, but they offer sufficient proof that everything can be taken from a man but one thing: the last of the human freedoms – to choose one's attitude in any given set of circumstances, to choose one's own way.
— Viktor Frankl

If we could read the secret history of our enemies, we should find in each man's life sorrow and suffering enough to disarm all hostility.
— Henry Wadsworth Longfellow

Client: I'd like to feel confident and assured so that I could stand my ground and not be bullied.

Coach: Take a moment and go back and find a time when you were this way, confident and assured. You don't need to tell me about the time, just tell me when you have recalled it.

Client: (smiles and nods their head as they recall an experience of being confident and assured)

Coach: Now imagine being this way in the future when you are with the person and you have this new response of being confident and assured ...

And as you imagine being confident and assured, what are you seeing, and what are you hearing, and what are you doing? ...

And now be aware that you can be this way to stay safe rather than relying on resentment to protect you ...

Client: (nods their head and maintains their resourceful composure as they imagine the future)

Notice we do not waste time inquiring into the origins of the client's undesired response, nor consider how we could get the difficult person to change. The focus is entirely on the client and what they want to be able to do.

Accessing a Resourceful State

Resentment restricts choices and results in behaviors that often evoke additional negative responses from others. Our goal is to create a resourceful state that provides the client the freedom of greater choices in how they can respond and, especially in the context of forgiveness, the ability to be creatively compassionate rather than resentful.

For many clients who have completed the Growing Compassion exercise (page 78), accessing a resourceful state may be as simple as recalling their fierceness and having them imagine what fierceness would be like when they deal with the difficult person. If being judgmental toward the person is restricting the client's choices, then they may find it helpful to engage in the Transforming Judgmental Thinking exercise on pages 182 and 183.

In most cases the client will be able to find a past personal experience of how they want to be in the future. If the client is unable to access a

A Cherokee elder was teaching his grandchildren about life. He said to them, "A fight is going on inside me. It is a terrible fight, and it is between two wolves.

One wolf represents fear, anger, envy, sorrow, regret, greed, arrogance, self-pity, guilt, resentment, inferiority, jealousy and lies.

The other wolf stands for joy, peace, love, hope, sharing, serenity, humility, kindness, benevolence, friendship, empathy, generosity, truth and compassion. This same fight is going on inside of you and every other person too."

The children thought about it for a minute and then one child asked his grandfather, "Which wolf will win?" The wise one simply replied: "The one I feed."
— Cherokee Parable

personal experience they can be invited to find a role model of how they want to be and imagine how the role model would respond to the difficult person. Here is how you can invite the client to access the wisdom of a role model:

> *"Step into that role model's shoes and imagine what it is like to really be them, doing what they are doing, saying what they are saying, and feeling what they are feeling. Once you have done this fully, feel free to adjust what they did so that it fits with your situation and values."*

Once they have accessed their memory of the role model the client can then imagine being that way in the future. When using a role model the final step needs to focus on how the client will respond, not on how the role model would respond to the difficult person.

Checking the Ecology of the New Response

As we create the new resource we will also want to consider the ecology of the final state. For example, if a client is responding to a bully we don't want to "build a bigger bully." We want to ensure that the client's response is congruent with their deeper values and is something they would like to have done to them.

If the client gives a desired behavior or state that seems unrealistic or unhelpful, rather becoming judgemental, we can inquire into why that would be important to the person and how it would help.

When conducting the ecology check consider:

- How does this response align with the Golden Rule?
  Is this something you would like to have done to you?

- Are there circumstances when the new response would be unwise or inappropriate and if so, what would an alternative response be?

- Does the client, or any part of the client, have an objection to the new response, and what would satisfy that objection?

- Can the client learn anything from the difficult person?
  While we want to establish a resourceful way of responding we may not want to simply dismiss the person as there may be something to be learned from them.

On the following page are the steps to coach a person to create and rehearse a resourceful response to help them respond to a difficult person[7].

Courage is what it takes to stand up and speak; courage is also what it takes to sit down and listen.
— *Winston Churchill*

Man's mind, once stretched by a new idea, never regains its original dimensions.
— *Oliver Wendell Holmes, Jr.*

Instructions: The purpose of this exercise is to help a client establish a resourceful state to deal with a difficult person. Focus your attention on the client and what the client can change (namely themselves) rather than being distracted by the difficult person and what they are doing.

1. **Identify How Currently Respond the Difficult Person.**

   Think of a time when you were with the person ...
   As you remember that experience, what is it like being there? ...
   What do you see? ... What do you hear? ... What do you feel? ... What are you doing? ...
   Notice any other characteristics of the experience ...
   Notice what you are responding to ... What triggers your unhelpful response? ...
   Is it their voice? ... Their size? ... A specific behavior? ...

2. **Identify a Resource State.**

   Now think about how you would like to be around this person ...
   Remember a time when you were this way, probably in some other setting ...
   As you remember that experience, what is it like being there? ...
   What do you see? ... What do you hear? ... What do you feel? ... What are you doing? ...
   Notice any other characteristics of the experience ...

3. **Check the Ecology of this New Response.**

   Check with your inner wisdom to see if there are some situations in the future where this response wouldn't be wise ... or if there would be a wiser way to be ...
   If there are, create an alternative response for those situations ...
   Notice your flexibility to choose these different responses depending on the context ...

   How does this new response align with your values? ...
   Is this something you would like someone to do to you? ...

   Does any part of you object to being this new way around the difficult person? ...
   If so, what would satisfy that objection? ...

4. **Rehearse the New Response.**

   Imagine a future time when you have to deal with the person again. Put yourself in that situation now and find out what it is like for you to have this new response, easily and automatically available to you ...
   What do you see? ... What do you hear? ... What do you feel? ... What are you doing? ...

   Remember what triggered your old response, and as you recall that trigger imagine automatically and easily having this new response ...
   Practice having this new response in several different situations when you encounter them ...

   Would you like to have this response with other people you might encounter? ...
   If yes, imagine encountering other people in the future and be grateful to yourself that you can automatically choose to have this new response ...

7. **Check the Outcome.**

   Imagine being with the difficult person now. What are you experiencing now? ...
   Is this how you want to be? ... If not, repeat any steps to create the desired response.

Transforming Judgmental Thinking

Dealing with difficult people can evoke and sustain judgmental thinking, which leads to increasing levels of alienation. Judgmental thinking is based on several important skills that help a person make judgments about what to do. If we simply got people to give up being judgmental, they would lose access to these skills. We want people to be able to make judgements between options that may be safe or unsafe, helpful or unhelpful. What we don't want or need is someone making these determinations and then alienating others who make decisions or act in ways contrary to that person's judgments.

Here is the pattern of judgmental thinking that leads to alienation:

| Attention and Observation | ⇨ | Evaluation With Respect to Values | ➕ | Contempt | ⇨ | Alienating Attitude and/or Behavior |

When people make judgments, they pay attention to and observe events or actions in their environment. They then evaluate the data they have gathered with respect to their value system. This leads to the person acting in a certain way. While this process is presented in a linear fashion, in fact it is likely to be iterative, with multiple feedback loops.

The problem in this scenario is the addition of contempt for anyone who does not agree with the evaluation. This leads to what we, in our society, call "judgmental thinking," which results in alienating attitudes and behaviors. Feeling contemptuous of others who do not act in accordance with our values inspires, and in some situations appears to entitle, us to reject, alienate and punish them.

To transform judgmental thinking we need to replace contempt with curiosity to create an alternate pattern:

| Attention and Observation | ⇨ | Evaluation With Respect to Values | ➕ | Curiosity | ⇨ | Compassionate Response |

In this pattern the observation and evaluation is maintained, and in situations where people are acting contrary to the values, the person doing the evaluation becomes curious about what led the other to act this way. This curiosity can be used to explore several things:

- What happened before the event that led to the behaviors that elicited the resentment.

- The other person's positive intentions behind the behavior.

- How and where the other person learned this behavior.

I don't like that man. I must get to know him better.
— Abraham Lincoln

The major block to compassion is the judgment in our minds. Judgment is the mind's primary tool of separation.
— Diane Berke

The important thing is not to stop questioning. Curiosity has its own reason for existing. One cannot help but be in awe when he contemplates the mysteries of eternity, of life, of the marvelous structure of reality. It is enough if one tries merely to comprehend a little of this mystery every day. Never lose a holy curiosity.
— Albert Einstein

- When the judgment is focused on the client's own behavior that led them to violate their own values, they can be curious about what they will do differently in the future when confronted with similar situations.

- When the judgment is focused on another person's actions, the client can be curious about alternative responses they might make when people act in a similar manner in the future.

- Is there anything to be learned from the person we are judging? Judgments create a walls between people that restrict the sharing of any wisdom. In addition to being curious about how the other person came to be the way they are, you can be curious about any wisdom they may be able to share with you.

Becoming curious about the origins of how someone learned a behavior is not to excuse or blame someone else for that person's behavior, nor is it used to deny the hurt that one person may have inflicted on another. The goal of adding curiosity is to help provide some emotional distance between the initiating experience and the current reality to create a "space" of understanding that will allow the client to decide on a more resourceful response in the future. We want the client's final response to be one that sets both the client and the other person free to create a better future for both.

On the following page is an exercise to transform judgmental attitudes and actions.

*I have never met a man
so ignorant
that I couldn't learn
something from him.*
— Galileo Galilei

*Curiosity is
the very basis of education
and if you tell me that
curiosity killed the cat,
I say only
the cat died nobly.*
— Arnold Edinborough

Instructions: The purpose of this exercise is to help you achieve an open, curious stance that can support a compassionate response toward people who have hurt or offended you. In this process we will begin by transforming your judgmental thinking toward yourself and then apply that strategy to a person who has offended you.

Being curious is not meant as a way to excuse or blame ourselves or others for what we have done. Being curious is a way to put emotional distance between ourselves and the painful event and create a "space" of understanding that allows us to accept responsibility for what we have done and what we will do in the future.

As you lead someone through the process you do not need to know the content of the client's self-judgment. You are providing a guide to help them make the transformation, rather than analyzing or rationalizing what they did.

1. **Recall an Experience of Self-Judgment.**
   Take a moment and remember doing something that violated your values and hurt someone.
   I don't want you to tell me what you did, I just want you to remember what you did ...
   Play it through as a movie in your mind ...
   Notice what you feel as you remember what you did ...

2. **Adding Curiosity to Discover the Positive Intent.**
   Now "step back" in your mind so that you can see what came before that. What led up to you doing this thing? ... Allow yourself to become curious about what led up to this action ...

   With the same spirit of curiosity think about what you were trying to accomplish by doing what you did ...
   What was the positive intention behind what you did? ...
   (This may take several iterations, to mine into the intentions to find a positive intention, such as protection, or to teach the person not to do something again.)

   Take some time to be curious about how and where you learned to behave in this way to achieve that intention ... Where did you learn to act like this? ...
   Notice that what you did was the best you knew how to do at that moment to achieve your intention ... and you can learn other ways to be more effective in achieving that intention ...

3. **Create and Check the Ecology of an Alternative Strategy to Achieve the Positive Intention.**
   Think of other ways you could act to achieve that same intention ...
   Does any part of you object to doing that in the future? ...
   Is there any situation where that would not be wise or helpful? ...
   If there are situations where it wouldn't be wise, what will you do instead? ...

   Step into your present moment so you can look back on what you did and have learned, and now turn and look forward into the future ...

   Imagine yourself doing what you would prefer to do if you find yourself in a similar situation ...

4. **Check the Outcome.**
   Now recall the initial thing you did. What is the feeling you are now having as you remember what you did? ... How has your feeling toward yourself changed? ...

Instructions: In this part of the exercise we will use the same process to help a client become curious about the actions of a person who has injured or offended them.

Being curious is not meant as a way to excuse or blame others for their actions, nor to minimize or deny the pain that someone has caused. Being curious is a way to put emotional distance between you and the painful event and create a "space" of understanding that allows you to adopt a compassionate attitude toward the person who has injured you.

1. **Recall an Experience of Being Judgmental of Others.**
   Take a moment and remember what someone did that hurt or offended you ...
   I don't need to know what happened, I just want you to remember what they did ...
   Play it through as a movie in your mind ...
   Notice what you feel as you remember what they did ...
   And what you want to do as a result of that feeling? ...

   We are now going to add curiosity, which we used to transform self-judgment.

2. **Adding Curiosity to Discover the Positive Intent.**
   "Step back" in your mind so that you can see what came before that. What led to them doing this thing that hurt you? ...
   Allow yourself to become curious about what led up to this action ...

   With the same spirit of curiosity, think about what they were trying to accomplish by doing what they did ...
   I know you are not a mind reader, so it may not be accurate, but can you see a positive intention behind what they did? ...
   (This may take several iterations, to mine into the other person's intentions to find a presumed positive intention.)
   Be curious about how and where they learned to behave in this way to achieve that intention ...
   Where did they learn to act like this? ...
   Who do you think taught them to act like this? ...
   You may need to "step back" from the incident to see the entirety of their life to come to some conclusion ...
   Note: this conclusion is an opportunity to exercise your curiosity and may not be true ...

3. **They are Doing the Best They Can.**
   Can you see the person doing the best they know how to achieve their goal? ...
   This is not to excuse or agree with their behavior, just to create a space to understand them ...

4. **What Can You Learn From the Person.**
   Take some time to consider whether you can learn anything from the person ...

5. **Check the Outcome.**
   Step into your present moment so you can look back on what they did and be aware of what you are feeling now that you have gone through this exercise ...
   How have your feelings toward them changed? ...
   Is this an awareness you want to keep? ...
   If yes, take some time to imagine relating to this person in the future with this new awareness ...

Forgiving Yourself

The forgiveness process, with some modification, can also be used to help you forgive yourself. To develop a healing process we need to distinguish between guilt and shame – they are often equated, yet they are based on different internal processes and experiences.

Distinguishing Guilt and Shame

Guilt is the experience we have when we damage the social fabric by violating cultural norms that we also affirm, and we are motivated to repair the damage. When a person experiences guilt, they are saying:

"I have done a bad thing and I want to make it better."

"I hate what I have done and I want to make it up to you."

When we feel guilt, we are evaluating our behavior with respect to our values and standards. Guilt is an appropriate and helpful response to wrongdoing, as it helps rebuild and restore the community.

Shame, on the other hand, is rarely helpful. When someone feels shame they are saying:

"I hate myself for what I did."

"I am a bad person because I have done a bad thing."

"I am a bad person." *(The shame has been generalized)*

When we feel shame, we are evaluating ourselves and not our behavior. Because the emotional pain of shame is self-alienation rather than alienation between two people, the emotional pain is deep within the person at their core sense of self. This is typically more severe and crippling than guilt. The shamed person is often emotionally overwhelmed to the point that they are self-absorbed with little psychic energy to reach out to the injured person to repair the injury. They may further condemn themselves for being self-absorbed.

Upon examination, the "bad thing" the person did is often a violation of someone else's values rather than their own values. Beneath this feeling of shame is often an admonition: "You should feel ashamed of yourself." In many cases, shame can arise in response to very trivial social improprieties that have little to do with social moral codes of right and wrong.

Research on shame shows that when people feel ashamed they often feel small, vulnerable, naked, or exposed, and have a desire to hide from others[8]. These experiences of size distortion are apparent in the internal representations the person will have of themselves.

Our deepest fear is not that we are inadequate. Our deepest fear is that we are powerful beyond measure.

It is our light, not our darkness, that most frightens us. We ask ourselves, "Who am I to be brilliant, gorgeous, talented and fabulous?" Actually, who are you not to be?

You are a child of God. Your 'playing small' does not suit the world. There is nothing enlightened about shrinking so that other people don't feel insecure around you.

We were born to make manifest the glory of God that is within us. It is not just in some of us. It is in everyone.

As you let your light shine, you unconsciously give other people permission to do the same.

As you are liberated from your own fears, your presence automatically liberates others.

— From 'A Return to Love' by Marianne Williamson

The Uselessness of Shame

While guilt motivates people to consider others, shame orients people to be ego-centric. When someone feels small and vulnerable and wants to hide, they are not able to reach out to others and repair relationships. Shaming them will only make the situation worse.

The research on shame also shows that when someone is continually kept in shame, the shamed person will seek to destroy the shamer. The Treaty of Versailles that concluded World War I was designed specifically to shame Germany. One of the motivations underlying Hitler's actions was to right that shame and restore pride in the German people.

This research indicates that any social education programs, such as anti-racism training, or prevention programs for sexual harassment, teen pregnancy, or drug use that use shame as a motivational strategy are likely to be counterproductive and actually make things worse rather than better. A more effective approach is to focus on a positive, desired outcome and then teach people the skills to achieve that outcome, rather than shame them for doing what is wrong.

For example, imagine you are asked to design an anti-racism program. The first step is to define the problem from the perspective of your desired outcome. Is the problem in our society racism or is the problem a lack of cross-cultural cooperation for the benefit for all of society? I don't think it is possible to reduce the presence of a negative such as racism. I think it is possible to increase cross-cultural collaboration and so I would make that the goal of the program.

From an appreciative perspective the next step would be to discover how people are already collaborating across cultures and then explore how they could increase their collaboration. Notice that this approach does not look back to find the cause of racism, but looks forward to identify a preferred future, a society where collaboration across cultures is the norm, and then looks back to find the resources to create that future.

When we recall that shame makes people feel small vulnerable, naked, and exposed, with a desire to hide from others, and in extremes to kill the shamer, we can ask how shaming someone for their racism would improve cross-cultural collaboration. In fact, evoking shame will do everything to maintain the cultural hostility and increase the lack of collaboration.

Defeat is not bitter unless you swallow it.
— Joe Clark

One of the great mistakes is to judge policies and programs by their intentions rather than their results.
— Milton Friedman

A victim lives in fear. A Survivor endures. A victim is weak and powerless, paying for what was not her doing. A Survivor has grown strong because she knows the price is not hers to pay, the sin is not hers to atone.
— Unknown

What We Can't be Forgiven For

In many abuse situations people feel deep shame for what others have done to them. This overwhelming shame often leads the abuse victim to endlessly confess and seek absolution for what was done to them without any sense of relief. We cannot be forgiven for other people's sins or what they have done to us. We might have to forgive ourselves for allowing somebody to do that to us, but we cannot be forgiven for those things that were beyond our control.

When we work with adults who were abused as children we may also need to clarify and correct their perception of control. Small children often have a highly distorted understanding of responsibility and what they can control. We need to help these clients find healing for the distressing memories of what was done to them, before working to resolve their shame and resentment.

Making Amends

Since guilt includes a desire to repair the damage done to a relationship, we need to include making amends as part of the forgiveness process. Making amends may be as simple as apologizing to someone, or it could be something extensive as you correct what you have done. When making amends, it is important to consider your motivation for the amends. Making amends is not about buying forgiveness, or paying for our errors, or trying to correct the past. Making amends is about creating a better future for the person and the community that we have injured.

We also need to ensure that the recipient of our amends is free to reject our offer. Sometimes the amends can be used inappropriately to manipulate the person we have hurt. We need to be clear that we are not trying to buy their love, or influence how they think of us; we are simply taking responsibility to repair the hurt we have caused.

Satisfying Your Objections to Forgiving Yourself

As we do when forgiving others, we will also need to discover and satisfy our objections to forgiving ourselves. Exploring the effectiveness of guilt and shame to achieve a moral objective may be helpful. In my experience, guilt and shame are rarely effective in achieving a desired outcome. However, letting go of these objections often creates fear that we will fall back into being the person we don't want to be.

One of the objections that you may have is a fear that if you "went easy" on yourself you would be come a slacker and never amount to

You cannot be lonely if you like the person you're alone with.
— Wayne W. Dyer

What have you got to lose? If hating yourself hasn't made you a better person try loving yourself.

No one can make you feel inferior without your consent.
— Eleanor Roosevelt

anything. If so, ask yourself how effective your self-resentment or guilt has been in helping you to be a creative, loving person. You could also explore times when you have been creative and productive and discover what motivated these times of excellence that you want to replicate. If self-hatred does make you a loving, creative, productive person, then don't stop hating yourself! If on the other hand, as I suspect, self-hate makes you miserable, unloving, and unproductive then I suggest you begin the process of forgiving yourself.

Forgiving yourself is not an example of going easy on yourself. Self-forgiveness is about taking responsibility for your actions, and using these experiences of failure to teach yourself how to be a better person in the future. In the self-forgiveness exercise we will spend time developing and practicing a preferred behavior that we can use in the future. Failing and letting people down is often painful. We don't want to waste the price we have paid for failing by ignoring what we did or dismissing it. Self-forgiveness is about taking personal responsibility and learning new ways of living congruently with our values.

Another obstacle to self-forgiveness is the belief that forgiveness has to be earned. Forgiveness is a gift. Trying to earn your own forgiveness is a waste of time. There is nothing in your life that can dim the light of God's love for you. Who are you to disagree with God? It is sheer arrogance to think you are beyond forgiveness. Rather than trying to forgive yourself, take a step forward and look back and see yourself through the eyes of unconditional love. Self-forgiveness is joining with love to see yourself and the world through the eyes of love.

The Joy of "Shouldless" Living

Living life from a series of "shoulds," "oughts," "musts," or other imperatives imposed on us by others is a really effective way to stay miserable. While some "shoulds" may contain a valid moral outlook, they are powerless to help you be moral. "Shoulds" also dangle a carrot out in front of us. In some cases the carrot is of a future reward, as in: "If you do what you should then you will be loved." In other cases, the "should" is related to avoiding a bad thing like being sent to hell.

Should thinking is at the heart of St. Paul's conundrum that he describes in his letter to the Romans as he describes the relationship between the law, sin, and grace[9]. St. Paul describes how the harder he tries to do what he should do the more he fails to do it. And the harder he tries to not do what he shouldn't do the worse it gets.

What would happen to our churches if they stopped doing what they "should" do and simply became places to support people to do what they love to do?

Of all tyrannies a tyranny sincerely exercised for the good of its victims may be the most oppressive.
— C. S. Lewis

A good motivation is what is needed: compassion without dogmatism, without complicated philosophy; just understanding that others are human brothers and sisters and respecting their human rights and dignities.
— Tenzin Gyatso

St. Paul's solution was to give up trying! When he realized that God's love as expressed in Jesus was more powerful, and not dependent on his keeping the "shoulds" he was free from their tyranny; and paradoxically, he then had the power to live the moral life he chose.

One strategy to break up "should" thinking is to recursively ask **why** we should do something. After repeatedly asking, "and why should you do that? ..." we will discover that the beneficiary of the "should" is not others but ourselves, as in:

> "I should love others because I want them to see me as a caring person."

We can then engage in radical honesty when we find ourselves doing something because we "should," by saying to ourselves:

> "The only reason I am doing this is to get people to think I am a caring person."

From personal experience, this radical honesty quickly dissipated my "should"-based motivation and paradoxically I found a genuinely loving, "shouldless"[10] reason to love others.

Transforming Personal Demands Into Preferences

Just as in the case of resenting and forgiving others, self-forgiveness involves transforming the demands we make on ourselves and converting them into preferences. Transforming a personal demand into a personal preference requires that we evaluate the values and standards we choose to live by.

As we go forward into our future we need to decide which standards we want to keep, and which ones we want to relinquish. This intentional choosing of standards is important if we are to authentically own and live our standards because they are right for us, rather than being burdened or shamed by the standards of others. Keeping our standards as personal preferences also compassionately acknowledges that we are finite creatures who may fail to keep to our standards.

Self-Forgiveness Exercises

In the following set of exercises, the first step is to clarify whether the experience the client is having is guilt or shame, as these will require somewhat different strategies to resolve.

Unlike the guilt exercise, the shame exercise includes steps to correct distortions in their self-image and steps to clarify their values and standards as distinct from the values and standards of others[11].

Sometimes I lie awake at night, and ask, 'Where have I gone wrong?' Then a voice says to me, 'This is going to take more than one night.'
— Charles M. Schulz

But if a man carries his own light within him, he need not be afraid of the darkness.
— Martin Buber

Instructions: This exercise is designed to distinguish guilt from shame as a precursor to creating a healing strategy. Invite the client to do this with a spirit of curiosity rather than judgment. You can lead the client through this process without knowing the content of their bad feelings.

1. Remembering the event.

Take a moment and remember what you did. Play it through as if you are watching a movie of yourself doing what you did ...

Notice what also comes to mind as you see yourself in the event ...

Guilt:
The event that evokes distress is likely to be specific and discrete. It may have occurred over a period of time, but it is related to a specific person.

Shame:
While there may be a specific event that evokes distress, it may be quickly connected to a myriad of similar behaviors. These behaviors may also be of a trivial social nature.

2. How do you see yourself in the event?

Notice how you see yourself and see others in the event. Notice any difference in how you represent yourself and the others ...

Guilt:
The client is likely to be the same size and clarity as the other people with minimal distortion.

Shame:
The client's self-representation is likely to be different than the way they represent others.
The client is likely to be small, obscure, fuzzy, distant in contrast to the the others.

3. Notice what you want to do.

As you see yourself, observe what you feel like doing ...

Guilt:
The client is more likely to be oriented to reaching out to the person they hurt. They may be sorrowful or downcast but they can "stay present" in the scene.

Shame:
The client wants to hide, or have the "floor open up and swallow them" so they can disappear.

4. Whose values or standards were violated?

Notice what values or standards were violated. Whose values are they? ...

Do you want to keep these values? ...

Guilt:
The client will own the values or standards and will want to keep them. They may say: "I want to be honest in the future."

Shame:
The values and standards belong to someone else and may be represented in a series of should statements: "You should be ashamed of yourself." The client may be ambivalent about the values as they go forward into the future and say: "I should be honest in the future."

5. What is the focus of your emotion?

As you observe yourself having the distressing emotion notice the focus of your emotion ...

Guilt:
The client will be sorrowful for what they have done and how they hurt or offended the other person.

Shame:
The client will be self-loathing, hating themselves for what they have done and/or distressed over the way others hate them because of who they are.

Instructions: This process is designed to resolve guilt. If the client is experiencing shame, use the shame protocol. When leading someone through the process, you do not need to know what they did. As the coach, you can simply ask the client when they have completed each step. The process may not be linear, nor sequential, but iterative, especially when satisfying objections.

1. **Establish a Loving Foundation for Forgiving.** *(See exercises on page 65)*
   Take a moment and re-member yourself in the midst of unconditional love. Remember that there is nothing you have done or will do, nor anything anyone has done or will do to you, that can separate you from that unconditional love. Rest for a moment in that love and from that foundation of love proceed with the following steps ...

2. **Identify the Positive Intention Behind Your Behavior.**
   Recall the incident that evokes the feelings of guilt ...
   Notice what led you to doing what you did ...
   What was happening just prior to the event? ...
   What were you hoping to achieve by doing what you did? ...
   This is not meant as an excuse, just as a way to understand your actions so you can take responsibility for doing something different in the future ...

   Discovering the positive intention may take several iterations of inquiry to discover the underlying positive intention and how that intention is of value to the client.

3. **Identify an Alternative Strategy to Achieve this Positive Intention.**
   What will you do differently in the future to achieve this positive intention? ...

   Take a moment and think of a time when you have taken a stand and done the right thing because it was the right thing to do ... a time perhaps when it would have been easier to go with the crowd but you stayed true to what you knew to be right ...

   Imagine being in the future using the alternative strategy in the same way as you did when you did the right thing ...
   Do you think you will be able to do that, or do you need some additional resources to achieve that intention? ...

   Continue to rehearse possible actions and resources until the client feels confident they can achieve the positive intention.

4. **Check the Ecology of this Alternative Behavior.**
   Are there any situations where this alternative behavior wouldn't be appropriate? ...
   If so, what would you do instead in this different situation? ...

   Imagine someone doing this to you ...
   Is this something you would like to have done to you? ...

   Does any part of you object to doing this alternative behavior? ...
   If so, what would satisfy the objection? ...

   Make any modifications to the alternative behavior to ensure that it is ecologically sound

5. **Making Amends.**

Is there anything that you need to do to heal the relationship or bring the relationship to a peaceful end? ...

This may be as small as an apology or something more substantial to ensure, where possible, that the person doesn't have to carry the consequences of your actions into their future ...

Check the motivation behind the amends.

Is it to correct or pay for the past, or is it to create a better future for yourself and the person you hurt? ...

If necessary, modify the amends so it is "clean" from motivations of punishment or attempts to influence or manipulate the other person.

Does any part of you object to doing the amends? ...
Satisfy any objections before continuing ...

6. **Identify the current demand in your resentment.**

As you think about your resentment, what is the demand you are making of yourself about your past actions? ...

7. **Transform the Demand Into the Preferred Alternative Strategy that You Have Practiced.**
What would you have preferred to have done? ...

8. **Seek and Satisfy Any Objections You Have to Releasing Yourself From the Demand.**
Does any part of you object to setting yourself free this demand? ...
Satisfy any objection before continuing ...

9. **In Your Imagination, Release Yourself From Your Demand.**
Say to yourself: "I would have preferred that I would have ... and now I release myself from this demand that in the past I would have, or should have, or shouldn't have ..."

Now turn to the future and see yourself doing the preferred behavior ...

10. **Return to Your Awareness of Unconditional Love.**
Re-member yourself in the midst of unconditional love ...
Imagine it flowing over and through you ...
Surrender yourself into that love and allow it to wash away any residual feelings of guilt ...
See the person you hurt also surrounded by that love and surrender them into that love ...
Return to your awareness of being surrounded by unconditional love ...

11. **Check the Outcome.**
Now recall the situation that evoked guilt. See if the you can feel guilty as you remember what you did ...

When the client can't get the feelings back invite them to try harder to get the feelings back. If they are still able to feel the guilt, ask them if they have any additional objections to being set free from the guilt.

Repeat any steps necessary until the incident can be remembered without the guilt.
If the person continues to experience guilt use the shame process on the next page.

Resolving Shame

Instructions: Use this process to help a client resolve their shame. Because shame often involves a distortion of self-image and ambiguous values, steps to resolve those distortions and values clarifications are included.

When leading a client through the process you do not need to know the content of their experience or what was done to evoke their shame response. The process may not be linear, nor sequential, but iterative, especially when satisfying objections.

1. **Establish a Loving Foundation for Resolving Shame.** *(See exercises on page 65)*
   Take a moment and re-member yourself in the midst of unconditional love. Remember that there is nothing you have done or will do, nor anything anyone has done or will do to you, that can separate you from unconditional love. Rest for a moment in that love and from that foundation of love proceed with the following steps ...

2. **Discovering the Structure of a Shaming Experience.**
   Close your eyes and remember the situation where you did something and felt ashamed ...
   If the person has numerous experiences, invite them to choose the most shaming as an archetypal expression of their shame.
   What do you see as you remember what you did? ...
   Check any differences in the way you represent yourself and the way you represent the others that you see ...
   Are you bigger or smaller? ... Where are you standing/sitting in relationship to the others? ... Are there any other difference between how you see yourself and you see the others? ...

   As you attend to the representation, where is it located in your mental space? ...
   Point to where you see this picture ...

   As you view the picture of what happened, listen to any dialogue or commentary about what you did that you can hear ...
   Whose voices are saying what? ... What is their tonal quality? ...

3. **Discover a Resource State.**
   Because the feelings of shame arise from breaking someone's rules we need to find a time when you broke someone's rules and felt OK and resourceful.
   Think back over your life and remember a time when you broke someone's rules because you didn't agree with their rules and you felt OK, or felt a sense of assurance inside of yourself because you knew what you believed was right ...

   How are your representing that experience in your mind? ...
   Notice how big you are in relationship to others in the representation ...
   Where are you located in relationship to others in the representation? ...

   As you attend to the entire representation, point to where it is located in your mental space ...

4. **Transform the Shamed Experience to the Resource Location.**
   Transform the shaming image so that you have the same size and aspect as you do in the resource state ...

   Now move the image from here ... (point to the location of the shame image) *... to here ...* (point to the location of the resource image) *...*

---

5. **Identify the Demands and Clarify Standards.**

   What values, standards, or rules did you break? ...

   Whose values and standards are those? ...

   Are they values or standards that you want to keep? ...

   Listen to any demands that you are making on yourself about what happened in the past ...

   Sort through all the demands and injunctions to find any values that you want to keep ...

   Convert these demands into preferences for how you would have been and how you want to be ...

   If necessary convert the tonal quality of a harsh demand to a loving preference ...

6. **Creating a Preferred Behavior To Respond to Other People's Demands.**

   How do you want to respond in the future to people who try to impose a standard on you that you do not value or agree with? ...

   (If necessary do the exercise Dealing with a Difficult Person on page 179)

7. **Creating a Preferred Behavior To Honor Your Values and Standards.**

   From the clarified values and standards that you want to keep create a preferred behavior of what you would have preferred to do in the past and what you will do in the future when you find yourself in a similar situation ...

8. **Check the Ecology of the New Response and Preferred Behavior.**

   Are there some circumstances where this response wouldn't be appropriate? ...

   If so, what would you do instead? ...

   Check your preferred behavior against the Golden Rule: is this something that you would want others to do to you? ...

   Does any part of you object to responding in this way? ...

   If so, ask the part what would satisfy the objection ...

   Make any adjustments to satisfy any objections and then imagine yourself responding and doing what you prefer in a variety of future situations ...

8. **In Your Imagination, Release Yourself From Your Demand.**

   Say to yourself: "I would have preferred that I would have ... and now I release myself from this demand that in the past I would have, or should have, or shouldn't have ..."

   Now turn to the future and imagine yourself doing the preferred behavior ...

10. **Return to Your Awareness of Unconditional Love.**

    Re-member yourself in the midst of unconditional love ... Imagine it flowing over and through you ... from the beginning of your time ... up through your life ... through this present moment ... and into the future ... Allow love to wash away any residual feelings of shame ...

    In that love imagine being yourself doing your preferred behavior as an expression of that love ...

    See the others also surrounded by that love and surrender them into that love ...

    Return to your awareness of being one with all the love in the universe ...

11. **Check the Outcome.**

    Now recall the situation that evoked shame and see if you can get the feeling of shame back ...

    If they can't get the feelings back invite them to try harder to get the feelings back.

    Repeat any steps necessary until the incident can be remembered without the shame.

Resolving Organizational Resentment

Once upon a time a man was shipwrecked on a small island and he stayed on the island all alone for many years before he was rescued. Being an industrious and creative fellow, he spent most of his time on the island building a house for himself and replicating many of the other buildings that were in the town where he had previously lived. Before he was taken from the island he took his rescuers on a tour of the town he had built. He showed them the first small house he had built, and then the bigger house he had built and moved into as he became adept at working with the limited resources on the island. He showed them the store where he stored his food and on one street he showed them two churches he had built. "This is where I worship," he proudly said as he showed them one of the churches with intricately carved pews and statues. "What is this other church?" his rescuers asked as they pointed to the other church. "Oh, that church," the man said disgustedly, "that's the church I would never set foot in."[12]

As well as personal resentment, a group of people can also engage in corporate resentment that can become part of their ongoing identity. They will teach newcomers to adopt the same attitude and will ostracize or reject people who will not hold the same resentment. In some situations, the original precipitating event that led to the resentment may be forgotten. but the subsequent generations "just know" that the other group are to be resented and not trusted. This group resentment may appear between churches, businesses, family clans, or entire nations.

Responding to large scale group or national resentment is beyond the scope of my expertise. However I do want to offer several resources for dealing with organizations such as churches where the members find themselves in patterns of resentment and conflict rather than forgiveness, reconciliation, and collaboration.

Resentment Within an Organization

When an organization such as a congregation has gone through a difficult event or had a troubled leadership relationship, the individual members may become resentful towards one another and form alliances within the congregation based on their shared resentment. Imagine a church that has been in conflict with a pastor who is subsequently fired or leaves under duress. Some people will resent

Attitudes are contagious. Are yours worth catching?
— Dennis & Wendy Mannering

Blessed are the flexible for they shall not be bent out of shape.
— Robet Ludlum

No one can whistle a symphony. It takes a whole orchestra to play it.
— H.E. Luccock

the pastor. Others will love the pastor and resent those who sought the pastor's removal. If the pastor was removed for misconduct, some will resent the pastor; others will resent the victims of the misconduct. Some will use a rush to forgive as a way to avoid or deny what has occurred. As time unfolds, those who have forgiven may resent those who haven't. People will form alliances depending on their shared resentment. These alliances will be reinforced and maintained through the repeated telling of stories that justify their stance. When a person finds forgiveness, they may be seen as disloyal to their group and may be subject to additional resentment and ostracism.

Because the members will have an ongoing relationship with each other, the goal of any intervention will include:

- Helping individuals within the organization find personal forgiveness toward those who have hurt them.

- Disrupting the patterns of resentful storytelling that nourished the resentments.

- Reconciling the members so that they can work collaboratively on their preferred future.

Teaching Congregations How to Forgive

There is a huge difference in teaching people they need to forgive and teaching them *how* to forgive. The first will add injury to the insult that elicited the resentment. The second will set people free. Many of the exercises that I have offered in this manual can be taught as a class or series of sermons. In every parish I have served I taught classes on forgiveness, as I believe forgiveness is a basic Christian skill and no one needs to go through life carrying the burden of resentment. As their leader, it seemed to me that one of my responsibilities was to teach them how to manifest in the world one of our deepest core values.

Many people have reported success in letting go of resentment simply by discovering the demanding nature of resentment, and transforming the demand into a preference during a Sunday sermon. Others have found it necessary to meet individually with me to resolve a specific resentment. As I have used the content-free structural process of forgiving, it is relatively easy to teach groups of people to forgive by leading the entire group through the process, with each person working on their own personal resentment and forgiveness. Forgiving one another is a precursor to the work of reconciliation.

*When I give food
to the poor,
they call me a saint.
When I ask why
the poor have no food,
they call me a communist.*
— Dom Helder Camara

*If you hug to yourself
any resentment against
anybody else, you destroy
the bridge by which God
would come to you.*
— Peter Marshall

*You can only protect
your liberties in this world
by protecting the other
man's freedom.
You can only be free
if I am free.*
— Clarence Darrow

Conflict, Resentment, and Reconciliation

While often found together, conflict and resentment are different, and each can evoke the other. On the other hand, not all conflict will lead to resentment and not all resentment will lead to conflict.

People go into conflict when a value is threatened or compromised. To understand the nature of conflict, we need to discover the values that are in conflict. To resolve conflict and become reconciled, we need to enable the people on both sides of the conflict to have or be able to pursue what they value in a way that does not compromise the "other side's" ability to access what they value. Compromise is not part of reconciliation. Any reconciliation that is built on a compromised core life-giving value will not be sustainable. At its best, compromise is only a temporary way station on the journey to reconciliation.

When values are in conflict, we need to go deeper into the underlying values to see if we can find a shared value that affirms what both sides find life-giving. This shared value can then be used as a foundation for reconciliation.

Some conflict is an essential part of our struggle for human dignity. It is appropriate to be in conflict when human rights are denied and injustice is perpetrated against ourselves or others. These are conflicts of the foundational core values of the right to exist and to live in freedom. These values cannot be ignored or compromised if we are to be reconciled. However, we need to pursue these issues of justice compassionately, rather than resentfully or angrily. St. James taught us that our anger would not bring about the righteousness of God (*James 1:20. See also Ephesians 4:17-32*). It is only in love that we can be reconciled and empowered to create a just future.

Sadly, from my experience, many of our church conflicts have little to do with issues of justice or our deeper core values. In most cases, church arguments are over trivial issues of power and status or in protecting personal images of gods that are so puny they need protecting by the mere mortals that the gods supposedly created. These types of conflict are energy-sapping distractions from the task of sharing God's love with our neighbors and ourselves.

Just as group resentment is sustained by the sharing of specific stories, reconciliation can also be achieved by sharing stories. The task is to discover the outcome of the storytelling and invite people to tell stories that will lead to reconciliation and not to resentment. The Appreciative Inquiry process of shared storytelling around what

---

Defining identity by comparison is found at the heart of all human conflicts, and the path to resolving those conflicts is always to start focusing attention on the similarities that unite the two sides, noticing all the ways they are the same, instead of the ways in which they are different.
— Steve Andreas

Most church arguments are over trivial issues of power and status or in protecting puny images of gods that are so puny they need protecting by the mere mortals that the gods created.

You don't have to attend every conflict you are invited to.
— Tim Scudder

people value and find life-giving will aid in the process of achieving a sustainable reconciled relationship.

Defining the Problem and Solution

When resentment and conflict abound in an organization the task is often described as "conflict management." This is a hugely limiting idea that I fell victim to early in my career. For a time I even listed conflict management on my business cards as one of the things I offered people. I look back and think, "How foolish – why on earth would I want to **manage** someone's conflict?" Even if I was really effective at managing their conflict, at the end of the day they would still be in conflict.

We need to define the goal from the perspective of the desired outcome, and not from having less of the problem or managing the problem. The problem in the church (or the Middle East, or other places where conflict abounds) is not that there is too much conflict. The problem is that there is not enough collaboration between the parties for the benefit of each other and the wider community. Within the church, we have been entrusted with a ministry of reconciliation and not a ministry of conflict management. We need to find and grow places of acceptance rather than trying to reduce the amount of alienation in the system.

Making it Safe to Talk: Dealing with Elephants

Conflict in organizations can be overt or covert. In many churches people want to be liked by others and often seek to avoid conflict. In these situations conflict is likely to go "underground" rather than be dealt with openly.

The phrase "there is an elephant in the room" in organizational behavior means that there is something of a critical nature that people are unwilling or reluctant to talk about because it will only lead to hurt and conflict. The presence of the "elephant" saps energy as people are constantly on guard and distracted from other tasks. Intentionally not talking about the elephant is a form of negative focus: it keeps the elephant in the front of our consciousness. Elephant avoidance can cause people to be trampled.

However, the critical issue in dealing with elephants is not to force people to talk about that which they are not willing to talk about. If people are forced to talk about something they are not willing to talk about, they will feel violated and the situation is likely to get worse

We have been entrusted with the ministry of reconciliation not a ministry of conflict management.

The problem in the world is not that there is too much conflict. The problem is that there is not enough cooperation.

Forcing people to talk about the elephants in the room will just create more elephant manure for you to clean up.

rather than better. When people are unwilling to talk about something it is probably because it is not safe to talk about the situation. Creating safety, rather than forcing to people to talk, will be the first step to helping people resolve these situations.

The following coaching vignette shows one way to create a safe place for people to discuss the conflict:

Coach: It seems to me that there are some things that it is not safe to talk about ...

(If that statement is true, many in the room will nod their heads in agreement.)

Coach: Rather than talking about the "elephant in the room," what I would like to do is to have a conversation about this: What do we need to make it safe enough to talk about the elephant? ...

The things people mention can be listed as a social contract and used as resources to create safety. Once the resources have been identified and the situation is safe, the people can be invited to discuss the elephant. In many situations, the presence of an outside facilitator may make it safe enough for people to have the conversation.

When I conduct mediation events I begin my consulting conversations with a question:

"We have *(amount of time)* today. What would a successful outcome at the end of this time be?"

Asking "what's the problem" will evoke ideas of blame and judgment and lead to conversations that rarely help. Moving the conversation to what we value and what we want more of is likely to be emotionally safer than conversations about problems and their causes. These conversations about growing what we value and want more of will equip people to create a better future, and will ultimately prove more beneficial.

Organizational Reconciliation

Albert Einstein once said that we can't solve a problem from the mindset that created the problem. Trying to manage or have less conflict is trying to solve the problem from within the mindset of the conflict rather than the mindset of the solution. However, simply trying to reconcile the people to one another or have them collaborate with one another is also likely to be unhelpful because

---

Father, forgive them; for they do not know what they are doing.
— Luke 23:34

Every gun that's made, every warship launched, every rocket fired, signifies a theft from those who hunger and are not fed, those who are cold and not clothed.
— Dwight David Eisenhower

A good heart is better than all the heads in the world.
— Edward Bulwer-Lytton

we are still working within the interpersonal mindset where conflict and collaboration exist.

To truly help a group of people who are in conflict, we can't simply get them reconciled to each other. We need to reconcile them to something that is beyond their immediate interpersonal experience. Is there a larger reality that holds both sides of the conflict? Does the organization have a "higher" unified purpose that can hold the conflicted parties? We need to reconcile the parties to this higher purpose before we can reconcile them to each other.

In my experience as a church consultant, very few churches have a clear sense of their purpose. In these congregations we need to begin by helping the people discern a purpose that they can all affirm.

In the Appreciative Inquiry process, core purpose is discerned by inviting church-wide conversations about people's best life-giving experiences in the congregation. This results in the people affirming a purpose that:

- Has been clearly demonstrated and experienced in their past.
- Contains what they value and find life giving.
- Is shared and "owned" by all the members and isn't simply imposed by one sub-group upon the rest.

When people within the organization are unable to affirm or accept the purpose, they will be in a continual state of conflict that is beyond reconciliation. In these situations it would be best for all concerned for the parties to separate and go their individual way. This is an example of the situation that Jesus described when he said: "When you go into a house say peace to the house. If your peace is not returned shake the dust off your feet as you leave." (Matthew 10:13-14.)

What in God's Name is Going on Here?

For many years I worked as a transitional pastor serving congregations during their transition from one senior pastor to another. Some of these congregations were in conflict, some had their pastor removed for misconduct, and some were in the midst of transition because their clergy had been called to other positions or had retired. Regardless of the reason for the transition my first sermon was always entitled "What in God's Name is Going on Here?"

It was interesting to watch the parishioners' reaction when I would ask that question from the pulpit – and then just pause. In one

The practice of peace and reconciliation is one of the most vital and artistic of human actions.
— Thich Nhat Hanh

*The very purpose of
religion is to
control yourself,
not to criticize others.
Rather, we must criticize
ourselves.
How much am I doing
about my anger?
About my attachment,
about my hatred,
about my pride,
my jealousy?
These are the things which
we must check in daily life.*
— Dalai Lama

situation where the pastor had been removed for misconduct, some parishioners appeared smug and all knowing, others appeared ashamed, others looked angry, and some were confused as to why I was there and their pastor was not. My response to all these thoughts and ideas was: "All these things you are thinking right at this moment are none of my business, and are actually none of your business, because they weren't happening in God's name. My task, and our task together, is to discover what *in God's name* is actually happening here, and join God in doing more of it."

This is an example of beginning to call the people to, and reconcile them with, their higher purpose. It is also an example of where to join a group of people. We don't want to join with them in their conflict, and become part of their conflict; we want to join with them in their higher purpose.

Joining a Group In The Midst of Trauma

When a traumatic event occurs in the life of an organization, the members are likely to be in very different emotional places. Our challenge as leaders is to work with the group collectively but not assume or act as though everyone is having the same uniform experience. When the leader is part of the traumatic event, an external facilitator is recommended as the leader is likely to be identified as part of a sub-group within the organization, and others in the organization will find it difficult to believe that the leader understands their experience.

As a facilitator, one way to join with a group while honoring their individual experiences is to engage them in a group process that includes:

- A clear statement of what has happened. This is not meant to create gossip but to create a shared understanding of what has transpired and the purpose of the gathering. For example, if a pastor has been removed by the Bishop or adjudicatory for misconduct we need to state that without elaborating the aspects that are part of an ongoing legal inquiry. For example:

  "The bishop has suspended Fr. Tom following allegations that he has been involved in sexual misconduct. Because these allegations are under investigation I cannot provide any additional information. The purpose of our meeting is to talk about what we are experiencing today in response to this information and not to elaborate on the sexual misconduct."

The public have an insatiable curiosity to know everything, except what is worth knowing.
— Oscar Wilde

We cannot hold a torch to light another's path without brightening our own.
— Ben Sweetland

In a controversy the instant we feel anger we have already ceased striving for the truth, and have begun striving for ourselves.
— Buddha

- The next step is to join with people in their present experience: I do this by imagining all the possible feelings that people may be having:

> "I imagine that you are feeling a variety of emotions as you have heard this news ...
>
> I imagine some of your are feeling shocked ...
> I imagine some of you are feeling, sad ... hurt ... bewildered, angry ... afraid ... or just numb ..."

As I mention all the possibilities I can imagine, I expand on the thoughts that may evoke the feelings. I also watch for affirming head nods, and nod in return. Once I have a head nod it is time to move to another aspect, we don't need to mine into those troubling emotions any further. The head nod indicates that the person knows that I know what they are feeling, and we can move on.

Doing this publicly helps people feel understood and allows other people to have very different responses. Since the misconduct is likely to have been alienating, accepting people where they are and allowing others to be where they are will rebuild acceptance and trust within the community.

In church settings I will often embed their experiences in Biblical stories. The Old Testament in particular has numerous stories of people struggling with rage, grief, loss, and every other human experience. The task is not to change what the people are feeling but to acknowledge that they are not alone, that the people of God have struggled with these emotions from the beginning of time.

- Invariably the topic of forgiveness is likely to come up, to which I will respond:

> "Some of you are thinking that we need to forgive, others are likely to be thinking that you will never forgive and just thinking about forgiving gets you angry.
>
> Let's not rush to forgive. Right at this moment we may not have all the facts, and more importantly we don't know all the consequences of what has happened, and what we will need to forgive."

This is designed to give people the freedom to be where they are emotionally and not to feel pressured to be somewhere else. Trauma is alienating; forcing people to forgive before they are ready deepens the alienation. The statement is also designed to

---

Without forgiveness there can be no healing.
— Archbishop Desmond Tutu

Anyone who proposes to do good must not expect people to roll stones out of their way, but must accept their lot calmly, even if they roll a few more upon it.
— Albert Schweitzer

Holding onto your anger is like clutching a vibrating pole. The harder you clench, the more every part of your being vibrates in reaction.
— Kare Anderson

*I never see
what has been done;
I only see
what remains to be done.*
— Buddha

*When will our consciences
grow so tender that we
will act to prevent human
misery rather than try to
avenge it?*
— Eleanor Roosevelt

*A dream is just a dream.
A goal is a dream with a
plan and a deadline.*
— Harvey Mackay

raise forgiveness in consciousness as a future goal. I am not telling them not to forgive, I am telling them not to rush to forgiveness. If they agree with that statement then they will have agreed to the underlying assumption that they will forgive at some point.

- If it seems helpful I might invite people to reflect on previous difficult times and what internal resources they relied on to cope during those times.

  "I imagine that you have gone through other difficult times ... Take a moment and remember what resources you relied on to get through those times ... And how you can use those resources now to help you get through this experience ..."

- Traumatic events create tunnel vision, and the trauma consumes all the space in consciousness. After talking about all the possibilities we can step back from the immediacy of the event and put it in a larger context.

  "We may feel so hurt that we find it difficult to be conscious of God's presence. We may wonder what God is up to or where God has gone or whether we can have a future together. Our task now is to begin to wonder how we can be God's people despite what has happened."

The goal of all of these steps is to help people accept what has happened and accept their emotions in relationship to what has happened. The goal is not to change the way they are feeling or make them feel comfortable. We need to help people access their resources of acceptance and faithfulness to deal with something that is uncomfortable, rather than making it seem like it didn't happen.

In the midst of adversity we can build community by helping people see that they are not alone and that there is a future for the organization. It is the realization of the presence of an ongoing community, and that they as individuals and as a community can survive this experience, that will restore them to hope.

Reconciliation: Restoring the Organization to Hope

Hope and reconciliation are based on a shared understanding of how we will live together in the future. What enables us to be reconciled is to have a shared set of values that we will live by as we co-create a shared future based on what we mutually find life-giving. As we seek reconciliation we need to ensure that we are not simply reconciled to each other, but that we are also reconciled to a vision of the future that contains what we value and find life-giving.

The task of leadership in these situations is to call the people to their purpose and to align their actions with their values. In the midst of conflict people often lose sight of their values and act in ways that violate their values and ultimately cause more harm.

Using resentment to create a loving future will not be effective or sustainable. The path to the future must be consistent with the future. If our purpose is to share God's love, then sharing God's love needs to be both the path and the destination.

As coaches working with groups in conflict, our task is to manage the process and not the outcome. When managing the process we need to call people to live their values even when it is difficult. We also need to call people to their higher purpose. As they consider various actions we can ask:

- How will this help you manifest your purpose?

- Is this in alignment with, and an expression of, your values?

- As you pursue this course of action, will anyone be deprived of what is life-giving to them?

- Does anyone object to pursuing this course of actions?
  If so, what would satisfy that objection?

When all hearts are clear they can proceed with love, courage, faith, and hope.

We do not believe in ourselves until someone reveals that deep inside us is someone valuable, worth listening to, worthy of our trust, sacred to our touch. Once we believe in ourselves we can risk curiosity, wonder, spontaneous delight or any experience that reveals the human spirit.
— *E. E. Cummings*

> *I have walked that long road to freedom.*
> *I have tried not to falter;*
> *I have made missteps along the way.*
> *But I have discovered the secret that after climbing a great hill, one only finds that there are more hills to climb.*
> *I have taken a moment here to rest, to steal a view of the glorious vista that surrounds me, to look back on the distance I have come.*
> *But I can rest only for a moment, for with freedom come responsibilities, and I dare not linger, for my long walk is not yet ended.*
> — *Nelson Mandela*

A Final Blessing

Here is my prayer for you as you journey into your future, free from grief and resentment, and sharing hope with those you encounter.

Watch over your friends, O God, so that they can look forward to the days when they can look back and behold with wonder the great things they have co-created with you.

The God of Truth bless you with discomfort at easy answers, half truths, and superficiality so that you live from deep within your heart.

The God of Understanding make you tender in the face of pain and rejection so that others can know the comfort of your acceptance.

The God of Justice make you fierce in the face of oppression and exploitation so that others can live with dignity in the midst of your respect.

The God of all Wisdom bless you with enough foolishness to believe that you can make a difference in this world, so that you can lead others to do what many claim cannot be done.

And the Blessing of God Almighty, Creator, Redeemer, and Life Giving Spirit be amongst you and all those whom you love and delight in now and for ever. Amen.

RESOURCES, ENDNOTES, AND REFERENCES

Additional Resources

When you register your copy of **Restoring Hope: Appreciative Strategies to Resolve Grief and Resentment** at www.appreciativeway.com/hope you will have access to the following web resources:

- Audio recordings by Dr. Voyle of all the exercises.

- Downloadable copies in .pdf format of each exercise.

- Updates and revisions.

If you purchased your copy online at the *The Appreciative Way* web site your copy will automatically be registered and you will receive a password in the confirmation email. If you purchased your copy at another bookstore please register your copy at: www.appreciativeway.com/hope

Your Registration Key is: **RHGR-10a**

Endnotes and References

Author's Note

I do not consider myself a scientist or academic inquirer who is making original discoveries. I think of myself as an engineer who applies and adapts the discoveries of others to daily living. Very little of the material in this book is original to me. As I mentioned in the Acknowledgments, most of this material was gathered at workshops and conferences, often as asides or comments during workshops, when tiny seeds were planted in my consciousness that went on to flourish into trees of skillfulness. Where possible, and my memory recalls, I gratefully acknowledge the source of my ideas and also point those who find reading helpful to their written materials.

What is original to me is the synthesis of the knowledge I have gathered from others and every client session in which I have used the material. Every client is unique and every session is original as the processes are adapted to meet their needs. It is in the use of the material that my skill and understanding has been developed and the synthesis has occurred.

Acknowledgments

.1 *(page 9)* Steve Andreas and his wife Connirae Andreas have been prolific writers and developers in the field of Neuro-Linguistic Programming (NLP). His books include:
Six Blind Elephants: Understanding Ourselves and Each Other. Volumes I and II. (2006).
Transforming Yourself: Becoming Who You Want to Be. (2002).
And with Connirae Andreas:
Heart of the Mind. (1989).
Change Your Mind and Keep the Change. (1987).
Connirae Andreas and Tamara Andreas also wrote:
Core Transformation: Reaching the Wellspring Within. (1984).
These books were all published by Real People Press, Boulder, Colorado and can be found along with videos and other resources at: www.realpeoplepress.com.

.2 *(page 9)* Andy Austin is a creative and provocative thinker in the world of psychotherapy and NLP specifically. He is the author of *The Rainbow Machine: Tales from a Neurolinguist's Journal.* Real People Press, Boulder, Colorado. (2007). It is a delightful collection of stories and reflections on how to really help clients who are ensnared in the web of both their own problems and the mental health systems attempts to help them.
Andy Austin's work can be found at: www.23nlpeople.com

.3 *(page 9)* Milton Erickson's approach to working with clients was unique and complex. He had acute powers of observation as he discovered "how people did" their problems and what they needed to do to be set free. Unlike many psychotherapists, he did not require his clients to gain insight into their problems, but created strategies to help them develop more resourceful ways of living. He used a combination of hypnosis, storytelling, paradox, indirect suggestion, confusion, utilizing the symptoms, and many other strategies to join with clients and help them co-create new outcomes. He taught his students in these same indirect ways so that it is difficult to describe in any linear fashion how to replicate what he was doing. His work came to public attention in Jay Haley's book: *Uncommon Therapy: The Psychiatric Techniques of Milton H. Erickson, M.D.* W. W. Norton, New York. (1973). Numerous authors have subsequently published books on his approaches and have edited his papers and recordings of his client sessions. These resources can be found at the Erickson Foundation in Phoenix, Arizona or online at: www.erickson-foundation.org

.4 *(page 9)* Stephen Gilligan's work can be found at: www.stephengilligan.com

.5 *(page 10)* Bill O'Hanlon's work can be found at: www.billohanlon.com

.6 *(page 10)* Steve Lankton's work can be found at: www.lankton.com

.7 *(page 10)* I only attended one weekend retreat, "Unconditional Love and Forgiveness," with Edith many years ago in the mid 1980s, before the advent of web sites, email, or desktop publishing. Her teaching and the workshop had a profound impact on me personally and professionally. Her process of forgiveness was based on the teachings of the Essenes, a spiritual community in Palestine during the days of Jesus. There is considerable theological speculation that Jesus, John the Beloved Disciple, and John the Baptist may have had contact and or been involved with the Essenes. Though she has died, Edith's approach and teaching live on and can be found at: www.maryhayesgrieco.com/about/stauffer.asp

1: Introduction to the Appreciative Way

1.1 *(page 15)* David Cooperrider's landmark essay, "Positive Image; Positive Action," can be found in *Appreciative Management and Leadership: The Power of Positive Thought and Action in Organizations,* edited by Suresh Srivasta, David Cooperrider and Associates. Jossey Bass, San Francisco. (1990).

For a concise and clear understanding of Appreciative Inquiry in organizational settings see Hammond, *The Thinbook of Appreciative Inquiry.* Thinbook Publishing, Bend, Oregon. (1996).

For a description of the origins of Appreciative Inquiry and its use in organizational development see Watkins and Mohr, *Change at the Speed of Imagination*. Jossey Bass, San Francisco. (2001).

See the Appreciative Inquiry Commons, http://appreciativeinquiry.case.edu/ for a wide variety of online articles and resources on Appreciative Inquiry.

See the Clergy Leadership Institute web site, http://www.clergyleadership.com, for Appreciative Inquiry-based training and resources for coaches and church leaders.

1.2 *(page 30)* Comment made at the International Erickson Conference in Phoenix in 2004, which I have subsequently discussed with Steve and with which I concur.

1.3 *(page 31)* I discovered the four motivations in Percy's *Exploring Spirituality Going Deep in Life and Leadership*. Inspired Production Press, Scottsdale, Arizona. (1997). In a personal communication, Percy reported he was not the originator of the four motivations and he was unaware of their origins.

2: Core Processes and Resources

2.1 *(page 38)* See Beck, A.T., Brown, G., Berchick, R.J., Steward, B.L., & Steer, R.A. (1990). Relationship between hopelessness and ultimate suicide: a replication of psychiatric outpatients, *American Journal of Psychiatry, 147, 190-195.*

2.2 *(page 39)* Understanding how we represent and structure our experiences and time in consciousness are core aspects of Neuro-Lingusitic Programming that I have learned from Steve Andreas and which can be found in his previously-listed books. I have used these understandings to to help people distinguish between temporal and eternal qualities, and to experience unconditional love and compassion.

2.3 *(page 59)* Contrary to popular opinion and thinking the research on optimism, pessimism, and cancer survivability is very unclear and non-predictive. See Coyne, J.C., Stefanek, M, & Palmer, S.C. (2007). Psychotherapy and survival in cancer: The conflict between hope and evidence. *Psychological Bulletin 133, 367-394.*

2.4 *(page 68)* I was introduced to the Goodness of God by a Clinical Pastoral education supervisor, Dr. George Markham, when I was in the midst of a major misery that had gone on for several years. He was the first person to actually help. Everyone else I had sought for help wanted to know **why** I was miserable. George wasn't interested in my misery; what he was interested in was **how** I "did happy," and he taught me how to be happy. George was a student of Thomas Hora, a psychiatrist who developed metapsychiatry, which in part was based on the idea and reality of the Goodness of God. The work of Thomas Hora (now deceased) can be found at www.pagl.org.

2.5 *(page 72)* Stephen Gilligan mentioned the three faces of compassion as an aside at the beginning of a class on Ericksonian hypnosis at the International Erickson Conference in Phoenix in 2001. I have no idea what else he said during the class as I immediately became entranced and spent the next hour recalling all the Gospel stories of Jesus and beginning to see them through these frames. It has now become a foundational aspect of the way I think about working and relating to people. Gilligan describes the faces of compassion in: *The Problem is the Solution: The Principle of Sponsorship in Psychotherapy*. In B. Geary & J. Zeig (Eds.), *The Handbook of Ericksonian Therapy*. MH Erickson Foundation Press, Phoenix. (2001).

2.6 *(page 76)* Dr. King's speeches can be found at: www.mlkonline.net.

3: Resolving Painful Memories

3.1 *(page 88)* Andy Austin presented the idea of painful memories being a distortion in perceived time by engaging participants in the exercise of adding brief "video clips" before and after the event at the 2009 Advanced Mastery Training in Winter Park, Colorado.

3.2 *(page 98)* The process for resolving traumatic memories can be found in Steve and Connirae Andreas's book *Heart of the Mind*. Real People Press, Boulder, Colorado. (1989) Steve also has a recorded demonstration of the process, *Resolving PTSD Flashbacks,* available at: www.realpeoplepress.com.

4: Resolving Grief

4.1 *(page 117)* Elisabeth Kubler-Ross first presented the five stages in her book, *On Death and Dying,* in 1969. A complete listing of her work can be found at the web site dedicated to her work: www.ekrfoundation.org/

4.2 *(page 134)* Dannie Beaulieu demonstrated this strategy during a presentation on Impact Therapy at the at the 2010 Advanced Mastery Training in Boulder, Colorado. Dannie's work can be found at: www.impactacademy.net/en/

4.3 *(page 137)* The structural process to resolve grief can be found in Steve and Connirae Andreas' book *Heart of the Mind*. Real People Press, Boulder, Colorado. (1989). In addition to the chapter in his book Steve Andreas also has available a DVD, *Client Session: Loss and Depression,* in which he treats a client suffering from grief. It can be found at www.realpeoplepress.com.

4.4 *(page 155)* This story was told to me by a fellow passenger on a flight to Portland. He was an electronics engineer who had worked for the company. I have forgotten his name and the name of the company but the essence of the story has stayed with me.

5: Forgiveness

5.1 *(page 157)* The International Center for Prison Studies at Kings College, London, report that the United States has 748 people per 100,000 in prison. The next highest is Russia, with 598 people per 100,000. The International Center for Prison Studies can be found at: www.kcl.ac.uk/schools/law/research/icps

5.2 *(page 157)* See previous note 1.2.

5.3 *(page 159)* The "demand" characteristics of resentment and extending unconditional love were adapted from Edith Stauffer's work presented at an Unconditional Love and Forgiveness workshop in Santa Monica, California in the mid 1980s.

5.4 *(page 160)* Robert McDonald has a parable, "My Friend John and the Tiger," which describes the need to forgive and remember in the book *Tools of the Spirit: Pathways to the Realization of Universal Innocence* by Dilts and McDonald. Meta Publications, Capitola, California. (1997).

5.5 *(page 164)* See the Death Penalty Information Center at www.deathpenaltyinfo.org for details. For the last 10 years states without the death penalty have averaged approximately 40% less deaths by murder than states with the death penalty.

5.6 *(page 170)* The structural process to forgive was demonstrated by Steve Andreas at the International Erickson Conference in Phoenix in 2004. A transcript of a session of Steve helping a woman forgive is included in his book *Six Blind Elephants: Understanding Ourselves and Each Other. Volume II.* Real People Press, Boulder, Colorado. (2006).

5.7 *(page 178)* Creating a Resourceful Response was synthesized with help from Steve Andreas from a series of exercises in his book, *Transforming Yourself: Becoming Who You Want to Be.* Real People Press, Boulder, Colorado. (2002).

5.8 *(page 184)* See Tangney, J. P., Miller, R. S., Flicker, L. & Barlow, D. H. (1996) Are Shame, Guilt, and Embarrassment Distinct Emotions? *Journal of Personality and Social Psychology, 70, 1256-1269.*

5.9 *(page 187)* St. Paul's conundrum of "should" thinking is presented in the theological language of law, sin, and grace and can be found in Romans 7:7-25. St. Paul graphically describes the torment that arises when the law (or a "should"), which may contain a good thing, leads to failure and guilt because it does not have the power to help a person keep the law. The power to keep the law is found by living in grace or love, over which there is no law.

5.10 *(page 188)* I was introduced to the "joy of shouldless living" by George Markham, who learned it from Thomas Hora. See 2.2 for details.

5.11 *(page 188)* The structural process to resolve shame was developed from *Recovering From Shame and Guilt* in Steve and Connirae Andreas' book *Heart of the Mind.* Real People Press, Boulder, Colorado. (1989). Steve also has a DVD, *Resolving Shame,* in which he treats a client suffering from shame. It can be found at www.realpeoplepress.com.

5.12 *(page 194)* I have seen and heard variations of this story in a variety of formats over the years. I am unaware of its original source.

RESTORING HOPE

Appreciative Strategies to
Resolve Grief and Resentment

Rev. Robert J. Voyle, Psy.D.
2010

The Appreciative Way
ENABLING INNOVATION AT THE *SPEED OF LIFE*

www.appreciativeway.com

Restoring Hope:
Appreciative Strategies to Resolve Grief and Resentment

Register Your Copy

When you register your copy of **Restoring Hope: Appreciative Strategies to Resolve Grief and Resentment** at www.appreciativeway.com you will have access to the following online resources:

- Audio recordings by Dr. Voyle of all the exercises.
- Downloadable copies in .pdf format of each exercise.
- Updates and revisions.

Please register your copy at: www.appreciativeway.com/hope
Your Registration Key is: **RHGR-10a**

Restoring Hope: Appreciative Strategies to Resolve Grief and Resentment

Author:

Robert J. Voyle

Editing:

Elizabeth Farquhar

Format and Design:

Kate Shirley, Stellar Designs

Cover Photo:

Diego Rojas, istockphoto

Published by:

The Appreciative Way
24965 NW Pederson Rd.
Hillsboro, Oregon 97124

Visit us at:
http://www.appreciativeway.com
ISBN-13: 978-0-9787076-4-4